VOLKSWAGEN

Beetles, Buses & Beyond

James M. Flammang

Published by

 **krause
publications**

700 E. State Street • Iola, WI 54990-0001
Telephone: 715/445-2214

Please call or write for our free catalog of automotive publications.
Our toll-free number to place an order or obtain a free catalog is 800-258-0929
or please use our regular business telephone 715-445-2214
for editorial comment and further information.

Library of Congress Catalog Number: 96-76687
ISBN: 0-87341-419-5
Printed in the United States of America

Cover Photos: 1959 Volkswagen Beetle (Photo: James M. Flammang — Owner: Kim and
Chuck Fryer). Concept One (Photo: Rodney Rascona, for Volkswagen of America).

TABLE OF CONTENTS

ACKNOWLEDGMENTS

Without the assistance of Phil and Penni Hall of Wauwatosa, Wisconsin, a Volkswagen history of this magnitude could not have been written. A widely-read automotive writer and longtime collector of Volkswagen material, Phil kindly offered the full use of his collection of factory photographs, press releases, and other valuable materials. Furthermore, the Halls generously invited me into their home to select whatever was needed. No author could ask for easier cooperation, or for a more gracious host.

Very special thanks, too, go to the members of the public relations staff at Volkswagen of America, in Auburn Hills, Michigan. Tony Fouladpour, Maria Leonhauser, Maureen Terry-Morehead, and Karla Waterhouse were generous with their time and knowledge during my visit. They also made available the complete Volkswagen photo files, allowing me to select whatever was required.

As is the case with each of my auto history books, thanks go to Marianne E. Flammang. From this book's inception all the way through the final stages, she contributed not only her editorial skills, but ideas for improvement.

While researching this book, I had the good fortune to meet a number of Volkswagen owners and enthusiasts. Some provided photographs and other materials; others contributed tales and opinions. Many thanks to all of them, but especially to:

Mike and Ann Fornataro — Jacksontown, Ohio
Chuck and Kim Fryer — Marengo, Illinois
Tina Gibson — Columbus, Ohio
Conrad Holcomb — Watertown, Wisconsin
Pat Miketinac — Brooksville, Florida
René Rondeau — Corte Madera, California
Richard Rymer — Kent, Ohio
E.C. (Erv) Smith — Salem, Oregon
Kurt Wendt — Island Lake, Illinois
Dave Wigglesworth — Kansas City, Missouri

Special appreciation is due to Chris McCarthy of Chicago, who gave me my first ride in a Volkswagen Beetle, in the mid-1950s. That exposure—and Chris' early enthusiasm for the make—helped instill an interest not only in VWs, but in foreign automobiles generally. That interest eventually resulted in the purchase of a 1957 Beetle sedan, followed later by a '61 bus.

A unique debt of gratitude also goes to Ernest F. Schulz. When the engine of that '61 stopped dead on a Chicago street one night long ago, prompting total disgust with all things Volkswagen, Ernie took the bus off my hands. With my assistance, he removed and rebuilt the 40-horsepower engine, and wound up getting several more years of dependable service out of the old bus. Both of us learned plenty about VWs along the way.

Finally, I enthusiastically acknowledge the guidance and patience of the editorial staff at Krause Publications: especially Patricia Klug, Deborah Faupel, Ron Kowalke and John Gunnell. Without John's suggestion that this book be written in the first place, and his recommendation that I be the one to undertake that task, it would never be in print today.

James M. Flammang
Chicago, Illinois

INTRODUCTION

What Is It About the Beetle?

Legendary auto writer Ken Purdy had a lot to say about automobiles. He said it memorably. Writing about the Beetle in *Look* magazine in 1962, after the car had established itself as a no-holds-barred sensation, Purdy looked back at the car's inception in the early postwar years.

"One of the epic wrong guesses of all time," Purdy wrote, "was registered in 1945 by the British Officer who advised his government not to pack up the Volkswagen factory and ship it to Britain as part of war reparations. He said the Volkswagen was a silly-looking little beetle with no future."

That unimaginative officer wasn't the only observer who erred in judgment at the time. "One of the most astute U.S. dealers," Purdy added, "a foreign car specialist, saw no hope for the Volkswagen...when the first few trickled into this country. No one ever blew an easier chance to become a millionaire."

Designed by Ferdinand Porsche, developed during Adolf Hitler's Third Reich, the Volkswagen (which translates directly to "people's car"), appeared to have died with the defeat of Germany. Instead, it eventually brought motoring to postwar Germans—and to millions of other Europeans. More surprising yet, the Beetle also helped change the way *Americans* thought about the automobile.

VW's success is even harder to grasp when viewed against its Nazi-era origin. After all, the first production Volkswagens emerged from the rubble-strewn Wolfsburg factory shortly after a vanquished Germany—despised by most of the world—had begun a slow recovery from the ashes of war.

What other automobile make had ever suffered such a dreadfully tarnished image? How could the Beetle's Third Reich connection possibly be overcome?

But overcome, it did. Just as American drivers of British-built sports cars in the 1950s shared a camaraderie, so too, did early VW owners feel a kinship. Their "joie de driving" was often expressed by hand waves and horn toots, when encountering any other Beetle on the road.

By the time the first Volkswagens ("people's car") were designed and tested, prior to World War II, the familiar Beetle shape was established. Early prototypes lacked a rear window. (Volkswagen)

In the Beetle's heyday, millions of motorists loved the little beast. Additional millions detested it—a shocking commentary to the car's fans, but true nonetheless. Some Americans couldn't get past the car's German origin—and Nazi past. Others simply deplored foreign cars in general, or mistrusted the Volkswagen's distinct—but radical—technical features.

Just two VWs arrived in New York in 1949. Early growth proved modest, but after a few ho-hum years, the Beetle blasted off into the sales stratosphere. The car's reign of glory lasted two full decades. Millions of Americans, sooner or later, were "bitten by the Bug," which was also known as the "Vee-dub," "Volks," and by other fond (or occasionally, contemptuous) nicknames.

Beetle sedans were exported to the United States as late as 1977, while its Karmann-built convertible companion lasted two years longer. Even though manufacture came to a halt in Germany earlier in that decade, Beetles remained in production elsewhere in the world into the 1990s, and have been especially popular in Brazil and Mexico.

This book won't tell you how to repair or restore your VW. Plenty of other books serve that purpose. You won't find a minutely detailed breakdown of technical details, pointing out every tiny change that the company made to the Beetle in its program of "continuous improvement." That term, incidentally—which became an auto industry "buzzword" in the 1990s—virtually defines the Volkswagen company's mentality 40 years earlier.

No, the purpose of this book is to try and isolate what might be called the *essence* of the Volkswagen. We want to ponder just why so many Americans—and their motoring colleagues worldwide—embraced the Beetle so tenaciously.

Why did so many—male and female—speak of their Beetles in affectionate, even loving terms? Why did owners feel such a kinship with other Beetle drivers? Why did the Beetle succeed so resoundingly in the U.S. market, when so many competitors—British, German, Italian, French—ultimately failed? (And in many cases, failed dramatically.)

Few people who were alive at the time of the Beetle's rise to prominence need to be reminded of its appearance. Many described the basic two-door sedan, with its doubly rounded profile, as an "ugly duckling." (Volkswagen later capitalized upon that supposedly derisive label, rather than make any vain attempt to dispute it.)

As everyone would eventually realize, however, that strange shape was destined to change little over the next three decades. Volkswagen promoted its continuous sequence of mechanical and detail improvements, but the long-lived flock of VW sedans looked roughly the same from the 1930s into the 1990s.

Who could have imagined back in 1949, when that pair of Beetles arrived in New York, that in 1972 the Beetle would beat the Model T Ford's record for production. And later yet, even after the Beetle ceased to be marketed in America, that the 20-millionth example would roll off one of VW's global assembly lines.

Not unlike that Model T Ford of 1909-27, air-cooled Volkswagens weren't limited to ordinary driving. Some were transformed into dune buggies and Baja Bugs, rail dragsters and hopped-up hot rods. VW engines found their way into airplanes, lawnmowers, and farm vehicles. Scores of replicars employed the VW's air-cooled, horizontally-opposed four-cylinder engine, and the car's platform frame.

Collegians stuffed themselves into Beetles. Daredevils piloted them across waterways. Instantly recognizable by nearly anyone in the world, they even turned up in musical productions and works of art.

After taking a close look at the past, we need to find out why, two decades after the last Beetles went on sale in the United States, thousands of collectors are pursuing them as hobby vehicles. We also want to learn why ordinary motorists still seek them out as regular transportation. And most of all, why both groups cling to their Beetles just as avidly as did the original owners, decades ago.

There are plenty of practical reasons why VWs have enjoyed such a surge of revived popularity, and remain collectible today. Some of them are the same reasons why they gained favor in the *first* place: reasonable price, easy availability of parts, rugged construction. Surprising numbers of young people still want a Beetle as their first car—just like their parents or grandparents might have done, when those very same Beetles were brand new.

Beetles were the prime choice for collectibility in 1976, when the Vintage Volkswagen Club of America was formed. They were virtually the *only* choice back in 1955, when the Volkswagen Club of America came into existence, soon calling itself the "fastest growing automobile club in the world." Not only did that group publish an informative newsletter (*VW Autoist*), which continues today, but it chartered a succession of local clubs.

Some contemporary organizations focus solely on the air-cooled era—which includes the luscious Karmann Ghia coupes and convertibles of 1956-74. Others open their doors to all comers.

Purists prefer the first-generation Beetles: especially the split-window sedans, but also the oval-window models of 1953-57. Many scoff at Volkswagens with square rear windows, which debuted in 1958. They don't even want to hear about VWs with water-cooled engines, or front-mounted powerplants. Super Beetles of the early 1970s, while sought-after by some as practical daily drivers, are scorned by others as overblown aberrations of Dr. Porsche's original design. In their eyes, a Super lacks the basic Beetle's charms.

Microbuses have their own eager following—especially the early DeLuxe models, with their two-tone paint jobs, multi-pane skylight windows, and fabric sun roofs. Early camper buses, with their birch wood trim and fitted sinks, also draw continued interest. So do such oddities as VW's seldom-seen six-passenger pickup trucks.

Some of the remaining buses are even customized in the style of the "hippie" era, when Microbuses were the transport of choice for out-of-the-mainstream folks from Haight-Ashbury to Woodstock. Through the 1960s, in fact, VW buses became a virtual "trademark" of the burgeoning

Volkswagen caused a sensation at the North American International Auto Show in Detroit, in January 1994, by exhibiting a modern-day rendition of the Beetle. To everyone's surprise, VW later decided to bring the Concept 1 into production—and call it the New Beetle.

counterculture, popular for their blend of economy and practicality—and also for the ease with which their slab-sided bodies could be adorned with colorful decorations.

Then too, who could ignore "The Thing," an open-air vehicle derived from Volkswagen's military Kübelwagen. Soundly derided by safety advocates in the 1970s, it nevertheless has established a base of avid owners.

Customized Beetles—"Cal-look" sedans and low riders, for instance—have their own collectibility niche. Even the water-cooled Rabbits—especially sporty GTIs and fancy Cabriolets of the 1980s—have their adherents.

At the same time, we need to delve into reasons why the Volkswagen company has not been able—or willing—to produce any other vehicle that even began to approach the popularity of the Beetle. Why didn't the Rabbit catch on? Or the Scirocco and Corrado, with their appealing blend of fun and performance? Those latter-day cars have their fans, but far smaller in number than those who revere the original design.

In short, how did that plain little critter, the Beetle, turn into what many consider to be the most phenomenal—if bizarre—success story in automotive history?

No other single car model, after all—with the exception of Ford's Model T—has played such a major role in changing the automotive world. More than any other make, the Volkswagen Beetle paved the way for the import invasion of the 1950s and '60s. That success, in turn, affected the types of vehicles turned out by Detroit's automakers—starting with the compacts and broadening later into subcompacts.

No other import automaker even came close to Volkswagen's sales totals in the 1950s and '60s. Only the Japanese succeeded in threatening the domestic automakers, and not until much later.

Homely? To most eyes, the Beetle certainly was—yet millions saw it as cute, and even cuddly. The subject of jokes and derision? Beetles suffered them all, emerging nobly in the end. Nothing quite like it ever came out of the automotive world. Most likely, nothing ever will. Let's, then, look back. Let's remember.

Chapter 1

How It All Began

Promised to the German citizenry during Adolf Hitler's odious regime, the Volkswagen (literally, "people's car") not only survived the horrors of war, but rose to become a global cultural icon. As Germany struggled to establish a foothold in the postwar world, no one would have believed that this homely little sedan—an orphaned relic of Nazi history—had any future whatsoever. Only a fool, in the late 1940s, would have foreseen a star-studded destiny for the humble Volkswagen.

That the VW survived at all was due to a curious blend of chance and circumstance. Volkswagen development through the years prior to World War II had made good sense to Germany, but its rebirth in the postwar era ranks as little short of a miracle.

Porsche Ponders a Small Car for the Average Family

Credit for the creation of the Volkswagen goes squarely to Ferdinand Porsche, the renowned designer best known for rear-engined sports cars that appeared after the war. Without the prodding of Hitler himself during the 1930s, though, the project never would have borne fruit. And without the nearly-miraculous guidance of Heinz Nordhoff *after* World War II, it never would have become more than a footnote in automotive history.

Porsche was not alone in coming up with the concept for a people's car—one that could be owned by the mass of German citizens. Those citizens had endured severe economic hardship during the 1920s, as inflation soared to unheard-of levels. Then came the Great Depression, felt around the world.

To the ordinary working person in Germany, even more than in most other European nations, car ownership seemed a far-off fantasy.

Once development began, Porsche took advantage of ideas from other experts. They included engineer Hans Ledwinka (who'd developed the rear-engined Tatra in Czechoslovakia), as well as aeronautical pioneer Edmund Rumpler.

Hitler and Porsche reportedly first met, briefly, in 1924—at a race near Stuttgart, when Hitler was a minor political figure. His rise to power was nearly a decade away. At the time, in any case, Porsche was occupied with far different tasks. Late in 1930, Porsche formed a new company: *Dr.-Ing. h.c. Ferdinand Porsche GmbH*. Porsche's start-up staff included body designer Erwin Komenda and air-cooled engine expert Joseph Kales, as well as his own son, Ferry Porsche.

Working largely on his own, in 1931 Porsche sketched a vehicle dubbed Project 12. He wanted it to be powered by an air-cooled three-cylinder engine. After a few detours and false starts, that basic notion would eventually evolve into the Volkswagen Beetle.

Most of the car's basic elements were defined early in the process. Designers chose a rear-mounted engine, for one, partly because it eliminated the need for a long, heavy driveshaft. To install a rear engine without harming safe weight distribution, however, such an engine would have to be lightweight. That meant extensive use of aluminum and magnesium castings.

A horizontally-opposed (flat) cylinder configuration allowed a short crankshaft, and would mate neatly with the proposed rear transaxle (an integrated transmission and differential). Known as the "Boxermotor," which suggests two pugilists throwing endless blows back and forth, the flat engine would become a Volkswagen hallmark—and later find its way into Porsche sports cars, exotic Ferraris, and even Japanese-built Subarus.

Air cooling allowed omission of a radiator. Owners would never have to worry about coolant freeze-ups.

Instead of a separate body and frame, the car would have a platform-type chassis with a central backbone and integral floorpan. Torsion bars were chosen for the suspension, complemented by swing axles at the rear. Porsche registered his own torsion-bar patent on August 10, 1931. Torsion bars were an old idea, having been used on British army vehicles as early as 1906, but Porsche's version was innovative.

Early Prototypes, for Zündapp and NSU

Rather than pursuing this small-car project further right then, Porsche took on work for such companies as Wanderer and Zündapp. Dr. Fritz Neumeyer, head of Zündapp

Dr. Ferdinand Porsche, an early proponent of air-cooling, designed this Zündapp Type 12 prototype in 1932, with a water-cooled five-cylinder radial engine. Mounted behind the rear axle, the 1200-cc engine developed 26 horsepower. (Volkswagen)

Motor Cycle Works at Nüremberg—one of the biggest makers of motorcycles—liked Porsche's Project 12 idea. However, Neumeyer preferred a water-cooled, five-cylinder engine to Porsche's proposed air-cooled, three-cylinder unit.

In 1932, Porsche built his first prototype for Zündapp, named *Volksauto* (which *also* translates to "people's car"). The result was a far cry from the configuration that would later become familiar. Oh, the fastback shape already showed touches of the eventual Beetle; but mounted behind the rear axle was the requisite water-cooled, 1200-cc radial five-cylinder engine. The gearbox sat ahead of the rear axle.

Three prototypes were produced, in a shroud of secrecy. Reutter, a Stuttgart coachbuilder, created the wood/aluminum bodies, and prototypes were ready in April 1932. (A third prototype was a cabriolet, rather than a sedan.)

Initial tests were not promising. The engine overheated and was not readily accessible for repairs. Transmission troubles were noted, and several torsion bars broke. Not that it mattered. Neumeyer quickly cancelled the project, deeming it too costly.

Late in 1932, Fritz von Falkenhayn, the managing director of NSU—another motorcycle builder—hired Porsche to further develop his own small car. That became the Type 32 (though prototype construction did not begin until January 1934).

Again, three prototypes were built, but clearly exhibiting what would later evolve into the basic Beetle shape. The first two Project 12 NSUs were built by Drauz, using "Wey-mann" construction techniques (artificial leather atop a wood superstructure). The third was all-steel, done by Reutter. Equipped with 1.5-liter air-cooled, horizontally opposed four-cylinder engines that developed 20 horsepower, the NSU prototypes reportedly could reach 72 mph.

Various features were destined to arrive on the production Beetle later on, including a central tube platform, fully independent suspension, and torsion springs with a swing rear axle. The NSU cars were bigger and roomier than the Zündapp project vehicles, their floors sitting higher off the ground.

Most important, they could be built cheaply. On the negative side, the air-cooled engines were noisy—a flaw that would not be fixed for quite a while. (And which, to more delicate ears, never would be fully acceptable.)

Due to legal problems with Fiat, NSU could not go into the automobile business at that time. Instead, it returned to a low-cost "people's" motorcycle.

Porsche then turned to design of Auto-Union's rear-engine Grand Prix racing cars. One of those won the Vanderbilt Cup in Long Island, New York. Still interested in the low-end market, as well as in racing machines, Porsche visited Michigan, to observe inexpensive cars being built.

Adolf Hitler and the People's Car

Hitler took over as Chancellor of Germany in 1933. At that year's Berlin Auto Show, he hinted at the prospect of a car for the masses. Not only did Hitler yearn to create the

Autobahnen (high-speed highway network), he wanted a "people's car" for the ordinary workingman's family.

Although Adolf Hitler enjoyed automobiles, he never drove himself—not uncommon in those days, for people of importance as well as ordinary citizens. More significantly for propaganda purposes, Hitler knew full well that the very idea of car ownership—even *potential* ownership—was powerful. Promise the German worker a motorcar at some ambiguous near-future date, and he just might more readily accept certain hardships—or even horrors—in the interim.

During his rise to power, Hitler relied on Jacob Werlin, a Mercedes agent, for automotive advice. Because Werlin was on the Daimler-Benz board, he knew about Porsche's talents. In autumn of 1933, Werlin and Porsche met in Berlin. Hitler himself joined in that meeting, at the Kaiserhof Hotel. In talks with Porsche, Hitler presented his own ideas for the project.

Porsche was chosen for the job, in part because of his prior design work on those Auto-Union racing cars. One obstacle appeared almost immediately. Hitler insisted on a maximum price for the car of 1,000 Reichsmarks (about $400). That was barely half the cost of the cheapest regular automobile available in Germany.

Opels came closest to that target figure. At the 1937 Berlin Motor Show, in fact, Opel exhibited a 1,400-mark automobile, billed as the "economical car for the small man." As development progressed, rival German automakers did not look kindly upon the Porsche design—or the whole concept of a people's automobile—viewing the state-supported program as unfair competition.

Equivalent to the price of a small motorcycle in 1934, the 1,000-mark figure was based on a proposed production run of 50,000 cars. Calculating costs, Porsche figured his design would have to sell for 1,550 Reichsmarks—far too expensive for Hitler's plan.

Regardless of that discrepancy, before long Chancellor Hitler ordered the *Reichsverband der Duetschen Automobilindustrie* (Reich Association of the German Automobile Industry, or RDA) to have Dr. Porsche develop such a vehicle. Finally, at the 1935 Berlin Auto Show, Hitler announced that Porsche would design it.

Meanwhile, early in 1934, Porsche had issued a proposal to the Reich Ministry of Transport: an "Exposé concerning the construction of a German people's car." Hitler's order of June 1934 spelled out that the eventual vehicle had to meet the following requirements:

• Cruising speed of 100 kilometers per hour (62 mph), thus deemed "fit for the Führer's autobahns."

• Fuel economy of at least 30 miles per gallon.

• Four or five seats, "because we can't separate children from their parents."

• An air-cooled engine, because "not every rural doctor has a garage" to keep his car from freezing in winter. Of course, ordinary folk were even *less* likely to possess garage space.

The German "people's car" also would have to function with minimal repair and maintenance. European roads were harsh: typically narrow and winding, and suffering uneven pavement surfaces. So, a people's car had to be tough.

Porsche designed this prototype for NSU in 1933-34. Its 1450-cc, overhead-valve, air-cooled rear engine made 20 horsepower (DIN rating). Reutter built the wood/leather body. (Volkswagen)

Details had yet to be revised, but this 1935 prototype exhibited the Beetle shape that would later attract millions of car-buyers around the globe.

A true people's car also had to be easy to produce in vast quantities. Replacement parts needed to be cheap and easy to obtain. Not only would such an automobile have to be low-priced initially, it had to be inexpensive to operate. European incomes were considerably lower than those in the United States, despite the Great Depression that American workers were suffering. Gasoline and rubber had to be imported into Germany, too.

Even during the depths of the Depression, millions of American workers managed to own an automobile—though typically an older one. For most Europeans, auto ownership was a distant dream, at best.

Because of the political ramifications, the Volkswagen had to be developed and tested (and financed) in a highly strict manner. Therefore, it became a project under the Society of German Automobile Manufacturers (even though that group wasn't really in charge). On June 22, 1934, Porsche got a contract from the RDA to turn out a prototype in 10 months, being paid 20,000 Reichsmarks ($8,000) per month.

Given a go-ahead, Porsche proceeded with an evolution of his Zündapp/NSU ideas. Early in 1936, Dr. Porsche and his son Ferry had the first prototype ready. Two "Series 3" cars (sedan and convertible) were built—a little late. Problems with engine overheating, and with the torsion-bar setup, had to be dealt with first.

Final prototypes were ready late in 1936, with body design generally credited to Erwin Komenda. Headlights re-mained in the nose, and rear-hinged ("suicide") doors were installed—still a common style, even in American automobiles. Extensive testing was planned, under the auspices of the German automaker's association. A large louvered area was deemed necessary for engine cooling, leaving no room for a back window. Early designs also had canted doors. Those were changed to vertical pillars, well before production commenced.

Ferry Porsche (wearing cap), son of Ferdinand, took the wheel of this V3 prototype convertible in 1935. (Volkswagen)

● Ferdinand Porsche (1875-1951) ●

Born September 3, 1875, in Maffersdort, Northern Bohemia (later Austria), Ferdinand Porsche served as an apprentice in his father's metalsmith shop. Early on, he took a liking to automobiles and electricity. Soon, he left the metals trade and took a job at Vienna Electrical Company. Porsche also took classes at a technical college.

Born in 1875, Ferdinand Porsche began design work in 1931 on a small, low-cost car for the general public. Result: the Volkswagen Beetle. Porsche became better known after his death in 1951, for the sports car that still bears his name. (Volkswagen)

Automotive work came early. In 1900, Porsche created an electric vehicle, with separate motors at each front wheel. Developed for Ludwig Lohner, a Viennese coachbuilder, this electric car went to the 1900 Paris World's Fair, and also to the Paris Exhibition. Front-wheel-drive, it had a range of only 32 miles, but managed a speed of 9 mph.

Drafted into the Austro-Hungarian army, Porsche served as chauffeur for Archduke Franz Ferdinand. A civilian again in 1905, Porsche became technical director of *Oesterreicher-Daimler Motoren Werke* (Austro-Daimler), replacing Daimler's own son, Paul.

Porsche's hurriedly-completed design for the Mixt deleted the former vehicle's batteries. Instead, he adopted a Daimler internal-combustion engine to generate power for the two electric "hub" motors. That one was capable of 55 mph. The Mixt sold well, and established Porsche's credentials as a designer.

The foremost Daimler motorcar at the time was the Maja, named for one of the daughters of financier Emil Jellinek, who'd helped secure financing for the company. (Jellinek's other daughter, Mercedes, was immortalized by the Mercedes-Benz nameplate.)

Even in his early years, Porsche favored a rear-mounted engine and rear-wheel-drive. That configuration simply made perfect sense, putting the power source right where it was used (at the drive wheels).

Three of Porsche's cars ran in the week-long Prince Henry rally, Berlin to Budapest, in 1909. Each vehicle had a driver and three passengers, and each finished without any penalty.

Porsche's next projects were air-cooled aircraft engines. In 1917, he received an honorary doctorate from Vienna Technical University.

After The Great War (World War I), Porsche foresaw the need for a small, cheap car for the masses. More important, he knew it could be accomplished, as technology improved. His proposal for such a concept fell on deaf ears at Austro-Daimler. The reason was simple: There was more money to be made in big cars—an obstacle that continues to plague development of low-cost vehicles, even in modern times.

Turning again to competition, Porsche designed a 1-liter sports car to run in the 1922 Targa Florio, in Sicily. His cars finished first and second. Next up: a 2-liter version, also built for Count Sascha Kolowrat, which hit 106 mph.

Porsche left Austro-Daimler and took it easy for a while.

Then, he became technical director at *Daimler Motoren Gesellschaft*, in Stuttgart. While there, he created a 7.2-liter touring car. He also further developed a 2-liter supercharged sports car, which won 21 of its 27 races.

Through the early 1920s, Porsche envisioned a small car for the average man. His vision inevitably included an air-cooled rear engine, swing axle, and torsion bar suspension.

Porsche saw the creation of small cars as a challenge. By the mid-1920s, he had an idea for a horizontally-opposed rear engine. Daimler and Benz merged in 1926, and Porsche remained as technical director.

For Daimler-Benz, Porsche designed a small, almost beetle-like car with an air-cooled, 1.3-liter flat rear engine and swing-type rear axle. Mercedes-Benz actually built such a machine in 1933-34: the Type 130. Daimler-Benz was ready for a small car, but this one was deemed too radical. So, they turned instead to a front-engined, water-cooled automobile.

Porsche returned to Austria in October 1929, and soon was named chief engineer at Steyr, in Vienna. Then, on December 1, 1930, Porsche opened his own consulting firm, *Konstruktionsbüro für Motoren-und Fahrzeugbau Dr.-Ing. h.c. Ferdinand Porsche GmbH* (in other words, the Porsche Bureau), on Kronenstrasse in Stuttgart.

Porsche's chief designer in the early 1930s was Karl Rabe. His first client was the producer of the Wanderer. That vehicle made use of Porsche's ingenious torsion bar design. Porsche also did prototypes that went into Auto-Union race cars—one a Beetle-like fastback, but with a front engine.

After developing the KdF-Wagen, which led to the legendary Volkswagen, Porsche's fortune faded for a time. After World War II, in July 1945, he was ordered to Frankfurt for interrogation by the Americans, regarding his Nazi connections. Throughout his life, before and during the Nazi regime, Porsche had been unwaveringly non-political. Nevertheless, both Ferdinand and his son Ferry were imprisoned in France for nearly two years.

After their release in 1947, father and son turned to the rear-engined sports cars that continue to bear their name. In addition to engine placement, some versions of those cars—including the early Type 356—show more than a hint of Volkswagen influence, and even Volkswagen componentry. One Porsche model, the 914 of the early 1970s, was in fact largely VW-based.

Not until September 1950 did Ferdinand Porsche see the Volkswagen factory for the first time. He died on January 30, 1951, at age 75.

One of Porsche's early creations was the Lohner Chaise, an electric vehicle with motors mounted inside the front hubs. Porsche won a Grand Prize for this design. (Volkswagen)

One of 30 prototypes hand-built in 1937, this sedan had a 985-cc engine that developed 23.5 horsepower at 3000 rpm. (Volkswagen)

Auto critics didn't all fall in love with the design. Some dubbed the cars "ugly ducklings," not unlike the barbs aimed at Beetles when they arrived in America, much later.

Visiting America for the second time, Dr. Porsche met with auto-industry leaders—including Henry Ford. During his visit, Porsche also sought engineers of German ancestry to come back and help set up the factory.

"Venetian blinds" not only provided a rearward view on prototypes from 1936 (right) and 1937 (left), but doubled as engine air intake louvers. An inside window separated the passenger and engine compartments. (Volkswagen)

By October 12, 1936, road tests began for the first prototypes: V1 sedan and V2 convertible (built by Reutter, with the "V" standing for *Versuch*, or experimental). After testing three "VW3" prototypes for 30,000 miles, the Society of German Automobile Manufacturers recommended production of 30 more test models. Their report indicates that the initial cars "showed qualities which appear to recommend themselves for further development."

That next batch of 30 cars was rigorously evaluated on the *Autobahn*, as well as on rural roads. Drivers charted mileage, fuel consumption and speed.

Later, in 1937, the original design progressed into Series 30, featuring shorter rear side windows. Thirty of those prototypes were produced at the Daimler-Benz plant at Sindelfingen, with that company's assistance. Some of the work was done by Reutter.

Before long, those largely handmade automobiles (including one convertible) were being driven throughout Germany—by Nazi storm troopers, no less. In all, 200 soldiers drove the early cars some 1.5 million miles, without serious problems. Though considered a secret project, the vehicles—still lacking rear windows—were seen by citizens all over Germany.

Production Is in the Cards—Factory Site Needed

By 1937, it had been determined that a separate government company would be needed to complete development and enter into production. Therefore, on May 28, 1937, the Association for the Development of the German People's Car (*Gesellschaft für Vorbereitung des Deutschen Volkswagens*) was formed. Porsche himself served as general manager of the development company, and the government provided 480,000 marks as start-up capital.

As *U.S. News & World Report* later explained it, "Hitler decreed that Germany must develop a cheap, sturdy automobile for the man of modest means. No ceiling was put on development costs, and they ran up to 21 million dollars."

The fledgling company was financed with 50 million Reichsmarks from the *Deutsche Arbeitsfront* (German Labor Front), run by Robert Ley, Hitler's Minister of Labor. Ley

Top speed of the 1937 prototypes was 62 mph. Subsequent prototypes gained a real back window and abandoned the early "suicide" doors. (Volkswagen)

Adolf Hitler (center) himself presided over the laying of the factory cornerstone on May 26, 1938. Cars were to be produced under the auspices of Kraft durch Freude ("Strength Through Joy"), a Nazi recreational organization. (Volkswagen)

Beetle prototypes in 1938 were ready for production, with front-hinged doors and a back window. (Volkswagen)

Dr. Ferdinand Porsche (right), heading the "Volkswagen" project at Adolf Hitler's direction, attended the cornerstone-laying extravaganza. Hitler (seated) promoted the "people's car" as one element in his propaganda campaign. Although development began as a private venture in Porsche's Stuttgart engineering offices in 1931, Hitler seized upon it for political purposes after coming to power in 1933. (Volkswagen)

At a glance, the 1938 Type 60 prototype looks little different from the Beetles that would roll out of the Wolfsburg factory after the war. (Phil Hall)

Three hand-built KdF-Wagen prototypes, including a convertible, appeared at the cornerstone-laying ceremony for the new factory in Wolfsburg, in May 1938. (Volkswagen)

Instruments sat toward the center of the dashboard in the 1938 prototype, matching a diagram of the four-speed transmission's shift pattern. (Volkswagen)

Ready for production in 1938, the air-cooled, horizontally-opposed engine of the KdF-Wagen displaced only 985 cubic centimeters and ran on 5.6:1 compression, developing 27.5 horsepower. (Volkswagen)

had headed *Autobahn* construction and now served as chief of the *Kraft durch Freude* ("Strength through Joy") movement—a Nazi recreational organization. Soon, the group's initials (KdF) would be immortalized on the nameplates of the first Volkswagen automobiles.

The long-familiar symbol (gear teeth surrounding "VW") was designed about 1937 by Porsche chief engineer Franz X. Reimspiess, who earned a 100 mark bonus for his efforts.

Hitler wanted to build 1.5 million cars per year, in what would be the biggest auto plant in the world. Dr. Bodo Lafferentz, an economics expert, was assigned to select the factory locale, which needed access to railroads and canals. The founding group settled on a factory site in the town of Fallersleben, along the Mitteland Canal in Lower Saxony (near Hanover).

Count Werner von Schulenburg, who owned the 14th century Wolfsburg Castle in that area, was forced to sell property to the government. A portion of an adjoining estate also was confiscated. Plant design was assigned to Peter Koller, an engineer at the University of Brunswick. Koller also planned the workers' city that Hitler had in mind, which was to contain residential facilities for 15,000 families.

That workers' town surrounding the plant was for a time called *KdF-Stadt*, or *Kraft durch Freude Stadt*. After the war, it would be renamed Wolfsburg—a name as familiar to VW enthusiasts as their own birthplaces.

On May 26, 1938, Adolf Hitler himself laid the cornerstone for the Wolfsburg factory. A massive ceremony drew 70,000 people. Hitler, of course, made extensive use of massive ceremonies as a propaganda tool, with plenty of pomp and circumstance. Naturally, this new "people's car" deserved no less.

A special convertible was built for the occasion. Hermann Goering, second-ranking official in the Third Reich, liked the convertible, but production was not contemplated. Hitler announced that the sedan would indeed be called the "KdF-Wagen."

Two days later, Hitler's troops entered Czechoslovakia, setting the stage for war. Nevertheless, work began on the plant at Wolfsburg in mid-1938, with the first cars scheduled to emerge late the following year. The factory was registered in October, as *Volkswagenwerk GmbH*.

Even before the Wolfsburg plant was completed in 1938-39, some 124 KdF-Wagens were assembled at the Daimler-Benz plant. After testing, they were sold to Nazi officials.

Manufacture of the 1938 prototype could have begun almost immediately, but the German aggression that brought about World War II called a halt to Hitler's notion of a car for every worker. (Volkswagen)

By the time production commenced in 1938, Porsche had been refining his design. Type 38 included a rear window, absent from earlier prototypes. Formerly protruding in style, the headlights now sat flush in the fenders. The hood lid was now full-length, and doors were front-hinged (no longer "suicide-style"). By now, the later-to-be-familiar profile was well-developed. Initial engines measured 985-cc and were rated at 23 horsepower.

A batch of Volkswagens (some with sun roofs) paraded in Munich in 1938. Italy's dictator, Benito Mussolini, even sent 3,000 unemployed workers to toil at the Wolfsburg plant in Germany.

At first, the KdF-Wagen was promoted for the requisite 990 Reichsmarks. Insurance and delivery charges added 250 marks more, despite the fact that the car would have to be picked up at the plant—if a person were fortunate enough to get one, that is. A sun roof added another 60 marks.

Equivalent to about $396 (U.S.), those 990 marks amounted to about 800 hours of toil for a German worker. How could such a worker come up with such a sum? He

VW-1410-5

After putting the civilian sedan on hold, the Wolfsburg factory turned to production of military vehicles, including the Kübelwagen (shown) and a companion amphibious Schwimmwagen. Bodies came from outside suppliers, but the rear-mounted engine and chassis were produced in Wolfsburg. Fewer than 50,000 were built from 1940 to 1945. (Volkswagen)

The amphibious Schwimmwagen used a 30-horsepower, 1131-cc rear engine. It used four-wheel-drive on land, and a retractable propeller on water. (Volkswagen)

couldn't. So, the company devised a coupon-purchase plan (see sidebar). Workers obtained 5RM stamps, attempting to save them until the 990RM total was reached. The company collected some $112 million in public subscriptions before the war, but not a single German customer got a car.

Still named KdF-Wagen, the cars appeared at the 1939 Berlin Auto Show. Official designation aside, the car quickly adopted the "Volkswagen" nickname that it had earned early on. German workers—like toilers elsewhere in Europe—obviously craved motorcars, even if destiny was about to prevent them from obtaining one.

World War II Ends Plan for People's Car

Whatever the name, serious production of the "people's car" was not meant to be—not under the Third Reich, at any rate. In September 1939, German troops marched into eastern Europe. World War II had begun. Along the menacing path to the dreadful destruction that followed, Hitler ordered that the KdF-Wagen prototypes be destroyed.

Before the plant was finished and ready to turn out sedans and sun roofs, the organization turned to military contracts—and to the production of Porsche-designed military vehicles. Production of KdF-Wagens ostensibly

began in April 1939, but only 210 cars left the factory before war production was fully underway in 1940.

Production shifted instead to the Type 82 Kübelwagen (which translates to "bucket car," or "tub car"), an all-terrain reconnaissance vehicle for the military. A total of 50,788 of those were built from 1940-45. Comparable to

Only a prototype of this Type 823 simulated armored vehicle was built. The strange creation evidently was designed as a tank dummy, for infantry training. (Volkswagen)

● Saving for a Volkswagen ●

Few Germans in the 1930s had the means to purchase and maintain a car of any kind. Even if a Volkswagen could be obtained for the requisite 990 Reichsmarks, how could the prewar organization hope to sell more than a trickle? The answer seemed logical enough: make the customer save the money first, and get the car later.

To accomplish this feat of making a car available to every German worker, the Nazi Labor Front initiated a stamp-purchase plan on August 1, 1938. In theory, at least, any worker could purchase stamps each week. Finally, when his stamp "card" was full, he'd become the owner of a Volkswagen.

Cash was unacceptable, and no dealers or distributors were involved. Cars could only be bought through the Nazi Labor offices, and only by presenting one's filled stamp book.

During the late Thirties, 336,668 Germans dutifully pasted stamps into their books, hoping for a car one day. Although the total number of "savers" was smaller than Hitler anticipated, it was still a sizable proportion of the employed populace.

At first, those workers bought a stamp each week for five Reichsmarks (about $2). Soon, the amount changed to $2 per month. Simple math reveals that at such a sluggish rate, it would take many years to save enough stamps to cover the 990 Reichsmark price.

Not that it mattered. Not a single car ever was delivered to any of the savers. World War II scuttled that goal, before civilian auto production ever got started. By then, some 280 million Reichsmarks ($112 million) had been paid into the company coffers, in installments. The average saver had deposited some 400 marks. That total sum wound up in the KdF account at the Bank of German Labor, which—due to its location just inside the Russian occupation zone—fell into Soviet hands after the defeat of the Third Reich.

Several years after the war, quite a few Germans presented their collections of saved-up stamps, insisting that the revived VW company honor its prewar commitment. Formed in 1948, The Society for the Relief of Former Volkswagen Savers was led by a former Nazi named Karl Stolz. The savers sued the postwar Volkswagen company, their efforts directed by attorney Gerard Richter. They demanded that VW pay them the difference between the prewar retail price of a car (had it gone on sale) and the production cost of a 1954 model.

Speaking for the company, Heinz Nordhoff insisted that the savers, "like all Germans who survived the war, will have to take certain losses." After all, he cautioned, those people had "put their money and their trust in the 1,000-year Hitler Reich. Why should they profit through this trust while others lost all they had?"

Late in 1954, the German High Federal Court at Karlsrühe rejected the savers' claim. The Supreme Court decided that the West German government, serving as trustee of the revived company, was not bound by the Nazis' promises or contracts. In the Court's opinion, the German Labor Front—which collected the funds—was not strictly an agent of Volkswagen. Therefore, it was declared "evident that Volkswagen shares no co-liability."

That wasn't the end of the case. Finally, in October 1961, Volkswagen allowed those people a 600 Deutschmark credit toward a new car—or 100 marks in cash. No court had ordered Volkswagen to make restitution, but the company elected to offer one anyway.

Though different in execution, and vastly divergent in ultimate result, Volkswagen's coupon savings plan is reminiscent of the way Model T Fords were sold for a time. American workers also pasted stamps into a book each week. One big difference: when those books were filled, an actual Model T Ford was waiting to be driven home.

the quickly-developed American Jeep and its offshoots, the Type 82 was a simple open box with totally slab-sided body panels.

Erwin Rommel, later dubbed the "Desert Fox" for his military exploits in North Africa, was an early proponent of the Kübelwagen. Rommel quickly envisioned its potential for desert warfare. The sturdy vehicles also proved useful during wartime Russian winters. (In a curious aside later in the war, which testifies to the vehicle's presumed durability, Allied GIs decided that as a medium of exchange, a Kübelwagen was worth *two* American-built Jeeps.)

The company also built 14,276 Schwimmwagens—amphibious vehicles with a propeller, engine and exhaust snorkels, and even a paddle (just in case). Named Type 166, these four-wheel-drive wet-or-dry machines used a 30-horsepower, 1131-cc engine. A KdF Type 87 sedan also was produced during the war. Beetle-shaped but with four-wheel-drive and tractor-style tires, it was called the *Kommandeurswagen* ("commanding officer's vehicle"). Some military vehicles—Kübelwagen or sedan—even were modified to run on gas generated by charcoal or wood.

Bombing of Wolfsburg began in 1940, but the plant suffered little harm in the early years of the war. Later, in April 1944, the factory was hit by three bomber flights, and badly damaged. "In the closing years of the war," said *U.S. News & World Report*, "the Wolfsburg plant became a primary target of Allied bombers."

By war's end, in May 1945, only about one-third of the plant was left standing. Who, then, could have dreamed that within those shattered walls lay the foundation for a global phenomenon? Who could even have predicted that 1,785 hastily-assembled cars would roll out of the factory door by the end of 1945?

American advertisers during World War II ridiculed the idea of a German "people's car," especially when it became part of the Third Reich's war machine.

OWNER COMMENTS: Richard Rymer

"In January 1953," says Richard Rymer of Kent, Ohio, "I was assigned to Germany by my employer, an American military electronics equipment manufacturer." Rymer went to Germany "to train technical personnel of the U.S. Air Force, the NATO air forces and, eventually, the German Air Force.

"In the summer of 1955," he continues, "my wife and I took an overnight train to Wolfsburg and toured the Volkswagen factory, where we took delivery of our first VW, a sedan. When we returned to the U.S. in July 1958, we brought with us a new VW as well as a new Mercedes-Benz.

"After buying some five or six more new VWs over the succeeding years, we bought no more after the Rabbit was introduced in 1980—partly because the new model did not have adequate headroom for my 6'4" frame, but mostly because the 'magic' of the original car had been lost.

"I have owned some fascinating cars over the years but, for me, the original VW as designed by Ferdinand Porsche remains the most enchanting car ever to come off a drawing board. I have been under its spell ever since I saw one for the first time on the last day of January 1953. Perhaps it was a case of love at first sight."

Rymer owns an unrestored 1957 sedan, "the last year for the 'classic' models with the oval rear window, with low mileage and all the paperwork since it was delivered by South Import Motors of Chicago. The car is original, just as it came from Wolfsburg, with black finish and red interior." It's stored through the winter.

After retiring in 1993 as a university psychologist, Rymer became more active in several antique auto clubs. He's a member of VVWCA, VWCA and AACA, and a director of the Goodyear club.

Chapter 2

Beetles Go Into Production

When the German army finally surrendered to the Allies, in May 1945, the country lay in shambles. So did the factory at Wolfsburg—no longer known as KdF-Stadt. Germany was split into three zones by the Allied occupation forces. The Wolfsburg plant sat in the British zone, about 100 miles west of Berlin—but only a few miles from the Russian sector.

After a brief takeover by American troops, the plant went under British military control. Meanwhile, it had suffered additional damage from vandalism by newly-liberated forced laborers. In August 1945, the Royal Electrical and Mechanical Engineers set up a vehicle repair shop in that derelict KdF-Wagen factory.

As part of the aftermath of war, the plant was headed for demolition—so ordered by the British Commission in charge of the area. After all, no one had any reason to believe that it could be worth much. In an attempt to avert that threat, the remaining workers hastily began to assemble a couple of vehicles. As they followed orders to clear away the rubble, they also gathered usable, leftover components for that seemingly futile assembly task.

"Volkswagen's comeback began a few months after the war's end," *Time* magazine later explained. At that time, "some of its workers secretly brought the old prewar dies out of storage, and used a surviving heavy press to make two complete cars before the British, who controlled the occupation zone, were aware of it."

Instead of abandoning the site—and altering the course of automotive history in an incomprehensible way—it was transformed into a repair and assembly center. British Major Ivan Hirst, who ran the shop, quickly put his people to work building cars. Colonel C.R. Radclyffe was placed in charge of production.

Ferdinand Porsche was in Austria at this time and knew nothing of the situation. Not until the 1960s, when the British VW magazine *Safer Motoring* ran stories on the subject, did the general public learn fully of the British contribution to Volkswagen development.

Mechanics thus began to turn out Volkswagens in the final months of 1945, using repairable machinery and tooling, initially for use in the British motor pool. Much machinery had survived the war but was in bad shape. For instance, no overhead conveyors were available. Material shortages during that first winter forced a temporary plant closing.

In these early postwar years, workers lived in barracks. All of the first 1,785 vehicles were produced for military use, going to the Control Commission for Germany.

These first postwar automobiles continued the Type 38 design. The 1945 and early '46 models actually qualified as Type 51, however, with Kübelwagen axles and reduction gears, and high ground clearance. During the war, the original 985-cc engine had grown to 1131-cc size, to meet military specifications. That turned out to be a sensible displacement for the first civilian sedans.

Meanwhile, both the Russians and the French considered taking over the Volkswagen plant as an element of war reparations, but negotiations faltered. "British occupiers," *Time* later noted, "offered the remains of the equipment to British automakers and other businessmen of the Commonwealth. They all turned it down."

According to a British spokesman, not only was the VW ugly and noisy, it did not even "meet the fundamental

Soon after World War II ended, workers began to assemble sedans using leftover components, following the prewar design. Only 1,785 cars were produced in the final months of 1945. (Volkswagen)

Major Ivan Hirst, one of the two British officers in charge of early postwar production, drove the 1,000th Volkswagen off the Wolfsburg assembly line in March 1946. (Volkswagen)

technical requirements of a motorcar." Said Heinz Nordhoff, later to become savior of the operation: "Volkswagen didn't even smell good enough for the Russians."

Henry Ford II met with Colonel Radclyffe in March 1948, to consider buying both the plant and the rights to the car itself. Ford was even offered the VW factory for nothing. Ford chairman Ernest Breech reportedly declared that he thought it was "not worth a damn," and too great a risk for the American company.

Thus, the youthful grandson of the original Henry Ford tossed away an opportunity to get in on the ground floor of a phenomenon. Of course, that phenomenon would not take hold for another decade. Only a tiny handful of far-sighted observers could envision any prospect for VW's ultimate success.

Long before Ford's decision, in October 1946, the 10,000th Volkswagen had rolled off the line. Early models were sold mainly to occupation forces—mainly British and American—who snapped them up with a passion that would eventually be seen virtually everywhere in the world. Not until 1947 were Volkswagens offered to private parties.

Here's the shape that would become familiar to nearly everyone in the world over the next decade or two. This 1948 Beetle had semaphore turn signals and an outside-mounted horn.

Sales outside of Germany began early, if in modest numbers. In 1946-47, for instance, VW shipped 56 Beetles to Holland. By 1948, they were on sale in such countries as Denmark and Switzerland, the outlets growing steadily.

Rather than remaining in a collapsed state after the war, as many observers expected, the German auto industry began a rapid buildup in the late 1940s. Production included everything from the Goliath three-wheeler (with a two-cylinder engine) to the massive Mercedes-Benz, with Opels and American-style Hansas in between.

"When in the spring of 1949 the money reform occurred in Germany," said *Automotive News* in January 1950, "the industry swung into action like a well rehearsed team." Already, Volkswagenwerk was the biggest German producer, turning out 6,000 vehicles per month, with sales/service outlets "in almost every European country."

Nordhoff Arrives—True Production Begins

If the Volkswagen was to become a serious production automobile for sale to civilians, British officers weren't the best men to head the operation. An expert in engineering and marketing was needed. London was ready to turn the plant over to German management, under the leadership of the best available man.

Colonel Radclyffe found a perfect choice—Heinz Nordhoff—and called upon him to revitalize the Volkswagen factory and add some muscle to its production totals. By now a civilian, Ivan Hirst appointed Nordhoff, intending for him to take full charge as of August 1949 (when Hirst would leave permanently).

A former executive for Adam Opel AG, a General Motors subsidiary in Europe, Nordhoff (see sidebar) had traveled widely in the United States before the war, and spoke near-perfect English. Ironically, he'd had little contact with Volkswagens. Worse yet, he'd stated that he was "scornful" of the make, adding: "I wanted nothing to do with that cheap competition."

In fact, Nordhoff once described the original Volkswagen car as "a poor thing, cheap, ugly and inefficient." Its engine, he noted, had a life of only 10,000 miles, and exhibited "a noisy death rattle."

"If the British could have foreseen how Nordhoff would drive their own cars off the export markets," *Time* magazine accurately proclaimed several years later, "they might never have given him the job." Just as Volkswagen

At the Volkswagen factory in Wolfsburg, in the late 1940s, crankshafts were subjected to 100-percent inspection. (Volkswagen)

Workers test engines on stands at the Wolfsburg factory, late in the 1940s. (Volkswagen)

reached its Golden Age in the late 1950s and early '60s, compact British cars—surprisingly popular for a decade after World War II—were destined to fade into the footnotes of auto history.

When he took the helm on January 2, 1948, according to *Time*, Nordhoff "found the plant turning out four different models. To cut costs, he trimmed Volkswagen's design to only one engine and one chassis which would fit any one of five different types of bodies." The new director had "some of the original Porsche designs redrawn ten times," *Time* noted.

In the words of *Newsweek*, Nordhoff "rebuilt the Volkswagen plant along U.S. mass-production lines," initially living in a room in the factory. Working long and hard himself, Nordhoff led close to 7,000 workers, who could turn out 6,000 cars a month.

Nordhoff gave liberal benefits to workers, boosting pay scales as production rose. Among other goals, he wanted to improve Volkswagen quality, and to reduce the time required to build each car.

Nordhoff also installed a rigid cost-accounting system. "I told them their working methods and production were miserable," Nordhoff explained in 1954. "It was taking us 400 man-hours to produce one car. I told them we would cut this to 100 hours. They laughed at me. But today we do that."

On June 20, 1948, the Reichsmark was replaced by a new Deutschmark. This new currency exchanged at a little more than four to the U.S. dollar (one Deutschmark for every 10 old Reichsmarks turned in). If Volkswagen were to keep growing, the company had a compelling need for foreign currency. Therefore, Nordhoff gazed longingly toward the United States as a possible market. But not just yet.

In September 1949, the Control Commission for Germany withdrew, and British Occupation turned the factory over to the Federal Republic of Germany. By then, Beetles were rolling out of the factory gate at a rapidly-escalating rate. Volkswagen production hit 46,594 cars after one year, then doubled in 1950. The 100,000th car was assembled in March of that year. Output for 1951 totaled 135,970 cars (45 percent of all German production).

The half-millionth VW was produced in July 1953. To mark the occasion, a huge roulette wheel, with cars in place of numbers, was used to raffle off a host of prizes—including five VWs.

By now, the Volkswagen name was copyrighted, and the KdF-Wagen nomenclature forgotten. Not quite so dim in the public memory was the company's Nazi past. How could Volkswagen overcome the obvious drawback of being manufactured in Germany, when memories of World

● Heinz Nordhoff (1899-1968) ●

In one of many ironies that dot Volkswagen history, its rebirth occurred under the leadership of a man who'd called the early, cobbled-together Beetle "a wretched, ugly thing, a car with more defects than a dog has fleas."

Not everyone today remembers the name of the man responsible, during the early postwar era, for transforming Volkswagen from a barely-discernible manufacturer into a global sensation. Born in 1899 at Hildesheim in Lower Saxony, Heinz Nordhoff was the son of a small-town banker. After attending technical high school and serving in World War I, Nordhoff graduated from Berlin-Charlottenburg technical university in 1927, as a mechanical engineer.

First stop: a job with BMW, working on aircraft design. In 1929, Nordhoff applied at Opel, which had just been bought by General Motors. His first job at Opel was writing service manuals. Through more than 17 years before his Volkswagen connection, as described by *U.S. News & World Report*, Nordhoff served as "an engineer, salesman and manager in the automobile industries of Europe and the U.S." Visiting American GM factories in the 1930s, he'd studied both production and sales/marketing techniques.

During the war, Nordhoff had headed a truck factory in Brandenburg. After V-E Day in May 1945, he was just one of millions of Germans and other Europeans without a job or a home.

Despite his lack of familiarity with—and interest in—the Volkswagen, Nordhoff was chosen by the British to head the new organization. On January 2, 1948, Nordhoff took charge of the Volkswagen plant as Director General, and would remain in that role for two decades, until his death in April 1968.

Economic Minister Ludwig Erhard acted as trustee, while Finance Minister Fritz Schaffer represented shareholders. They appointed an 18-member committee to assist Nordhoff.

Nordhoff knew success would come only with a top-notch sales/service network. That was Step One. He needed foreign exchange, too, so exports escalated right away.

"The most important job was to take the car out of the atmosphere of austerity," Nordhoff noted in the early 1950s. "People said, 'We like it technically, but we can't afford to be seen in it.' Austerity touches neither the heart nor the pocketbook."

After those early doubts about the value of the Beetle, Nordhoff transformed himself into a true believer. "As an engineer who knows many cars," he explained late in 1967, "and quite apart from the fact that I am a Volkswagen man, I would always rate the good old Beetle as one of the happiest combinations amongst the automobiles of the world....

"The star of the Beetle is still shining with undiminished brightness and you see for yourselves every day what vitality there is hidden in this car which has been pronounced dead more often than all these designs of which hardly a memory remains. I am absolutely sure that our Beetle will be produced for a very long time to come." How true.

Heinz Nordhoff served as Director General of Volkswagenwerk GmbH from early 1948 until his death 20 years later. Without his heroic efforts, the company might never have survived, much less become a cultural phenomenon and economic powerhouse. Here, Nordhoff (left) greets a teenage participant in the annual Youth Exchange Program, introduced by his daughter, Barbara. Mrs. Heinz Nordhoff (far left) looks on. (Volkswagen)

At the body drop station in Wolfsburg, a Beetle body meets its chassis, assisted by a group of workers. The first post-war cars were haphazardly built, but once Heinz Nordhoff took over in January 1948, quality became a byword. (Volkswagen)

Volkswagens soon earned a reputation for versatility. This late 1940s Beetle sedan, complete with roof rack, was called a Holzbrenner (wood burner) and ran on char-coal—as had some vehicles produced during the war. Per-formance was weak, but fuel shortages made such conversions necessary. (Volkswagen)

War II remained fresh in so many minds? Something would have to be done about that, if the cars were to sell outside Germany—and beyond Europe.

Split-Window Sedans (1945-1953)

To some VW Beetle fans, the only cars worth keeping are the early models—the ones with the distinctive split rear window. Others extend the desirability range into—if not beyond—the oval-window era that ended after 1957.

Except for engine size, Volkswagens saw no drastic changes from the split-window period until 1958. Early on, however, the company established its principle of making changes when necessary—or desirable—rather than to follow a strict, preset pattern by model year.

The split-oval rear window (also known as "pretzel window") had a rather thick pillar between its tiny panes. American cars had abandoned runningboards before World War II, but VWs kept them—though they weren't the kind that anyone could stand on.

These first production cars exhibited virtually no bright-work. Hubcaps, bumpers and guards were painted—though later models got nipple-shaped chrome hubcaps. Headlights sat behind glass covers. Seats were uphol-stered in humble cloth, as were the door panels, which lacked any storage pockets. The driver faced a simple three-spoke steering wheel with a center horn button. Open gloveboxes stood at each end of the dashboard.

What some referred to as an "upside-down and back-ward" speedometer sat at the center of the instrument panel, registering as much as 120 kilometers per hour (73 mph). Just above the speedometer, the driver could reach a lever to actuate the lighted turn-signal semaphores, which popped out from the door pillars.

A circular gauge that matched the speedometer dis-played the gearshift pattern. The gearshift lever itself still was embossed with the KdF symbol.

Only the driver enjoyed a sun visor, made of simple plastic. An interior light went between the split rear win-dow panes. Doors held no vent windows.

A Volkswagen fuel tank held eight gallons, including a one-gallon reserve supply. Instead of a fuel gauge, VWs from the start had a lever on the firewall. As soon as the engine began to exhibit signs of running out of gasoline, the driver reached over with his foot and rotated that tap, to let the extra gallon flow toward the carburetor. The gas tank sat under the hood, which meant the hood had to be raised with each fill-up. Earliest models even included a stick to measure fuel in the tank. Basic, at best.

In case the engine failed to start, the driver could em-ploy a starting crank—a device that had disappeared from most automobiles in the 1930s, as self-starters became more reliable. A notch below the rear bumper permitted insertion of the hand crank. The crank wouldn't last past October 1949 on VWs, but Renault kept one for its little 4CV well into the 1950s.

Early engines had been rated at 24 horsepower, which grew to 25 bhp by 1947, and 30 bhp the next year. Volks-wagen's 5.8:1 compression ratio was well below that used for most conventional engines at the time. Brakes were mechanically-operated for the first several years—and later than that, for European models.

An under-dashboard pull cable replaced the former locking-handle hood release as the 1949 model debuted, and a Solex carburetor became standard for the engine.

For the first production models, Volkswagen claimed gas mileage of 37.5 miles per gallon—when running at a steady 34 miles an hour. Top speed was billed as 65 mph, and the car weighed about 1,550 pounds.

Dashboards were essentially unchanged through 1951. Until October 1952, Volkswagens also had a roof indentation above the windshield, serving as a platform for the available radio.

Earliest examples were cobbled together and poorly painted. That unfortunate situation was the result of excessive improvisation—a far cry from VW's subsequent reputation for high quality and top-notch engineering.

In addition to their homely shape and personality, the first Beetles were noisy and stiffly sprung. No matter. Their owners quickly grew to love these little machines, even if neighbors found them homely and unappealing.

This early chassis was called Type 1. Broken down, the sedan was Type 11, and the sun roof sedan that soon joined the lineup was Type 13. A two-seat convertible would be Type 14, and the later-arriving Karmann four-seat convertible earned a Type 15 designation.

Beetles Go DeLuxe

Already in 1948, one-fourth of Beetles were exported. By July 1949, Volkswagen was turning out not only the Standard models, but also a growing number of DeLuxe editions. DeLuxe versions had an inside hood release, versus an external latch handle for Standard sedans. A chrome horn sat behind the fender on DeLuxe cars, but behind the bumper on Standard models. Chrome hubcaps decorated the DeLuxe.

Upgraded interiors on Export versions included grab handles and an inside light. Rear armrest cushions went into European models in 1949 (but not until 1951 on Exports).

Tiny round taillights remained well into the 1950s—a hard-to-see style that would bring shivers to modern-day safety advocates. The instrument panel, steering wheel, and most knobs still were painted black. Early models had an oval rear view mirror, but a rectangular shape arrived by 1950.

Export and DeLuxe models got an ivory-colored, two-spoke steering wheel for 1950, along with ivory-colored plastic control knobs. Those knobs remained black for several more years on Standard cars.

An optional clock could replace the gearshift diagram, but semaphores continued to be operated by a center-mounted switch. Interiors contained ashtrays on the dashboard and the right rear quarter panel.

The 1951 DeLuxe sedan had vent shutters ahead of its doors. Note the semaphore-style turn signals in the door pillar. (Volkswagen)

● Early Years in the Wolfsburg Plant ●

Work began on the factory at Wolfsburg, Germany, in mid-1938, with the intention of having the first cars ready to emerge late in the following year. By then, World War II was underway. Initially, the plant was run by Robert Ley, head of the *Kraft durch Freude* ("Strength through Joy") organization.

After the war, the plant stood in occupied West Germany, just 17 miles from the Soviet zone. Rising from the rubble of war, the Wolfsburg facility became—in just a few

Split-window Volkswagens reach the body drop at the Wolfsburg factory. (Phil Hall)

short years—the largest auto plant in Europe.

From a total of 10,000 cars built in 1948, production rose to 10,000 per *month* by 1952. In fact, nearly 47,000 VW vehicles were exported in 1952, to 43 countries. By 1953, the assembly lines were turning out 135,000 vehicles per year—550 Beetles each day, soon rising to 700 (versus just 165 per day in 1952).

One year later, a Volkswagen was rolling out of the factory door every 80 seconds, destined for 83 foreign nations. In the early 1950s, Volkswagen topped the German

"Big Five" automakers, which also included Daimler-Benz, Ford and Borgward.

"Assembly lines are among the most modern, fastest (a car every 90 seconds) on the continent," *Business Week* insisted in 1953. The mile-long factory in rural Wolfsburg consisted of more than five million square feet, with a capacity of 300,000 cars yearly. Its press room was the largest in Europe, holding 125 machines. By then, about 2,900 machine tools were in use (one-fourth of them obtained from the United States).

Nobody "owned" the company through the late 1940s and '50s. Instead, it was run by a council that represented workers, managers, and the Bonn government, with Heinz Nordhoff as managing director. Dr. Karl Feuereissen managed sales, distribution, and parts. The plant might have been in rough shape, but at least Nordhoff had no stockholders to answer to.

One-third of Wolfsburg's population worked at the VW plant in the 1950s. It amounted to a complete company town. In addition to supplying 4,000 housing units, the company grew its own wheat, vegetables—even cattle—for use in factory canteens. Employee benefits ranged from pensions and insurance to a skating rink on the premises, and rest camps in the Hartz mountains and on the North Sea.

Wages in 1953 were among the highest in German industry: 2.30 Deutschmarks (about 51 cents) hourly. Even so, *Business Week* noted, at DM 4,400 ($1,050) a Beetle was "too expensive for most of the Germans to whom it was promised." Being realistic, that price was the equivalent of 2,000 hours of work. So it was no surprise that only about 350 of the 20,000 employees owned a Volkswagen. Most workers rode bicycles.

In 1953, Volkswagen also had assembly plants in Brazil, Ireland, and South Africa, and was planning one for Australia. In addition to the Wolfsburg facility, there was also the convertible plant at Osnabrück. By 1954, Volkswagen was the fourth largest auto manufacturer in the world, trailing only the American "Big Three."

Women made up a small, but significant part of the workforce. By 1962, some 9,560 women worked in plants at Wolfsburg and Hanover (12.3 percent of the total of 78,000-plus workers).

Seeking to establish a tighter connection with the growing American market, Volkswagen bought the four-year-old Studebaker-Packard assembly plant at Brunswick, New Jersey. After months of rumors, the deal went through in August 1955, VW paying an estimated $5 million.

Some observers believed that it really was to be little more than a parts/service depot, but Nordhoff had visited the United States to try and line up suppliers for the factory. Nordhoff believed that VW needed U.S. manufacturing facilities to meet the growing demand for cars, and also was concerned about the cost and availability of shipping fleets across the North Atlantic. Nordhoff also liked the idea of building cars where they would be sold. Dies would come from Germany, but VW considered buying machine tools from U.S. suppliers. Nordhoff even hinted at a stock issue.

Production in New Jersey was supposed to begin by October 1956. Alas, that plan failed to materialize. Analysts learned that higher American wages—and a shorter work week—would send unit costs too high to make an American-built Beetle affordable. Early in 1956, Volkswagen announced abandonment of plans for New Jersey. "Rather than increase prices or sacrifice to the slightest degree the high quality that has been largely responsible for the success of our product," Nordhoff explained, "we will be compelled to continue our present system of operations."

After the U.S. plant fizzled, Volkswagen arranged long-term leases on ships for the 14-day run from Bremen or Hamburg. Not until the mid-1970s would Volkswagen make another stab at an American plant (see Chapter 18), for the front-engine Rabbit.

As Beetles gained popularity worldwide, the Wolfsburg factory became quite a tourist attraction. In 1969, for instance, the plant hosted 100,000 visitors.

From the bombed-out rubble of World War II, the Wolfsburg plant became the largest auto factory in Europe in just a few years. (Phil Hall)

Ben Pon (left), a Dutchman responsible for bringing the first few Volkswagens to America, observes the unloading of a Beetle in January 1949. Only two of these cars were sold in the United States that year. (Volkswagen)

DeLuxe Volkswagens switched to hydraulic brakes and gained runningboard trim. The engine added a heat riser, and the gas tank grew to 10 gallon capacity.

Some cloth upholstery for 1950 had contrasting vinyl piping. Heaters became quieter, as a result of the addition of duct mufflers. A thermostatically-controlled throttle ring provided automatic air cooling. Fenders were insulated from the body by contrasting-color welting. Volkswagens could be ordered with a sun roof option—a body style destined to last for decades.

A Wolfsburg crest was added to 1951 VWs, mounted above the hood handle. Windshields added a bright chrome molding. Kick-panel vent flaps were installed inside, ahead of the doors—for this year only. Front passengers now enjoyed door-mounted armrests.

More serious changes arrived for 1952—actually in the period from March 1952 to March 1953. In October 1952, for instance, chrome trim was added to the split rear windows. The speedometer moved to the left side of the dashboard, ahead of the steering wheel, for easier read-

ing. The turn-signal actuator moved to the steering column—a far more convenient spot.

Crank-up windows required only 3-1/2 turns, versus a tiresome 10-1/2 turns for earlier models. A rotary heater knob replaced the former pull-type unit, and a T-type decklid handle supplanted the earlier loop-style handle.

Brake lights were incorporated into taillights, replacing the former single fender lamp and rear-deck stoplight. New 5.60x15 tires replaced 16-inch rubber, easing the ride a bit. Most important, a synchromesh transmission (Porsche patented) was installed in Export models. This welcome change replaced the original "crash box," enjoyed only by hardy drivers. All forward gears except first were now synchronized.

VWs Arrive in America

Before official importation began, and many years before the Beetlemania craze hit its stride, the first Beetles came to the United States. They accompanied returning servicemen, who'd taken a liking to the curious machines. Discharged or transferred military men also brought a host of other European vehicles to American shores—from economy sedans to full-fledged sports cars. A military man who'd grown fond of an Anglia or VW—or a Jaguar or MG roadster—simply made arrangements to haul his favorite machine stateside when he headed back home.

Early Volkswagens sold for about $645, through the U.S. military's Post Exchange System. Supply fell far short of demand, so a lottery was used to distribute the hard-to-get vehicles. Not every buyer was happy. Some were disappointed with the car's modest performance and high noise level. Nevertheless, back to the States they went, on the next boat.

Even non-enthusiasts may be aware that only two Volkswagen arrived for sale in the United States, to no fanfare whatsoever, late in 1949. That forlorn fact was mentioned frequently in ads, after VWs grew more popular.

Actually, a solitary 1948 Volkswagen had landed at the port of New York *earlier* that year, accompanied by Ben Pon. Ben and his brother Winjant, of Amersfoort, The Netherlands, had taken the first consignment of Volkswagen sedans into Holland in October 1947. Despite strong anti-German sentiment in his home country, Pon was successful at selling the curious little Beetles. Most important, Pon demonstrated that Volkswagens could sell outside Germany.

Therefore, on January 17, 1949, Pon had arrived from Holland by ship (the Holland-America Lines' Westerdam) to promote the Volkswagen in America. His premier effort faltered completely. No dealers or importers took more than scant notice of the homely little German machine. In fact, Pon soon had to sell his single sample car at a bargain price, to pay his $800 hotel bill.

Because Heinz Nordhoff definitely needed dollars to invest in American-built equipment, to meet growing production demands, he soon visited the United States himself. Alas, his efforts to take up Pon's aborted cause also met with failure. Prospects for sale in the U.S. market, currently enamored by the new hardtop coupes and high-compression V-8 engines, looked bleak. Said Nordhoff: "We will have to make our own way in the world without American dollars." A skilled visionary in so many ways, in this particular prediction he was obviously grossly mistaken.

In 1950, shortly after that first pair of VWs had arrived on American shores, Beetles began to trickle in regardless. Twenty cars (in four models) had a private showing in New York, before appearing at the First U.S. International Trade Fair in Chicago, in August 1950. In all, some 220 German companies exhibited at the Trade Fair.

English language VW sales brochures now were available, but those didn't help the sales charts much. Not yet. Word-of-mouth appeared to be the main selling tool.

"Germany's new Volkswagen hit the boom right on the nose," according to *Business Week* magazine in its July 29, 1950 issue. It was one of a series of little European machines that began to capture the attention of sophisticated American drivers.

On the previous Monday, Hoffman Motor Car Co. had put a batch of Volkswagens on sale. By the close of business Tuesday, there were dealer orders for 250 cars. One Washington (D.C.) dealer—with a single demonstrator car—took orders for 32 Beetles in a single day.

"In a modern mile-long factory," said Tom McCahill, the rotund and rambunctious auto tester of *Mechanix Illustrated* in October 1950, "Volkswagens are now being turned out like hot dogs at Swift & Company." Max Hoffman, an immigrant from Germany, had "established himself as America's European car Czar," with a showroom in Chicago as well as two in New York. As McCahill observed at the time, "the floors of his plush Park Avenue, New York showroom were cleared for the cocktail party debut of the little Volkswagen."

Hoffman, who ordinarily handled such imported exotic motorcars as Jaguar and Lea Francis, became the first official importer—the distributor for the eastern states. He managed to move 330 cars in 1950. A Standard Beetle sold for $1,280, while the DeLuxe brought $200 more. A VW with sun roof went for $1,550, and the rarely-seen convertible could be driven home for $1,997.

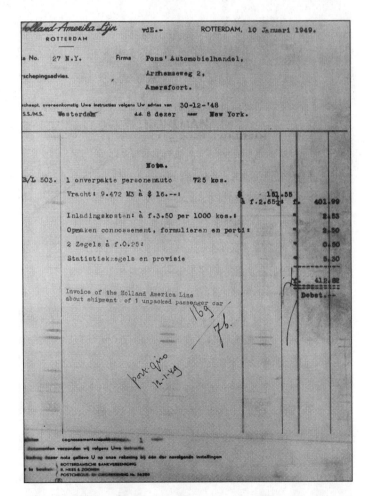

Already successful at selling Beetles in his home country, Ben Pon had a Volkswagen shipped from The Netherlands to New York, on the Holland America Line, early in 1949. Pon failed to interest American dealers in the curious little vehicle. (Volkswagen)

A Beetle sedan gets a final inspection before a 10-mile test run at the Wolfsburg plant, in 1952. (Phil Hall)

As early as November 1950, *Motor Trend* noted that VWs were fast becoming an outstanding success. Hoffman Motor Car Co. also was described as the agent for "the sensational Porsche car now being manufactured in Germany."

Early in 1951, *Business Week* reported that Hoffman was selling 600 cars a month, through 120 dealers. A Standard Beetle sold for $1,295 in the United States. Most

Early test drivers complained about limited visibility through the split rear window, but that design is the most sought-after today by collectors.

shoppers opted for the $1,480 DeLuxe model, if not the $1,550 sun roof sedan. Convertibles were seldom seen, partly due to their awesome $2,296 price tag.

Prices for the Standard model rose by $100 for 1952, and the DeLuxe brought $1,595. Convertibles edged upward to $2,395. The first Beetles arrived (officially) in Canada in autumn of 1952.

By early 1953, said *Newsweek* magazine, Nordhoff felt he had "about saturated the European market," and had "fixed his gaze on the United States." In a bizarre irony, Max Hoffman's contract as a VW dealer was not renewed that year.

Simplicity and technical prowess of the Volkswagen's engine became a top selling point. "That little air-cooled powerplant seldom stuttered" during the war, *Popular Science* pointed out in 1954, "whether in Africa's heat or Russia's cold." The Volkswagen had become "a symbol of West Germany's industrial recovery [and was] just what the doctor ordered for Europe."

Noting that the Beetle already was being called "Europe's Model T," *Popular Science* retorted: "That's an injustice to the car. It's more properly a Model A." Whereas the Model T had introduced the motorcar to the American mass market, it was technically primitive. While unknowing critics may have branded the Beetle *similarly* primitive, in reality it was refined and advanced in engineering—characteristics comparable to Ford's Model A.

What Kind of People Bought Early Beetles?

Before long, the Beetle would be appealing to a wide variety of customers, from *avant-garde* all the way into the mainstream. Early VWs were another story.

Quite content with their Fords and Chevrolets, Chryslers and Cadillacs, most Americans gave foreign cars little thought. The Austins and Anglias that turned up now and then in the late 1940s were viewed as curiosities. Surely, the servicemen who'd brought them back from Europe soon would come to their senses and buy themselves *real* automobiles: big, powerful, imposing, impressive. Oh, some of those sports cars looked like fun—if you liked that sort of thing. But an economy sedan? For a red-blooded American? Not on your life!

Opinions about the Beetle, when uttered at all, tended to be more scornful yet. Who could even speak of such a little "putt-putt" machine in the same breath as an American automobile? The war was over, postwar inflation and shortages were beginning to ebb, the future looked bright. Gasoline was cheap, so who needed an economy car—

Competition Motors was the first Volkswagen dealer in the Los Angeles area—but in the early 1950s, VW wasn't even listed among the makes offered for sale. Most early dealers also handled other imported makes. (Volkswagen)

Vent windows arrived during the 1952 model year. Even more important for VW drivers, the transmission adopted synchronized gears (second, third and fourth), a big improvement over the early "crash box." (Volkswagen)

Taillights were restyled in October 1952, but VWs stuck with the split rear window a little longer. Already, Volkswagen had initiated its well-known program of continuous improvement. (Volkswagen)

especially a silly-looking, unorthodox one such as that Volkswagen?

Besides, people insisted, those cars came out of Germany; and weren't they designed by the Nazis or something? Even if the Volkswagen's technical features were a little tempting, its national origin was enough to cross them off most shopping lists. Millions of Americans re-

Split-window sedans are highly prized. This 1952 Standard sedan appeared at a Central Ohio Volkswagen show in 1995. (Photo: James M. Flammang — Owner: Roy C. Mc-Cune)

called the war vividly, after all, including such items as a wartime cartoon that had depicted a Beetle (KdF-Wagen then) with a machine gun poking through its windshield.

Early sales suffered, too, from American mistrust of *all* small cars. Volkswagen performance was admittedly meager, and engine life of earliest models had been short—though that failing was rapidly remedied.

It took a certain kind of person to choose to be seen in a Beetle of the split-window or oval-window generation. This was the age of conformity, after all, and a Volkswagen didn't quite match the typical white- or blue-collar lifestyle.

To a large extent, then, the VW ownership list centered on people who didn't worry as much about the opinions of others. Just about anyone who shunned the "gray-flannel" mentality of the 1950s might give a VW a whirl. Students and academics gravitated to the Beetle early. So did folks who liked to be different, or considered themselves progressive. That out-of-the-loop list included a handful of hipsters—forerunners of the beats of the late 1950s and the hippies of the '60s.

Little by little, though, the list of customers began to encompass practical-minded, frugal motorists who simply recognized the car's quality and merits. "Vee-dubs" (another of the many nicknames) also gained favor with the growing number of do-it-yourselfers, who knew—or at least believed—they could repair it themselves in case of breakdown.

● Year-by-year changes, 1946 to 1953 ●
Beetles

Listed below are the significant changes in Volkswagen sedans, sun roof sedans, and convertibles through the split-window generation. Less-obvious improvements also were made continuously. In some cases, changes appeared first on European models.

1949
Standard and DeLuxe models available
Hebmüller convertibles start production
DeLuxe adds inside hood release (to replace locking handle), chrome horn behind fender, chrome hubcaps
Starting crank deleted (during year)
Solex carburetor made standard
Export interiors include grab handles and light
Rear armrest cushions (European models)
License plate identification on rear deck deleted

1950
Sun roof sedan available
DeLuxe and Export add hydraulic brakes; mechanical handbrake acts on rear wheels
Two-spoke ivory-colored steering wheel and ivory plastic knobs (Export and DeLuxe)
Optional clock may replace gearshift diagram
Runningboard trim and long bodyside trim strip on DeLuxe
Rectangular inside mirror replaces oval
Heat riser added to engine's intake manifold
Gas tank enlarged to 10 gallons
Fenders insulated from body with contrasting-color welting
All models have concealed horn

Ashtrays installed on dashboard and right rear quarter panel
Heat ducts add silencing mufflers
Thermostat throttle ring controls air cooling automatically

1951
Wolfsburg crest added (above hood handle)
Windshield adds bright trim
Vent flaps go ahead of doors
Door armrest added to passenger side
Taillights delete chrome surround
Rear armrest cushions installed (Export models)

1952 (March 1952 to March 1953)
Turn signal moves to steering column
Brake lights incorporated into taillights (formerly, single light at center)
5.60x15 tires replace 16-inch
Synchromesh installed for transmission's second, third and fourth gears
Crank-up windows require fewer turns
Torsion bar system modified
T-style rear hood handle replaces loop-type
Glove compartment adds door
Glass vent windows installed (formerly vent wings in body panels)
Rotary knob controls heater (formerly pull-type)
October 1952: chrome trim added to split windows; speedometer moves ahead of driver

Chapter 3

The Oval-Window Generation (1953-1957)

"Do you like the European look in automobiles?" VW's handsome sales brochure asked. "Are you fond of clean-cut streamlined cars? Are you keen on riding in easy comfort, yet would like to have a means of transportation that is downright cheap to operate?"

All this was yours, the brochure promised, if you bought a Volkswagen, heralded as the "leading European car in its field." Furthermore, the copy went on: "Technicians the world over say that the Volkswagen is the most sensible automobile ever built and that it is years ahead in de-sign...designed by a genius as unique in his field as Caruso was as a tenor."

Sure, some might question the "remarkably fast get-away" claimed by the copywriters. On the other hand, many new VW drivers agreed about the "smooth and safe driving thanks to marvelous suspension and a low center of gravity." They also appreciated the "short gracefully plunging Volkswagen hood [that] increases driving safety by permitting an unobstructed view of the road almost up to the front wheels."

A single-pane rear window replaced the initial split-glass design during 1953. (Volkswagen)

Adding another temptation, because the car was "so compact and maneuverable," you could always find a suitable parking space. Not only did a VW's "smart appearance and practical European lines charm the eye," but it also promised "a maximum of performance for a minimum of outlay...sparing of every cent spent on it."

High praise indeed, and the lush, distinctive illustrations in the sales brochures doubtless helped to attract attention to the vehicle. Unlike so much sales literature, VW's literature never "talked down" to its audience. Technical details were explained in clear, but not gushy, language. Marketers assumed that the reader understood what was important, and knew the rudiments of automobile operation.

Most noticeable of the 1953 changes was the installation of a single-pane, oval-shaped rear window to replace the low-visibility split-window design. At the same time, in March of 1953, vent-window handles added a lock button, and a separate brake-fluid reservoir moved from the master cylinder to behind the spare tire.

By this time, the top three gears were synchronized—a good thing for sales since few Americans, even those who disdained U.S. cars, cared to suffer the indignities of a "crash box." Double-clutching might be okay for truckers, but comfort-loving Americans wanted an easygoing gearbox (if not an automatic transmission).

Heart of the VW, of course, was its rear-mounted, air-cooled, horizontally-opposed engine—three characteristics found on no domestically-built automobiles. Even the fact that it had four cylinders set it apart from nearly all American vehicles, with their potent V-8s and heavyweight six-cylinder engines sitting atop the front ends.

The engine was so dependable, the brochure insisted, "that it is a source of constant wonder. You can do almost anything with the Volkswagen Marathon engine except spend money on it." In fact, the engine was "such a miser with gasoline, too, that you do not often have the opportunity of showing off your Volkswagen in a filling station."

Maybe so, but plenty of VW owners dearly *loved* to show off their cars to friends and neighbors, boasting about the Beetle's numerous—if not always obvious—virtues.

Bragging about the lack of need for antifreeze, for instance, could bring a mild grumble or two from a domestic-car owner who had to change that fluid periodically, and check it regularly throughout the winter. Many an amateur critic might have snorted and scoffed at the Beetle when it turned up next door in summer. A few months later, when winter winds began to blow, he'd be singing a different tune. That's when the 15-inch tires on the little VWs were able to sustain a tenacious grip on icy pavement, which no American sedan could match. After spinning his own car's wheels on glare ice, the owner of a Ford or Plymouth just might entertain a more approving thought about those eccentric, rear-engined German machines.

"There is not a mountainous highway in the world too hard for the Volkswagen to negotiate with ease," the brochures continued, focusing on the Beetle's performance skills under difficult conditions, and its rear-drive configu-

Installation of the single-pane window gave Volkswagen quite a boost in the U.S. market. Ernst Reuters created the dramatic artwork for early sales brochures, which were printed on thick, high-quality paper. In his paintings, VWs looked super-streamlined. (Phil Hall)

ration. "The steeper the grade and the sharper the curves, the better the Volkswagen can show what it can do. It is particularly when crossing high mountain passes that a Volkswagen is appreciated, thanks to its air-cooled engine mounted in the rear where its weight gives the rear wheels good traction at all times."

A combined instrument unit contained a speedometer (showing kilometers or miles per hour) and warning lights. The light-toned, twin-spoke steering wheel on DeLuxe models held a horn button featuring the black/gold VW emblem. Dashboards had space for an optional radio's dial and control knobs. To start the engine, the driver had to pull out a hand choke—a component that had already disappeared from most American automobiles. Volkswagens also had a large hinged ashtray and a lockable glovebox.

Individual bucket seats were rare items in American vehicles. With "a seat to himself...the driver of a Volkswagen feels just as much part of his mount as a cowboy does on his pony."

Flashing turn signals, mounted far out on front fenders, replaced the original mechanical semaphores in April 1955. Fabric slid all the way to the rear on sun roof sedans. (Volkswagen)

Dealers scurried to obtain cars in the early 1950s, once they realized that they could actually sell the little critters—easily. This Pennsylvania dealership became an authorized outlet for Volkswagens in 1955. (Volkswagen)

A DeLuxe VW in 1954 sold for $1,595 in the United States. A sun roof added just $80. The convertible, on the other hand, commanded a hefty $2,350 and weighed 250 pounds extra. DeLuxe models had a door pocket beside the driver's seat, as well as rubber floor mats.

"With a sweep of the hand," the brochure said of the Golde Sun Roof model, "you can fold the top back and enjoy the fresh air and sunshine." When closed, it's "just as weatherproof in bad weather as if it had a steel top."

Sun roofs, for the next two decades, drew customers who liked a little air but mistrusted a full convertible's likelihood to leak. Domestic makes steered clear of sun roofs through most of that period, though a handful of other imports adopted them.

Although it would draw no end of gripes from chilled occupants through the coming years, a heater was built into each and every Volkswagen. Because the engine was air-cooled, there was no coolant to flow through heater hoses. Therefore, the amount of warm air available to passengers was generally meager, at best.

As for windshield wipers, owners might have described them as skimpy, but the sales brochure called them "lively." DeLuxe models got self-parking, increased-capacity wipers.

Displacement of the flat-four engine grew from 1131 to 1192 cubic centimeters for 1954. Rounded off, that became the "1200" series. Coupled with a compression boost from 5.8:1 to 6.6:1, this yielded an output increase to 36 horsepower, from the prior 30.

Horsepower Note: By some measures, the horsepower hike was from 25 to 30. Some data sheets gave DIN (German) ratings, while others used the SAE measurement system. The source of the figure was not necessarily identified, prompting considerable confusion.

An oil-bath air cleaner replaced the felt-element filter in 1954. Taillight housings no longer had a top window. A key-type starter switch replaced the earlier dashboard push button, and a three-way dome light was installed. Engines no longer required a break-in period.

Prices dipped a bit for 1955, to $1,495 for the DeLuxe sedan and $1,995 for the convertible. Change was minimal, except for low, fender-mounted turn signal flashers to replace the original mechanical semaphore units. Semaphores might have been quaint, but they hardly fit into the American motoring scene of the mid-1950s. On non-U.S. Volkswagens, semaphores hung on for several more years.

On August 8, 1955, the one-millionth Volkswagen was assembled—painted in gold color. Not until that year did the Volkswagen company recognize official model years. At that time, a model year beginning on August 1 was established.

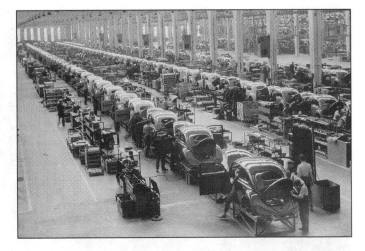

Fans of oval-window Beetles can only dream of seeing all these cars in one place. The Wolfsburg factory quickly became the largest auto plant in Europe. (Phil Hall)

Eventually, these seemingly-endless improvements would be promoted in full-page advertisements, intended to demonstrate VW's commitment to ongoing change. Not all of the changes necessarily took place at the start of a given model year, even after 1955.

Dual chromed tailpipes went into the 1956 models. Taillights sat two inches higher on the rear fenders. A reshaped gas tank yielded greater luggage space under the hood. Front seatbacks now could be adjusted, and the

Not too many oval-window sedans were as fully decked out as this example, seen at a 1995 VW show in Ohio. Note the fender skirts, bumper guards, and tailpipe decoration. (Photo: James M. Flammang — Owner: Dave Gallaher)

A fleet of 1954 Beetles were lined up at night, at the Wolfsburg factory, for this dramatic photo.

driver faced a new steering wheel with a lower (off-center) horizontal spoke.

Sun roofs now were made of nylon, not cloth. The heater knob moved forward from its former location in back of the front seats.

Volkswagen's first U.S. headquarters opened in 1955, at this building in Englewood Cliffs, New Jersey.

Tubeless tires were installed on 1957 models, following the lead of American manufacturers. With only a few exceptions among passenger cars, inner tubes became a relic of the past.

By now, interiors were mainly vinyl-upholstered, except for the headliner. Doors incorporated adjustable strikers. Front heater outlets moved toward the rear, within a foot of the doors, to improve heat distribution. Prices stuck at the 1955-56 level.

Going Global—and Selling in America

Volkswagen United States was established in New York in April 1955, as a subsidiary of Volkswagenwerk in Germany. Six months later, the name changed to Volkswagen of America Inc. The subsidiary's purpose: to coordinate importation, distribution, sales, and service standards.

Not only did Volkswagens begin to appear in countries around the world, they went into production outside of Germany. In March 1953, for instance, a new plant opened at Sao Bernardo do Campo, Brazil. For its first four years, Volkswagen do Brasil—headed by a Nordhoff associate, Dr. F.W. Schult-Wenk—used parts from Germany.

Transporters and sedans sold well in Canada, but only 1,500 VWs had found customers in America in 1952. Of the 29,299 foreign cars registered that year, only 600 were VWs. That was an improvement over the 157 sold in 1950, but the spurt had yet to arrive.

During the first half of 1954, on the other hand, Volkswagen leaped from sixth to first place in foreign car sales. By the end of that year, VW was the top-selling import in the United States, nearly doubling the total of its nearest rival (MG). VW's total reached 6,343 vehicles (up 412 percent), in a year when foreign car sales generally fell 12 percent—to 25,379.

In 1955, some 29,000 Volkswagen cars and 6,000 commercial vehicles were sold in the United States alone, out of 60,000 imports. Production reached 1,500 vehicles per day. Volkswagen issued a total of 330,120 vehicles in 1955, more than half of them for the export market.

To help push sales totals higher yet, the company was encouraging American dealers to go exclusively with Volkswagen, rather than pushing a variety of makes. "Show the car to young dealers who still have some ambition," Nordhoff advised.

In a 1954 news conference, soon after Volkswagenwerk announced price cuts for cars in France and Britain, Heinz Nordhoff had criticized the trend toward bigness. "The future of the automobile lies in the small car," he insisted. He pointedly addressed the growing size of American cars, "which have ten times more power than can be put to any use and thus violate every principle of engineering and technical science."

Volkswagen not only was leading the way into the compact car "revolution," but it stood far ahead of the pack. Could it keep up the momentum? For one thing, U.S. two-car families increased from 4.8 percent in 1948 to 13.8 percent in 1955, and the trend was still growing. Families in the West, and in the suburbs, were particularly good candidates for a second car—a Beetle. Then too, in 1955, a full 12.7 million families had no car at all. Wouldn't some of them be happy behind the wheel of a Bug?

● Year-by-year changes, 1953 to 1957 ●
Beetles

Listed are the significant changes in Volkswagen sedans, sun roof sedans, and convertibles through the oval-window generation.

1953
Single oval rear window replaces split window (March 1953)
Separate brake master cylinder reservoir installed behind spare tire
Vent windows add lock buttons
Third and fourth gear ratios revised

1954
Engine enlarged by 61 cc (to 1192 cc); gains 6 horsepower
Compression ratio rises from 5.8:1 to 6.6:1
Key-operated starter switch replaces push button
Engine gains oil-bath air filter element (formerly felt)
Engine break-in requirement deleted
Vacuum/mechanical distributor installed
Automatic three-way courtesy light installed

1955
U.S. models get turn signal flashers, delete semaphores
Tubular overriders (bumper guards) added

1956
Twin chrome exhaust pipes replace single outlet
Overriders made standard on U.S. models
New steering wheel has off-center bar
Fuel tank reshaped to add luggage space
Front-seat backs now are adjustable
Taillights sit two inches higher
Sun roofs switch from cloth to plastic
Heater knob moves forward

1957
Tubeless tires become standard
Heater vents move closer to door
Interiors are mainly vinyl (except headliner)
Doors add adjustable striker plates

Chapter 4

Early Offshoots: Convertibles and Special Bodies

Not much time passed before Heinz Nordhoff and his staff realized that their steadily-expanding company needed a product beyond the ordinary sedan. To attract the attention of a broader base of customers, something more dramatic was in order.

A pair of special two-passenger convertibles had been built for the British officers in charge of the plant: Colonel C.R. Radclyffe and Major Ivan Hirst. Even before the war, in fact, a convertible had been part of the festivities that marked the cornerstone-laying for the Wolfsburg factory. Obviously, then, offering an open-topped model to the general public—inside or outside of Germany—seemed to make good sense.

Hebmüller Cabriolets—Rare Earlybirds

Partly because the German police wanted an open car, in 1948 a project for 2,000 such vehicles wound up at the Hebmüller company in Wulfrath, Germany. In the late 1940s and early '50s, years before the stylish Karmann Ghia was penned, as many as 750 specially-bodied Volkswagen convertibles went to customers. Based upon the design of the two-seat convertible issued to Colonel Radclyffe, they offered a dramatic taste of what could be accomplished atop a basic VW chassis.

Created by the Hebmüller company, these sporty two-passenger cabriolets—essentially roadsters—featured

Before Karmann got an assignment to produce Beetle-based convertibles, as many as 750 Hebmüller Cabriolets were built, starting in 1948. The two-seaters are among the rarest, and most prized, VW collectibles. (Volkswagen)

For three decades, starting in 1949, the Karmann coachbuilding firm turned out convertibles on assignment from Volkswagen. Many early examples, including this 1950 model, were two-toned.

small, rounded side windows and a neatly-disappearing convertible top. Many observers felt the car looked its best with the top up. A scoop-like license plate light housing decorated the engine lid. Two-tone paint on many of the cars enhanced their sporty appearance.

Hebmüller convertibles employed stock body panels, adapting doors and rear quarter panels to fit. Doors were reworked to a cut-down style.

Because drivetrain components were shared with the basic Beetles, performance lagged behind the roadster's aggressive appearance. The 1131-cc engine developed the usual 30 horsepower. Top speed was about 63 mph and, as Volkswagen later described it, "the non-synchromesh transmission made driving more challenge than sport." The roadsters were 159.5 inches long, 60.5 inches wide, and 61 inches high, riding the usual 5.00x16 tires.

Hebmüllers were sold through VW dealers. Even before Hebmüller initiated production of cabriolets, Volkswagen turned to the Karmann company as a source for a four-passenger convertible model—the one that would eventually last three decades in the lineup. Later on, the Hebmüller firm also issued a solitary, one-off sports coupe of similar design.

Note: Many sources give total Hebmüller production as 696 cars, built from 1949 through the summer of 1952. Others suggest that as many as 750 were made. Either way, a serious fire at the Hebmüller factory, not long after start-up, held production far below what might otherwise have been possible.

Beetle Convertibles from Karmann (1949-1979)

Bulbous but strangely captivating, VW's four-passenger convertibles engaged for three decades in a flirtation with drivers around the globe. Young-at-heart folks who weren't content with a steel-roofed Beetle needed another, more romantic choice. Based solidly upon the sedan, Volkswagen convertibles soon became noteworthy for their unusually bulky soft tops (when folded).

Convertible bodies came not from the Volkswagen factory, but from the Karmann coachwork firm. Wilhelm Karmann had begun building car bodies in 1901, at Osnabrück. Through the 1920s and '30s, he'd turned out handsome convertibles for Adler, Minerva and Opel.

Back in business after the war, in 1948 he bought a Beetle. Before long, Karmann received an order for a full 1,000 four-seat convertibles.

Design was nearly identical to the 1938-39 prototype. By 1950, Karmann had delivered the initial thousand, and Volkswagen eagerly ordered more.

Sales brochures in the early 1950s pledged that "this uncompromising full convertible is a true sporting comrade for nature loving motorists. Closed, the thickly padded sound absorbing folding top, with its rear windows now enlarged almost by half, offers the same coziness and protection from the dust, wind and weather as the steel roof on the sedan."

Better yet, the brochure continued, "wherever you drive

Early sales brochures enhanced the already-luminous appeal of the convertible body style. (Phil Hall)

or park a Volkswagen Convertible, it attracts the admiring attention of all eyes." In fact, dealers were told that it was "hard to talk a woman into a Sedan when she has once seen the graceful lines of the Convertible."

While other designers tried hard to make their convertible tops virtually disappear into the deck, Volkswagen and Karmann took the opposite tack. With the top down,

the fabric bundle looked big enough to make the car practically tip backward. Rather than detract from its appeal, curiously, that tall stack actually illuminated the car's endearing traits.

As a bonus, the bulky top yielded more rear-seat space, but it hampered visibility. Unlike most convertibles, the Volkswagen actually looked no less distinctive with its top erected. *Road & Track* magazine noted in 1954 that the Beetle's well-constructed top was padded and weatherproof. Veering aside from convention in another way, the VW was one of the few plushly-fitted convertibles on sale in the United States to have evolved from an economy car, instead of a more extravagant machine.

Motor Trend took a less charitable approach, branding the convertible "dumpy but minutely finished." It noted of the Beetle in general that the "reconstructed Nazi has won few prizes for beauty." Naturally, many would disagree on both counts.

"If you drive a Volkswagen Convertible," the sales brochure insisted in 1954, "you will always look tanned and healthy as if you just got back from a long vacation. With the top down you get full benefit of every ray of sunshine." No sun block for those hardy VW owners!

Few convertibles reached the United States before 1955. Production totaled just 364 convertibles in 1949, jumping to 2,695 in 1950, and 3,938 in 1951. (Some sources, including historian Jan Norbye, insist that early output was greater.)

By 1960, the convertible had adopted nearly all the improvements that were making sedans sell so strongly, including new push-button door handles and a bigger back window. When folded, the fabric top stood unusually tall, adding to the car's charms. Not too many convertibles reached the United States until the mid-1950s. (Volkswagen)

A larger-yet rear window went on the 1963 convertible (left), with one-third more glass area. Much-needed heater modifications helped keep the interior cozy—to a point. Volkswagens drew harsh criticism for meager heat. (Volkswagen)

Distinguishing a 1964 convertible from the prior year wasn't easy. Inside, a deep-dish two-spoke steering wheel, with spoke-mounted horn, replaced the earlier horn half-ring. (Volkswagen)

By 1966, convertibles enjoyed the benefits of a 50-horsepower "1300" engine—which helped, because ragtops weighed more than sedans. Initially popular with celebrities, by the Sixties convertibles enjoyed quite a following among ordinary outdoor-minded motorists.

Front occupants got built-in head restraints in the 1968 convertible, as well as taller, stronger bumpers. Moving the gearshift lever three inches to the rear was supposed to make shifting easier. (Volkswagen)

Convertibles tended to be fully "loaded," equipped with many more options than a typical Beetle sedan. In some cases, new features appeared on the convertibles first, then trickled down to "lowly" sedans and sun roofed models—the latter serving as VW's compromise offering. Back windows got 45 percent larger in 1957, to match the new oval-window sedans, then grew again in late 1962.

Celebrities—including some who might not wish to be seen in a prosaic Beetle sedan—took more kindly to the convertibles. In fact, they became quite fashionable in certain quarters. Such well-known international figures as seductive film star Brigitte Bardot, actor Alain Delon, and fashion designers Pierre Cardin and Yves St. Laurent soon could be seen tooling around Europe in Volkswagen convertibles.

Ordinary folk, on the other hand, had a harder time coming up with the cash for a convertible, which consistently sold for considerably more than the sedan. They looked like fun, and were fine choices for motorists who liked to be noticed. Not unlike the revived Chrysler LeBaron convertibles of the early 1980s, the Beetle ragtops tended to be especially popular with women.

Volkswagen marketers called it "the car of your dreams," a passionate vehicle that was also practical. Not only was the convertible "absolutely impervious to rain, wind, dust and cold," but inside—as in all VWs—"not an inch of space is unexploited and every ounce of weight is put to good use."

Special and Custom Bodies

Long before the era of dune buggies and Baja Bugs, replicars and retrocars, custom coachbuilders laid their hands on Beetles. What they produced ranged from elegant and memorable to "eek"-inspiring and eminently forgettable.

Most of the earliest special bodies hailed from Europe—especially (logically enough) from Germany. Among the most notable was the Rometsch company—officially Karosserie Friedrich Rometsch, in Berlin-Halensee. One of the top German coachworks, Rometsch produced a series of luxurious sport coupes and cabriolets from the early 1950s to about 1961. The first ones were rounded and elongated—hardtop coupes as well as full convertibles. Among their curious features, both body styles had a single, transversely-placed rear seat. In all, about 500 Rometsch VWs were built.

Most Rometsch cars were imported to the United States by individuals. All body panels were worked by hand, using no dies. Finishing a Rometsch body took as many as 2,000 man-hours.

Twin carburetors added zip to the Rometsch convertible's rear-mounted engine, borrowed from the Beetle but modified.

A far different form of Rometsch conversion arrived by 1956, restyled along American themes—including two-toning and wraparound windshields, two popular trends of the day. They also got wide doors (which dipped forward under the cowl for easier entry/exit). Disappearing tops folded neatly into the coachwork, the metal boot serving as part of the body's profile. In the custom tradition, trim and exterior were left up to the customer.

Like various other manufacturers, Rometsch produced special-bodied convertibles based on the VW chassis. Spear-shaped body trim on this 1962 model was exactly what Volkswagen vowed never to offer, in one of its advertisements.

Volkswagen-based roadsters built by Carr Kometson had just a little of the Porsche look. Note the "suicide" door.

Rometsch also built approximately 50 four-door Beetles, which were used for a time as taxis in Berlin, and served similar duty at Alpine resorts in Switzerland. The very idea of a Beetle with extra doors sounds bizarre, but several manufacturers tried their hand at extended-wheelbase renditions, with an even greater number of entry points.

At the 1954 Geneva Auto Salon, showgoers got to see coupes and cabriolets from the Beutler Body Shop, of Thun, Switzerland. Priced at $4,000, these Beutlers used a few stock parts—hubcaps, bumpers—but little else was Beetle-like. Later models used no VW body parts at all. Like most custom machines, such details as body colors, special features, and interior fittings were chosen by the paying customer. (Beutler also built the first Porsche sports car bodies.)

A handful of other German companies turned out the occasional special body, based upon the VW platform. They included Dannenhauser, Eller, Drews, and Stauss. See Chapter 14 for details on performance-oriented Volkswagen transformations.

OWNER COMMENTS: Dave Wigglesworth

He bought his first Volkswagen when he was about 14. A '61 sun roof. Today, oldies capture the attention of Dave Wigglesworth, a Kansas City resident. His 1946 Beetle was "put together with scavenged parts." It had been purchased by an American military officer, who'd bought a lottery ticket that entitled him to buy a new Volkswagen.

"He drove it all over Europe," Wigglesworth recalls. "He was stationed there. Then he shipped the car to Kansas City, where he was from." Before that original owner returned to Europe, in 1953, he put the car up on blocks. Wigglesworth finally bought it in '71.

The '46 is "mostly all original," except for a repaint in Europe. Formerly gray, it was repainted a VW color, "between tan and gray." The first owner also put seat covers on it. Wigglesworth still has a "couple of original tires." The car was written about in the *Kansas City Star* in the late 1980s, and was taken to a show in summer 1995. Those were "the only two times it's been out."

Wigglesworth has owned a 1950 black/white convertible for about four years. Like most convertibles, this one has "got everything on it," Dave says. "Dealers usually put everything on them." Fenders, hood and trunk lid are black; bodysides are white. Seats and top are gray.

Chapter 5

Beetle Into Bus: The First-Generation Transporters

Could a boxy, slab-sided van conceal underpinnings borrowed from a humble, basic Beetle? At first glance, the notion seems almost preposterous. Yet, more than three decades before the concept of a car-like minivan filled the minds of designers at Chrysler Corporation, Volkswagen began to issue a series of Transporters with the same rear-mounted, air-cooled engine as the Beetle. Looking closer, we find that their platform, suspension, drivetrain—scads of mechanical components—were little different than the parts employed by their smaller brother.

If the very idea of a Beetle-based van wasn't far-out enough, who could have imagined that the Microbus would become a cultural icon on its own—as familiar around the world as the Beetle itself. Not only would it serve millions as utilitarian transport and cargo-hauler, but its destiny would eventually become intertwined with the counterculture of the Sixties.

VW vans hauled goods to stores, carried invalids to hospitals, dragged loads of Little Leaguers to playing fields, and conveyed countless suburban families to holiday sites. They packed surfboards and suitcases, musical instruments and machinery. At the same time, they also became the transportation mode of choice for thousands of flower children and their followers, gaily decorated with "flower power" paint jobs and unofficially dubbed "hippie vans." Transporters were just as much at home at Woodstock or Haight-Ashbury, as they were at a civilized campground or beach, or parked in a suburban driveway.

Startup Time

Ben Pon, the Dutchman responsible for getting the first Beetles to New York, had drawn a plan for a boxy Type 2 Transporter as early as 1947. He was convinced that such a vehicle would sell in his native Holland. Major Hirst sketched a commercial lift truck earlier yet, and several of those saw service in the factory. Engineers got busy, and turned out a design for a slab-sided vehicle that employed basic Volkswagen components and offered passenger car virtues. Yet, it looked nothing like a Beetle and offered a wealth of load capacity.

Eight Transporters went on display late in 1949. Production of the pioneering minivan began early in 1950.

By 1951, a handful of buses were trickling into the United States, priced just above $2,000—considerably higher than a Beetle, but not out of line in the U.S. market. Transporters carried the same engine used in the sedan, also mounted at the rear. They weren't officially exported to the United States until 1952 (when 10 were sold). A press release issued 30 years later claimed that Volkswagen "started the van craze in America while attracting its own fierce brand of loyalists."

Imports started off slowly, in fact, but buses easily found their own legion of devoted fans. Standard and DeLuxe models were available, the latter priced $137 higher, and carrying up to eight passengers. Prices for the Standard model dipped to $1,995 in 1952, when a DeLuxe Transporter commanded $2,169.

By the mid-1950s, passenger-carrying Transporters—commonly called Microbuses—were gaining popularity almost as fast as the Beetle sedans on which they were based. Both vehicles rode on the same wheelbase, and Transporters measured only a few inches longer overall. (Phil Hall)

Side and rear doors on this panel truck gave easy access to its 170 cubic feet of cargo space. By 1961, the VW engine put out 40 horsepower—enough to propel a Transporter to 59 mph. (Volkswagen)

From the beginning, Transporters were used for commercial purposes. Not many bookkeepers would have thought of taking to a Kombi to offer on-the-road accounting services. (Volkswagen)

Flatbed trucks weren't common sights, but they demonstrate the versatility of the basic Transporter concept. (Phil Hall)

In 1954, the Transporter sales brochure listed six models:

• Eight-passenger Micro Bus (available with Golde sun roof at extra cost).

• DeLuxe Micro Bus with Golde sun roof, all-round windows, and side observation panels in the roof.

• Kombi—offered with or without passenger seating (Golde sun roof available). Seats were removable, but a Kombi could carry as many as eight or nine passengers with all seats in place. Rear side windows pivoted outward for extra ventilation. Because center and rear seats could be removed in seconds, Kombis were intended for transportation of either passengers or merchandise, alternating between the two. Cargo areas lacked complete headlining and interior panels.

• Delivery Van with hinged double doors on the right (doors on both sides at extra cost).

• Pickup Truck, with or without a cover. Pickups included an auxiliary, enclosed load space beneath the main loading area—a feature seldom seen in other trucks. Fragile or perishable items could go into that enclosed "Treasure Compartment," between the axles, considered to be the "best sprung part of the vehicle."

• Ambulance—complete with stretcher and additional seat. Fire trucks also were available.

Note: Early Volkswagen literature referred to the passenger vehicles as "Micro Buses," but a single word—Microbus—was more commonly used. Like the passenger car sales brochures, those promoting the Transporters were technically oriented, devoid of glib, overblown claims.

A double door on the right side of the Microbus gave access to the center and rear seats—which could be removed in two minutes or so. DeLuxe Microbuses added extra curved glass panels along the roof and rear quarters, as well as a sliding cloth sunshine roof. Pre-1955 Transporters had a large door (sometimes dubbed "barn door") covering the engine, gas tank, and spare tire.

Nearly 100,000 vans already were in service by 1954. Transporters were billed as suitable "for every job in every line of business." Commercial vans were "economical light-duty trucks perfectly fitted for the job at hand so that delivery costs can be drastically reduced."

Transporters, the brochure explained, were "not just converted sedans offering relatively little load space for freight in lieu of passengers." Volkswagen touted the Delivery Van as "quick and maneuverable in city traffic and robust and dependable in the country."

Even better, the commercial vans seated three on a bench seat that was "as comfortable as [sitting] on a sofa." Perhaps not quite, but Transporter owners and drivers

Chrysler boasted about having doors on both sides of its 1996 minivans, but Volkswagen beat them to the punch, more than three decades earlier, with its panel trucks. This is a 1961. (Phil Hall)

generally found their vehicles surprisingly comfortable, once they got used to the distinctive driving position, facing a nearly-horizontal steering wheel.

Volkswagen touted five Transporter features in the mid-Fifties:

Not too many wagons or vans came with swing-open "Safari" windshields, which locked in any position. This is a 1957 Microbus, at a Volkswagen event.

1. They could haul a larger quantity of cargo, because two-thirds of the interior volume was load space: 170 cubic feet in all.

2. With the loading door on the side next to the pavement, they were designed for easy loading and unloading. The driver did not have to leave the sidewalk or "stand in the gutter." Furthermore, the double doors were wide, so he had no difficulty in handling even the bulkiest articles. A low floor meant easier loading of heavy items.

3. "Counterbalanced" weight distribution, leading to a smooth ride. Even when empty, Volkswagen promised, a Transporter "glides as smoothly over rough roads as a swan on a pond," courtesy of its Torsi-O-Matic suspension. (Even Volkswagen couldn't resist fancy terms for technical features, in the American mode.)

4. With no "superfluous weight," Transporters could "haul a payload almost as heavy as they are themselves."

5. Low fuel consumption—over 25 miles per gallon with a full load.

Volkswagen boasted that no other vehicle in this class was fitted with standard roof-mounted ventilation. Fresh air came through an inlet above the windshield—an arrangement that was called the VW "air-conditioning system." (In those days before true air conditioning became common, many manufacturers used that term to describe their ventilation systems.)

Transporters also promised "ideal weight distribution, with the driver in front, engine in the rear, and load in the center and best sprung part of the vehicle." In addition, the load floor extended "unobstructed from the cab panel right to the engine compartment." For added convenience, a full-width parcel tray sat under the dashboard.

"Like a pilot in a plane," VW said of the Microbus, "the driver has unobstructed vision in every direction." Safety was assured "whether darting through traffic, skimming along country roads or winding...through tortuous mountains." A tilting seatback in the center row gave access to rear seats. DeLuxe Microbuses included plexiglas lateral deck windows, a sun roof, two-tone paint, and a double chrome ornamental band.

All first-generation buses were takeoffs on the same principle, with the same structure surrounding the occupants and down below. Volkswagen's basic Transporter design lasted into 1990, when it was replaced by the front-drive EuroVan. Meanwhile, a second generation debuted in 1968 (see Chapter 16).

More Than Mere Convenience

Nearly two million vans were built between 1950 and 1967—the first generation—but sales did not take off in the United States until the 1960s. By 1962, Transporters were the second best-selling imported vehicles.

Buses began with the 1131-cc engine, just like the Beetles. As the years passed, they gained bigger flat fours—usually at the same time as their passenger-sedan counterparts.

A rear bumper became standard on 1953 DeLuxe Microbuses, but was optional on others until mid-1954. In March 1955, buses got a larger dashboard, and lost their "barn door" lid and turn signal semaphores.

The basic 1956 lineup included the Kombi, Microbus and DeLuxe Microbus. Kombis again lacked complete side glass, while the DeLuxe Microbus had windows around its entire body, as well as skylights above the side windows. An eight-passenger Kombi sold for $1,995 in the United States, while the Microbus went for $2,095. In contrast, the new Karmann Ghia coupe commanded $2,395. Tires were larger than those on Beetles: super-balloon low-pressure rubber in 6.40x15 size.

On March 8, 1956, bus production switched to Hanover, 50 miles away from Wolfsburg.

A DeLuxe bus, complete with sun roof, went for a hefty $2,576 in 1958, while the basic Microbus brought just $2,120 and a Kombi listed for only $1,955. Microbuses weighed considerably more than the Kombi: 2,447 pounds vs. 2,127 for the fewer-windowed Kombi. Transporters gained a fully synchronized transmission (all four forward speeds) in 1959, earlier than the Beetle.

Like the Beetle sedans, Transporters got a boost to 40

Wide-opening doors and fold-down seats made it easy to climb aboard a DeLuxe wagon in the early 1960s. The sliding sun roof and abundance of windows made it a great sightseeing vehicle. Lower-cost models lacked the small, roof-mounted "skylight" windows. (Phil Hall)

Small rear window marks this busy VW panel truck as a pre-1964 model. It carried up to 1,830 pounds, economically. (Volkswagen)

DeLuxe station wagons and other Transporters gained a wider rear door—and broader back window—for 1964, improving rearward visibility. The new spring-loaded door was more than four feet wide. With a 50-horsepower engine, the wagon could travel at speeds up to 65 mph. (Volkswagen)

horsepower for 1961. The standard bus (generally called a station wagon) went for $2,245, and the DeLuxe brought $2,495. The price for a DeLuxe model rose to $2,655 in 1962—$390 more than the standard edition, and $670 higher than a Kombi.

Changes for 1962, as usual, were subtle—yet important. All four turn indicators now flashed simultaneously for emergencies. Larger taillights included a second bulb for turn signals. Like the Beetle, the buses now had a gas gauge, and lubed-for-life joints reduced the need for lubrication.

Billed as "famous in 120 countries," the first-generation bus measured only 9 inches longer than a sedan, and had a 9.4-inch road clearance. Microbuses still offered 170 cubic feet of cargo space, and were able to cruise at 59 mph.

Larger round front turn signal indicators went into 1963 models, and a fresh-air heating system became available. Microbuses could get an optional "1500" engine during that year, which would become standard by the 1965 season. The new engine measured 1493 cubic centimeters (91.1 cubic inches), and put out 50 horsepower. That contrasted with 72.7-cid and 40 horsepower for the standard four-cylinder engine.

Brakes increased in size, too (from 96 to 159 square inches). Top speed was 65 miles per hour—six more than before. By 1963, Volkswagen claimed that more than 150,000 of its trucks and wagons were in use in the United States.

The 1963 lineup included a station wagon (Microbus), wagon with sun roof, DeLuxe wagon, Kombi with seats, Kombi with sun roof, panel delivery, pickup and double-cab pickup.

By 1965, van seats were air-permeable leatherette, and the windshield wiper motor was more powerful. Not exactly earthshaking changes, but in keeping with Volkswagen's philosophy of continuous improvement. Seat belt anchorages were new in 1967, and control buttons got soft plastic knobs. Safety door locks were another new feature.

Most vans before 1967 had gear-reduction hubs for each rear axle. All had four-speed transmissions, but with low ratios that helped hold down speed. Even more than with passenger sedans, many owners elected to swap engines, tucking a later model flat four into their older vans.

Lack of power had been a common complaint, and Volkswagen didn't care for complaints. For 1966, the bigger engine gained some extra oomph—now rated at 53 horsepower.

Who Bought the Buses?

When Transporters first arrived on the market, they faced no real competition. Americans had not yet discovered trucks as daily transportation. That wouldn't happen for several decades. A fair number of practical-minded folks, though, quickly grasped the virtues of a spacious in-

Wagon owners could pack plenty of gear inside, along with as many as nine passengers. A new third-gear ratio for 1967 improved hill-climbing, and the electrical system went to 12 volts. (Phil Hall)

Many Microbus owners kept their vehicles strictly stock, but some took the personalized route. While this checkered van had a legitimate use in military flight line service, "Hippies" and counterculture folk of the late 1960s and '70s adopted the VW van as their transportation of choice, often painting the bodies in psychedelic colors and patterns. (Volkswagen)

terior, substantial load capacity, easy maneuverability—and frugal running. After all, no conventional American truck could offer gas mileage in the league of a Microbus.

Arrival of the DeLuxe models with their sun roofs and multiple windows—including panes along the roofline—attracted a different sort of customer. These vans could carry as many passengers as a gas-hungry American station wagon, but their miserly four-cylinder engines took those occupants far more miles with each gallon of fuel.

Sure, the driver of a Microbus couldn't expect much in the way of performance—even when the vehicle carried no load at all. Fill it up with humanity, and the already-dismal acceleration figures rose to agonizingly long durations.

At the same time, the "Vee-dub" vans just kept on rolling—slowly, but surprisingly surely—even when the terrain got tough. A bus might struggle hard up a mountain road, but it wound up at the summit eventually, just like the overweight American dreamboats.

As the counterculture emerged in the mid-Sixties, the strangest type of customer took hard to Microbuses. Lineal descendants of the "beat" generation of the 1950s, thousands of "hippies" and "flower children" took to the highways of America in battered or gaudily-decorated VW buses.

Typically, these were people who *deplored* the automobile culture and all its trappings, and seldom hesitated to say so. Yet, they felt at home in a Microbus. Just as Beetle owners formed a subculture of their own, Microbus fans fell into several different, but equally avid, groups.

How come? What was the main attraction?

Was it the basic nature of the beast? Its ease of repair—exemplified by the late John Muir, the enthusiastic but nonconformist author of *How to Keep Your Volkswagen Alive*? Its adaptability? Its reliability?

Or was it the hippie vehicle of choice simply because it was "different?"

Whatever the reason—and it's doubtless a blend of all the above—no other vehicle is so closely identified with the counterculture movement of the 1960s and '70s. More surprising yet, the vehicle's popularity with out-of-the-mainstream folks never died, as witness the "deadheads" who followed the concerts of the late Jerry Garcia and the Grateful Dead—well into the 1990s.

Curious Appeal of the Campmobile

Americans had taken their vehicles off to the woods before. Motor camping became a hot trend in the Teens and Twenties—the Model T Ford era. Early on, it was a rich person's pastime. As public campgrounds began to fill with people of more *modest* means—including some who camped as a way to live cheaply—the affluent turned to other pursuits rather than share the facilities.

In those days, motels did not dot the landscape. Howard Johnson's and Holiday Inn had not been "invented" yet. Hotels tended to be either expensive or uncomfortable (if not both). Tourist cabins sprung up in the 1930s, but many travelers liked something a bit more rustic—or couldn't afford even the modest rates of the day. So, the idea of camping out in a vehicle that could carry a full set of gear—tent, cookware, bedding—proved tempting to thousands.

The postwar era brought the first motels, but they took a while to spread their tentacles across the nation. Some farsighted folks took a look at that ever-so-basic Volkswagen bus, gradually making its way onto the U.S. scene, and envisioned a rebirth of the motor-camping notion.

America was prospering. Workers were able to enjoy more leisure time than ever before. Whether they lived in a city or in one of the emerging suburbs, the prospect of weekend trips—and summer vacations—traveling the nation's byroads proved hard to resist.

Volkswagen's first Campers, converted from regular vans, were issued by the Westfalia company, founded in 1844. By 1956, a Kamper kit was available, which converted an ordinary VW bus into a vehicle that could sleep a small family and included ample storage and a pop-up top. In 1957, the $2,712 Camper bus was fitted with such extras as a folding table and fold-out beds.

Camper prices edged upward in the late 1950s and early '60s, reaching $2,982 in 1962. In the final year of the first-generation buses, however, the 1967 Campmobile

Suburban dwellers who used their 1966 wagons for shopping and other sedate pursuits would be shocked to learn that "hippie freaks" loved their merrily-painted VW vans just as much. Engines added three horsepower this year, and a front stabilizer bar helped reduce body lean through corners. Whether headed for "love-ins" or the commuter train station, VW vans and wagons offered practical, economical transportation. (Phil Hall)

By the early Sixties, thousands of outdoorsy folks were heading for campgrounds aboard a VW Camper. A side-mounted awning was just one of many accessories to make the outdoor life more palatable. Equipped with running water and other comforts, a Camper could sleep two adults and two youngsters. (Volkswagen)

Several styles of "pop-tops" could be installed atop a Volkswagen Camper. This 1967 model is well-fitted, giving the owner a compact combination of kitchen, dinette, living and dining room—and sleeping area. (Phil Hall)

carried a lower ($2,667) sticker.

By 1962, Volkswagen announced that 10 different campers were available, at a variety of prices, allowing owners of existing vans to convert to camper operation. No longer was it necessary to buy a brand-new, expensive Westfalia Camper, to enjoy the benefits of having a mini-home on wheels.

Eight of these conversion units were German-produced, by Westfalia. Two were American. Each was equipped with beds and other fixtures. Four of the Westfalias could be converted to regular use, and several included a standard luggage rack and skylight.

Removable versions (Series 22) could be used for standard or Kombi wagons. Permanent conversions (Series 33) were only for installation in the Kombi. Prices ranged from $399 for the most basic removable conversion, all the way to $1,088 for the top permanent setup.

As described in a 1962 issue of *Foreign Car Guide*, one of the Texas-made conversion kits started at $450, plus installation charges. Known as the "20-minute" camper—because the equipment could be removed or reinstalled in that time, after initial dealer-installation—it could be used with any VW bus except the pickup.

Typical installations included a closet (with door mirror), a medicine cabinet, partial wall paneling, floor covering, hinged dining table, door shelf, cushions and curtains.

Front and rear benches converted into a small bed. The deluxe version went for $700, adding full paneling, a two-burner stove, icebox, water tank (with spigot), and a chemical toilet under the rear bench seat. Each model slept two adults and two children. A sling could convert the driver's seat area into a third child's bed.

By 1963, *Motor Trend* noted that six Campmobile kits were available, each permitting "easy disassembly." Available for the Kombi or panel truck, the more elaborate kits included storage closets, magazine racks, cabinets, 14-gallon water tanks (with pumps and swivel spigots), toilets and gas stoves.

Campers, as usual, had special screened windows and curtains. Options included a roof-mounted bedroom that could sleep two or more adults, free-standing tents and awnings, a luggage rack/sun deck (with ladder) and even a shower. A Campmobile could sleep up to four adults and two children. A new 50-horsepower engine was optional.

Volkswagen vowed that the final edition of its first-generation Campmobile "packs just about everything but the scenery inside its quick-change interior." Furthermore, it was "just as much at home on a mountain road or dirt trail as it is on a beach [and its] eight-inch road clearance and rear-wheel traction 'levels' all but the most uneven ground." An optional 6'6" by 9'5" free-standing tent could be left behind at the campsite if you wanted to dash off to town, and provided the privacy of an extra bedroom at night—plus the convenience of an extra living room by day.

Electrical fixtures included wall lamps and an outside service connection. Five of the screened windows were louver-type, with safety glass sections cranking open. Water could be stored in a pump-equipped tank built into the portable icebox. A fiberglass "pop-top" was optional, providing extra headroom or fresh air. Measuring 36 x 40 inches, the pop-up roof sections had screens on three sides and could be closed for privacy, using built-in canvas flaps.

Counterculture folks, incidentally, tended to ignore the Campers. Such factory-created concoctions were deemed far too "middle class" to be of value to those living in voluntary poverty. Instead, the "hippie" generation preferred to outfit its vans more haphazardly, with cursory sleeping and dining gear rather than squeaky-clean sinks and cushy cots.

Chapter 6

Beautiful Beetles: The Karmann Ghias (1956-1974)

Elegance melded with utility when Volkswagen enlisted the services of Ghia—the renowned Italian coachbuilding firm—to try its hand at a stylish variant of the Beetle. Karmann Ghias blended the mechanical components and structure of the humble two-door sedan with a luscious 2+2 coupe body.

The idea for a shapelier model came early. On November 16, 1953, Heinz Nordhoff saw and approved the prototype Karmann Ghia. In September 1955, the hardtop coupe went on exhibit at the Frankfurt motor show, and it was on sale a month later—in the United States as well as in Europe. America, in fact, soon became the prime market for Karmann Ghias. Half of all the Ghias produced over the next two decades were exported, and four-fifths of those crossed the Atlantic to America.

At first, the car went unnamed. Dr. Wilhelm Karmann, Jr. came up with the name, which gave equal credit to the design studio and the coachbuilder. Yes, this was the same Wilhelm Karmann coach company that built the Beetle convertibles. Often hyphenated in print, the name as used in VW literature had no hyphen: just Karmann Ghia.

Personal credit for the design itself was seized by Virgil Exner (who did dream cars for Ghia at the time), but also by Mario Felice Boana (owner of Ghia). Squint a little, in fact, and the car could be an essentially downsized version of the Chrysler D'Elegance, lending some credence to Exner's claim.

Despite its modest-size glass area and rather high beltline, the sporty 2+2 displayed lovely proportions. Defying aging, the coupe's stunning shape looked as alluring two decades later as it did at debut time.

Actually, except for enlarged taillights and federally-mandated bumpers in the Karmann Ghia's mature years, little changed over its long life, which ended with the 1974 model year. Few cars, imported or domestic, can approach that record of consistency in design.

Final models, for instance, had wraparound bumpers with rubber inserts, larger taillight housings and bigger brake pads. But no knowledgeable Volkswagen enthusi-

ast would ever mistake a Karmann Ghia—whatever its vintage—for anything else on the road.

To produce the Karmann Ghia, officially known as Type 143, a conventional Beetle chassis was widened, to accept the hand-built body. That shapely shell had a sculpted line leading from the lower door, upward and along the rear quarter panel. Small rear quarter windows were installed, along with curved door windows.

Drivers sat lower than in a Beetle, occupying a driving position described by *Motor Trend* as "more like Porsche." Trim and controls were a cut above those in the sedan: similar, but not identical. Either cloth or leatherette upholstery was available. Karmann Ghias could have fitted luggage, and doors were said to make a reassuring thud.

Accurately described in *Popular Mechanics*, the Karmann Ghia was "completely streamlined, the low, sleek body...designed and built by one of Italy's most famous body shops." The battery sat in the engine compartment,

Styled by Ghia in Italy, built at the Karmann coachworks in Germany, the luscious Karmann Ghia coupe debuted as a 1956 model. A matching convertible arrived two years later. (Phil Hall)

Structurally similar to the Volkswagen sedan, the Karmann Ghia had the same air-cooled rear engine. Displacement and horsepower increases occurred periodically regularly through the Sixties, but Karmann Ghias never fit the definition of a sports car—though they handled better than Beetles.

Karmann Ghias changed little in basic shape over their two-decade lifespan. By 1963, the stylish 2+2 coupe and convertible had a 40-horsepower engine, just like the Beetle's. In fact, nearly all year-by-year technical improvements for the Beetle also appeared in the Karmann Ghia. (Volkswagen)

and the car used "standard VW chassis components with only those minor modifications made necessary by the drastic streamlining."

The coupe had "an almost universal appeal to the eye," said *Road & Track* in its 1956 evaluation. "If looks are paramount, there is little doubt that [the car] will find fertile soil." Their Ghia accelerated to 60 mph in 27.2 seconds. Slim pillars and ample glass made visibility superior.

Contributing commentary to Volkswagen's *Small World* magazine years later, J.R. Clement of Tulsa put it sweeter yet: "A Karmann Ghia is a Volkswagen that has been kissed by a princess."

A large, velour-trimmed section in the rear held an upholstered bench seat of sorts, capable of holding cargo or a couple of highly cramped passengers. Its seatback folded for additional storage space—double the volume, in fact. Still, this was essentially a two-seater. Extra features included fresh air vents on left and right, plus a defroster jet for the rear window.

Volkswagen initially claimed a 72 mph top speed and fuel economy of 32 mpg for the Karmann Ghia. The coupe stood 52.2 inches tall, measured 64.2 inches wide and 163 inches long, and weighed 1,782 pounds. *Motor Trend* suggested that 80 mph was possible, due to streamlining, and you could "cruise with your foot to the firewall."

Convertible Joins the Karmann Ghia Coupe

A similarly-sleek cabriolet (convertible) debuted two years later, in 1957. Karmann created the smooth, weatherproof, neatly padded tops. Convertibles would get a vinyl top in 1964 (as did the open Beetle) to fold more compactly.

Dubbed Type 141, the convertible sold for $2,725 in its first season vs. $2,495 for a sport coupe, and weighed only 66 pounds more than the coupe.

Not even the alluring words in the Karmann Ghia sales brochure of the late 1950s could do the car justice. Each reader was asked to "Imagine it is *you* seated" in the Karmann Ghia.... She's the very essence of Beauty wedded to Common Sense.

"Every line says quality...quietly. The easy curvature of the body, the large contoured windows tell a story of great skill in design, in engineering.... And what a ride! Sure and steady, she handles with consummate ease."

Volkswagen's brochure copywriters had no hesitation about giving the Karmann Ghia a female persona. The Beetle had no specific gender, but the Karmann Ghia coupe and convertible were regularly defined as female—and presumably, aimed at women. Ease of entry, for instance, was touted as a prominent feature. So were seats that adjusted easily "to suit your leg length, your most comfortable back angle."

The foot that pressed the rubber-encased gas pedal—not the old-fashioned roller—in one illustration was wearing high-heeled pumps. In another picture, the driver wearing snug-fitting gloves was unquestionably a woman.

"You like her...enormously," the brochure implored.

"You want her...tremendously. And why not? Nowhere in the whole world of automobiles can you find such a happy combination of appearance, performance, riding comfort, and operating economy."

And that was just the coupe. The new convertible was described as "a very dream of a car—bright, gay, and eager to let you learn again the real fun of driving—blue skies, radiant sun, the wind in your hair, and a streamlined beauty that fairly hums with delight as she breezes along mile after mile."

Sounds like excitement aplenty. The only thing you *failed* to get was vigorous performance. Volkswagen promised a top speed of 70 mph, and the "fun" of getting fuel mileage of 32 miles per gallon. But in no way could the automaker ensure acceleration that took anyone's breath away. Performance was billed as "dependable," mechanical elements "delightful," but no words to suggest a thrill when tromping the gas were employed for this "nobly styled" Volkswagen.

Was it a sports car? Not by the usual definitions. Was it a "sporty" car? Definitely—though that term would not take hold until decades later. Could a Karmann Ghia hold its own among authentic sports cars? No. All you got, really, was Beetle-style performance, with a bit better handling.

The convertible was billed as "sleek, low and racy," wearing a soft top that one person could put up or down, in one minute, with one hand, using a central handle. Half of the top folded down into the body, the remainder protruding upward only moderately.

Aware that visibility was a problem in many convertibles, VW touted the virtues of the "unusually large and low" back windows, the big curved side windows, the narrow corner posts, and the high one-piece windshield.

Seats were upholstered in a combination of fabric in the center and washable, fade-proof leatherette on the sides. Full "leather-like" upholstery could be ordered. Beetles still did without a gas gauge, but the Karmann Ghia included one on its handsomely laid-out instrument panel.

In 1964, as before, the Karmann Ghia convertible promised the "dependability of the familiar VW sedan," blended with the "sleek sportiness" of a more costly car. Though frugal with fuel, Ghias could reach 75 mph. (Volkswagen)

Improvements for the 1965 Karmann Ghia coupe were all inside the car, including more responsive brakes, quicker wind-shield demisting, and lever-type heater controls. (Volkswagen)

Styling definitely took precedence over performance in the Karmann Ghia, but the 50-horsepower engine introduced for 1966 gave the convertible—and its coupe cousin—a little more energy.

Volkswagen continued to promote the "hand-finished body" of its 1967 Karmann Ghia convertible, which gained a "progressive" rear suspension for greater ride comfort, and a slightly larger engine. (Volkswagen)

A short, straight "sports-type" gearshift lever added to the cockpit appeal of the 1968 Karmann Ghia coupe, but the low-slung two-seater still looked little different than it had during its debut, more than a decade earlier. (Phil Hall)

Like the Beetle, the Karmann Ghia could have an Automatic Stick Shift transmission for 1969, which permitted manual shifting but eliminated the clutch pedal. Despite boosts in engine output through the years, the Karmann Ghia coupe still was tepid in the performance department—but lovers of its delectable shape didn't much care, whether in 1969 or any other season. (Phil Hall)

Installing a new "1600" engine in the 1970 Karmann Ghia convertible gave it a little more "oomph" when passing. Volkswagen billed the long-lived two-seater as "the world's most popular coupe." (Phil Hall)

Flexible, opaque sun visors were contoured to the roof/window lines. The steering wheel contained a horn ring, not a basic button.

Quite a few early Karmann Ghias were hopped up, using anything from a special cam and high compression pistons to going all the way—stuffing in a Porsche 356 engine.

Only 2,452 Karmann Ghia coupes reached the United States in 1956, initially priced at $2,395 in New York. Nevertheless, the car became a popular item worldwide—and remained in that laudable state for close to two decades. Between 1955 and 1973, a total of 283,501 Karmann Ghia coupes and 80,897 convertibles were made—plus 23,577 coupes built in Brazil.

Finally, Karmann Ghias Are Advertised

Word-of-mouth sold the Karmann Ghia through the first half-dozen years of its life. Advertising was nearly nonexistent until 1961. When national print ads did begin to appear, the theme was generally the car's blend of exotic looks, atop an oh-so-humble chassis. By 1962, Volkswagen reported that about half of Karmann Ghias, referred to as a "stylish young sister," went to owners over 40 years of age.

In early-Sixties advertisements, the company noted that "very limited production of this model was absorbed almost casually by established Volkswagen enthusiasts." Because most customers had previously owned Beetles, they "knew just what they were getting."

"In the last 6 years," an early Ghia ad commented, "this car has mystified millions. People have called it everything from an Alfa Romeo to a Ferrari." Quite a compliment, if true; but the ad agency's copywriters declared—tongue firmly in cheek—that "we can't have people calling it by somebody else's name." By then, about 9,000 Karmann Ghias headed toward the United States each year.

Volkswagen further claimed—with a strong helping of truth—that the Karmann Ghia's body lines were "too sculptured for mass production methods. The curve in the fender alone has to be made in 2 sections. Then welded together. Then shaped down by hand."

More than 185 workers were needed at the Karmann facility to make the body alone, using a large measure of handwork.

"You can't find a seam anywhere," the ad continued. "Not even where the fenders join the hood. One lady said it looked as if it had been carved out of soap." Coupe buyers also enjoyed a "soundproofed interior, with an acoustical ceiling like a modern office."

Critics placed the Karmann Ghia on a styling pedestal not unlike that earned by the 1953 Studebaker Starlight

Not many automobiles wind up as serious art objects, but late in the Sixties, the Karmann Ghia coupe headed an exhibit of the world's 15 best industrial designs. This "Designed for Use" show was arranged by industrial designer W. Dorwin Teague. Here, the honored coupe is entering the exhibition at the John and Mabel Ringling Museum of Art, in Sarasota, Florida. (Phil Hall)

coupe and its successors. In 1964, industrial designer W. Dorwin Teague included the Karmann Ghia in a list of the world's 20 best designs, for *Saturday Review* magazine. Later, Teague marveled that the car was "still being built and sold in its original form. It is amazing for a sports car to remain in vogue for so long." In 1969, a display of 15 best industrial designs at the John and Mabel Ringling Museum of Art in Sarasota included the Karmann Ghia coupe—part of a "Designed for Use" exhibit.

Karmann Ghias with the newly-introduced, no-clutch semi-automatic transmission (see Chapter 12) gained a double-jointed rear axle in 1969. Because their front ends could not accept the Super Beetle's MacPherson struts, they stuck with the original front suspension.

Chapter 7

Golden Age of the Beetle—The Square-Window Generation

Most Americans didn't know it yet, but by 1958—well before VW's phenomenal advertising campaign got underway—the stage already was set for the Beetle invasion. Yes, even before the oval-window sedan gave way to the more practical square-window design, the Beetle had established a rapidly-expanding toehold in the American market.

Sure, those imaginative, new-style ads drummed up plenty of sales through the early Sixties. But they could have done so only if Americans already were primed to respond. By the time those other Beatles—the mop-haired boys from Liverpool—arrived in the United States for the Ed Sullivan Show in 1964, the VW Beetle would turn into an automotive legend. A legend in its own time, at that.

What other vehicle, after all, could boast a steady—and increasingly steep—upward climb in sales, year after year? From a minuscule 390 Volkswagens sold in the United States in 1951, the total grew to a more-than-impressive 79,524 in 1957 (64,803 of them passenger cars). No other foreign make came close to that level of growth.

Still, success—however modest—of rival import makes helped pave the way for Volkswagen to turn from a strong

Even the 1953-57 oval rear window restricted visibility, so Volkswagen responded with a much larger, rectangular-shaped pane for its 1958 models. Purists and collectors tend to prefer the earlier Beetle models, whether split- or oval-window. (Volkswagen)

seller into a marketing superstar. Emergence in the early Fifties of such minicars as the Renault 4CV (and later, the more modern Dauphine), the British and German Fords, the Italian Fiats—each one helped prepare the American marketplace for a full-fledged invasion of the foreign machines. Each new arrival made the very idea of an imported car a bit more palatable to people who, a year or two earlier, would never have *dreamed* of taking the wheel of anything made outside of the United States.

Of all those European imports, few cars other than the Renault 4CV could be considered technically or stylistically related to the Beetle. Though the 4CV's tiny engine was water-cooled, not air-cooled, it resided in the rear. And although it had four doors instead of two, the mini-Renault's overall concept was at least a little Beetle-like.

Many of the other imported sedans tended to look like scaled-down American cars. That trend soon would reach absurd heights, as they also adopted tailfins and gaudy chrome. In a vain attempt to match their bigger American counterparts, rather than capitalize on their distinctly individual merits, most of those imports sealed their own doom.

By 1958, the sheer number of imported cars available in America had grown appreciably. As the 1957 season ended, the U.S. market offered more than 25 import models priced below $2,000.

Sweden had begun to ship the first Volvos and Saabs to East Coast ports. West Germany was sending everything from motorcycle-like Messerschmidts and mini Isettas to conventionally-designed Opel Rekords (available at Buick dealerships) and innovative DKWs. France had the Simca and Panhard, as well as the Renault 4CV and Dauphine—plus the crude-but-charming Citroën 2CV and its futuristic DS-19 cousin. Italy sent Fiat sedans in two sizes. Britain still had a host of offerings, including Austins, Ford Anglias and Prefects, Morris Minors, Hillmans, and the new Vauxhalls (sold by Pontiac dealers). Even East Germany was getting into the act, with the Wartburg.

There was also a trickle of minicars from Japan—the first Toyopets (from Toyota) and PL210 sedans from Datsun. They amounted to no more than a tiny blip in the sales picture. The day of Japanese dominance was still a long way off. Yet these seldom-seen entrants, too, played a small role in making small cars acceptable.

Who Was Buying Those Foreign Cars?

Already in the late Fifties, marketing analysts were studying the imported car market, trying to determine who bought them—and why. With the exception of American Motors, which was enjoying impressive success with its compact Ramblers, Detroit had scoffed all along at the idea of small cars. Industry leaders were dead certain that only a tiny handful of American motorists would ever be content with anything smaller than a Ford Customline or Chevrolet Bel Air.

As the decade drew to a close, however, Detroit had belatedly recognized the inevitable. Each of the Big Three was preparing for the debut of a compact model, intent on

capturing sales from these upstart imports. So was Studebaker, with its new Lark series (introduced in 1959). No one would ever mistake a Lark, Valiant or Ford Falcon for a Beetle—or any other foreign car—but the import manufacturers were getting worried.

Chevrolet, on the other hand, appeared to borrow a thought or two from Volkswagen when it launched the Corvair as its compact car entry for 1960. Instead of the usual inline six-cylinder engine up front, Corvairs got a rear-mounted, air-cooled powerplant—plus a fully independent suspension.

Meanwhile, the late Fifties ranked as the Golden Age of small imports in general—even though many of those "foreigners" weren't destined to last more than a few years in the U.S. market. A major shakeout was inevitable, with Volkswagen to be declared the sales champ by a knockout. But for the moment, driving an import—*any* import—was losing its negative image. Onlookers weren't so likely to laugh and scoff anymore. Why, some former naysayers even began to *praise* the import owners' collective wisdom.

Why were foreign cars—Volkswagen and otherwise—growing in popularity? For one thing, nonconformity wasn't quite as unacceptable as it had been earlier in the decade. Unconventional behavior still drew angry glares and bewildered stares, but Americans—at least in some circles, especially in the big cities—were developing a gradual taste for imported merchandise and previously-alien ideas. Many families, for instance, were augmenting their basic meat-and-potatoes diets with more exotic edibles from afar.

As for the Beetle, better visibility for 1958—and then a full-fledged gas gauge in 1962—helped make the car less idiosyncratic. More important, Americans were finally beginning to see the virtues in VW technology, and even to fall for its homely profile.

Benson & Benson Inc., of Princeton, New Jersey, surveyed people who bought new foreign cars in February 1958. They'd driven home 29 different makes. As summarized in *U.S. News & World Report*, the survey—called "The Market for Small Cars Today"—found that foreign car customers had a median income of $8,100 (vs. $7,850 for domestic car buyers). A full 85 percent earned $5,000 a year or more, and 37 percent made above $10,000.

Foreign car owners often were perceived as likely to be unmarried, but three-fifths of the small car buyers surveyed were married with children, and a comparable number had another car. Close to half were under 35 years old. Three-fourths were business executives, business owners or professionals. Two-thirds of the surveyed families had at least one member who'd finished college—this at a time when college degrees were far less common than they would become a decade or two later. No less than 85 percent of their trade-ins were domestic makes, so these were relative newcomers to the import car fold.

The National Automobile Dealers Association (NADA) undertook an even broader survey of import ownership, questioning 10,000 people who had bought foreign cars in 1956, 1957 or 1958. "The average customer for an import," said the summary in *Business Week*, "is educated, fairly prosperous—and so satisfied that he's likely to buy foreign again." The NADA concluded that "the buyer of a foreign car belongs to one of the most powerful economic blocs in the country today."

Getting down to arcane specifics, that average imported car owner in the NADA survey was male, 37 years old, stood 5 feet 9 inches tall, weighed 166 pounds—and had a median income around $8,200. He was also likely to be an executive or professional with a university education (69 percent had some college credit). That imported car cost him about $2,200. Though used primarily for commuting, 83 percent of those VWs went on long trips.

Demonstrating the growth in import ownership, only 10 percent had bought their cars in 1956, rising to 27 percent who had 1957 models, and 63 percent who made their purchases in 1958.

A mere 11 percent of the NADA-surveyed buyers were single and not living with their families, again defying the conventional wisdom that suggested import owners were "loners." More than three-fourths headed a household—but only 14 percent were female. Close to half of the respondents already owned a lower-priced domestic car, but 58 percent bought the import as their sole vehicle.

All told, the imported car buyers were found to be educated, with a "tendency not to conform to general patterns of behavior."

Asked by NADA if they would have bought an import if a similar U.S. car had been available at the same price,

60 percent said no. Equally revealing, 86 percent said they thought their *next* car would be import. The NADA called this "an overwhelming vote of confidence" in imported vehicles.

Why did they buy foreign instead of domestic? Among 13 possible reasons given in the NADA survey, 88 percent checked "cheaper to operate." More than half marked "easier handling in traffic," "easier to park," "not as much annual depreciation" and "better workmanship."

Building a Better Beetle

The new 1958 Volkswagen Beetle was easy to spot—and easier to sell. Why? Mainly, because its back window was *vastly* bigger. It was also rectangular instead of oval. VW had finally done something about a foremost complaint against early models: the lack of rearward visibility.

A larger windshield was less noticeable, but also made a difference, helping to turn the iconoclastic Beetle into a practical machine for mainstream motorists. That change was accomplished by narrowing the A-pillars. Windshield wipers now covered a 33 percent larger area.

Women, in particular, were presumed to appreciate the new gas pedal—especially if they wore high heels. Instead of the unique but awkward roller, installed in all prior models, a conventional flat pedal operated the accelerator cable.

Turn signal lights moved atop front fenders for 1958, and a chrome screen covered the horn. Inside, the radio grille moved to the left, facing the driver.

In addition to the bigger back window and larger windshield, 1958 Beetles got wider brake drums for quicker halting. Technical improvements continued to arrive at a rapid pace. (Volkswagen)

● Year-By-Year Changes, 1958-1964 ●
Beetles

1958:
Enlarged, rectangular rear window
Larger windshield
Flat gas pedal replaces roller-type accelerator
Turn signal lights move atop front fenders
Radio grille moves to left of speedometer, facing driver
Brake linings widened
Chrome screen covers horn

1959:
Stronger clutch springs
Improved fan belt
Reinforced frame

1960:
Push-button door handles replace pull-style
Redesigned, dish-style steering wheel with horn ring (Standard models, elsewhere in the world, keep three-spoke wheel)
Sun visors now padded vinyl (formerly transparent plastic)
Front anti-sway bar added, to improve cornering
Steering damper added, for better handling
Generator output increased (from 160 to 180 watts)
Seats re-contoured
Front passenger gets footrest

1961:
Engine gains 4 horsepower (now 40); still 1192 cc
All four forward speeds now synchronized
Reshaped (flatter) gas tank for 65 percent greater luggage volume
Automatic choke installed
New pump-type windshield washer

Transparent brake fluid reservoir
Non-repeating starter switch installed
Key slots in doors now horizontal (formerly vertical)
Second sun visor added
Passenger grab handle installed

1962:
Fuel gauge installed; reserve tank and lever deleted
New spring-loaded, counterbalanced hood
Larger brake and taillights
Three seatbelt mounting points installed
Sliding covers over heater vents
Windshield washer now pressurized by spare tire
Worm-and-roller steering replaces worm-and-sector unit
Perforated vinyl headliner replaces cloth (late 1962)
Lubrication points cut from 15 to 8, due to lubed-for-life joints
New anti-smog (PCV) breather attachment
More fore/aft front seat adjustment

1963:
Wolfsburg hood emblem dropped
Floorboards add foam insulation
Window guides now made of nylon
Fresh-air heating unit installed
Leatherette headliner installed
Adjustable rear heater vents added
Sun roof adds folding handle

1964:
Smaller steel sun roof replaces vinyl
New perforated leatherette upholstery matches headliner
Horn now operated by thumb bar
Wheel cover emblems no longer painted
Enlarged license plate light

Is it a 1959 Beetle—or a '58? Only the photo caption writer knew for sure. All improvements for 1959 were beneath the surface. Sun roofs added a dash of extra zest to the basic sedan design. (Volkswagen)

Except for new push-button door handles, replacing the prior pull-type units, the 1960 Volkswagens looked the same as '59s—and '58s. Front seats got re-contoured backrests for a little extra comfort on the road. (Volkswagen)

By now, the Beetle was selling for $1,545. A sun roof sedan went for $1,625, while the always-costlier convertible brought $2,045.

Changes were less evident for 1959, but just as important: stronger clutch springs, a better fan belt, a sturdier frame. Those improvements joined the bigger brakes that had been installed a year earlier. As the advertising campaign went into full swing (see Chapter 8), potential customers already were beginning to be aware that Volkswagen kept getting better and better, in ways that counted most, even if they looked little different from before.

Cosmetic improvements for 1960 included push-button door handles (edging aside the old-fashioned pull-type handles). American drivers faced a new recessed steering wheel with horn ring. (Standard models, elsewhere in the world, kept the traditional three-spoke wheel with a horn button.) Sun visors were now made of padded vinyl—considered more modern than the former transparent plastic visors. The front passenger gained the comfort of a footrest.

Finding ways to increase comfort always got attention, so seats were re-contoured. On the technical side, a front anti-sway bar was installed, and a steering damper added—two vital changes to improve the Beetle's handling prowess.

Volkswagen advised that the 1961 model had 27 different changes, though not all were major. Still displacing 1192 cubic centimeters, the Beetle engine gained 4 horsepower, reaching a whopping 40. Not every driver noticed the difference, which yielded quicker acceleration in the lower gears.

Everyone could appreciate the modified gearbox, however. All four forward speeds, including first, now were synchronized. Thus, a driver could snap the lever into first gear while the car was still moving. The old "crash box" with non-synchro cogs was long forgotten. So was the need to pull out a hand choke in the morning. The new engine's carburetor incorporated an automatic choke. A transparent brake-fluid reservoir was easier to check.

Lack of luggage space had long been a complaint, so designers reshaped the gas tank to permit a little more usable room up front. A new pump-type windshield washer was installed, but would last only a single season. Front passengers faced not only a sun visor, but a grab handle. Side marker lights and a non-repeating starter switch were new.

One of the most crucial items arrived for 1962: a real fuel gauge. That outmoded reserve-tank tap was gone, too—along with its potential for allowing fumes to leak into the passenger compartment. A quirky, even charming device in the Fifties, the reserve tap simply didn't fit in as Volkswagens moved into the automotive mainstream.

For years, VW front hoods had suffered nasty creases—and even breakage—because they became twisted when opened by a ratchet setup. Not anymore. A new dual-spring mechanism raised the hood evenly and held it open stably.

Taillights grew larger yet, in an endless quest for greater visibility on the road. Turn signals got separate bulbs.

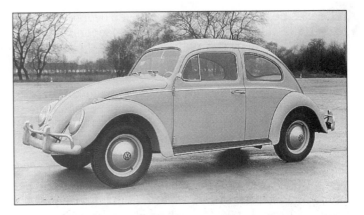

Volkswagens kept improving technically, and adopting cosmetic changes, as sales zoomed through the Fifties and early Sixties. The sales graph was on a steady uphill climb. The 1960 Beetles carried the last 36-horsepower engine. (Volkswagen)

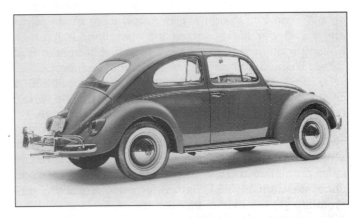

You wouldn't know it from outside, but the 1962 Volkswagens gained an item that few other modern automobiles had lacked—a gas gauge. Enlarged taillights promised greater safety. A more powerful (40-horsepower) engine had been installed a year earlier.

Shoulder belts could now be installed, on three-point mounting sites. Seats gained greater fore/aft and backrest adjustment.

Adding a little extra finesse to the interior, a sliding cover went over the heater vents. This year's optional windshield washer no longer was operated by a pump. Instead, it was pressurized by air from the spare tire—an innovation that never worked its way into general use among other makes. A hose connected its reservoir to the tire, to maintain pressure in the tank.

Whether European or American, automobiles still had to have periodic lube jobs. The task suddenly got easier, as new tie-rod ends were permanently lubricated. Those lubed-for-life joints and bearings cut the number of grease points from 15 to 8.

Worm-and-roller steering replaced the old worm-and-sector unit, but only the more dedicated, technically-focused drivers were likely to notice. As a sign of things to come, U.S.-market Volkswagens got a new "anti-smog" breather attachment.

Beetles destined for America had used hydraulic brakes for years, but elsewhere in the world, mechanical brakes hung on. No longer. The 1962 models were the last to employ this long-outmoded setup.

Years after American cars had switched to the 12-volt electrical system, VW stuck with 6-volt batteries. Promotional literature claimed that a 1962 Beetle could average 31.5 miles per gallon, drawing from its 10.6 gallon fuel tank. Both the sedan and the convertible could—according to the company—reach speeds of 72 mph.

Accessories—factory and aftermarket—continued to tempt Beetle owners. A set of four "Softafend" solid rubber bumper guards ran $19.95 in 1962, from International Automotive Imports. MW Specialties offered the Tilt-A-Seat, a nine-position reclining seat. A Travelounger recliner from Pemco sold for just $6.45.

Late in 1962, perforated vinyl headliner material replaced the familiar fabric. Up front, the Wolfsburg emblem was deleted for 1963, after decorating VW hoods since 1951. Floorboards added foam padding for a little extra insulation comfort. Window guides now were made of nylon, for longer life if not easier operation. A fresh-air heating system was installed. The sun roof handle now folded flush, and headlining was made of leatherette.

By 1963, Volkswagen of America had a staff of 250 at Englewood Cliffs, New Jersey, under Carl H. Hahn, who'd headed the American subsidiary since 1959. Educated in five countries, Hahn had earned a Ph.D. from the University of Bern, Switzerland, and later served as an assistant professor of economics. He joined VW as head of export sales promotion in 1954, and he served as Nordhoff's personal assistant. In 1964, Hahn returned to Wolfsburg, promoted to the board of management.

A lot of sun roof sedan lovers were disappointed by the 1964 models. The long, sliding-back vinyl roof was gone, replaced by a smaller-sized, crank-operated steel sun

Owners had been complaining about lack of heat for years. A new heating system for 1963 helped—but not much. By adding a new plastic headliner, interiors were now fully washable, usually requiring only a damp sponge for clean-up chores. (Volkswagen)

roof. Even if it turned out to be better at preventing leakage, the new sun roof was so much smaller that it gave the car a far less airy feel when opened up to the sun. Another concession to changing times and shifting American attitudes, the loss of a fabric sun roof might have dismayed traditionalists, but wasn't likely to hurt sales.

Prices had hardly changed at all through this period. By 1964, the Beetle sedan listed for just $1,595, and a sun roof added $90. The convertible brought $2,095—this at a time when a Ford Falcon ragtop started at $2,481, and an open Chevrolet Impala V-8 stickered for $3,025.

Looking Good—Even To Its Harshest Critics

Foreign car sales hit their peak in 1959. Volkswagen also had another good year, with 150,601 rolling into American dealerships (120,442 passenger cars and 30,159 Transporters).

In the late Fifties, enthusiastic customers didn't appreciate having to wait for weeks—or months—to get their Volkswagens. In some areas, the waiting period could be a year or more. Responding to that clamor for cars, a "gray market" developed. Ads for "bootlegged" Volkswagens promised no waiting, and no "red tape." The price might be higher, but a shady Beetle just might be available immediately, instead of months down the line.

For the 1958-60 period, the actual number of new VWs entering the country and winding up in consumer hands totaled about 20 percent higher than factory export figures. Those illicit cars were marketed by dealers who ordinarily sold other makes, and also by used car dealers.

Writing an introduction to one book on VW history, board chairman Carl Hahn noted that "the technical concept of the Volkswagen was so advanced that it remained one of the best in the world for half a century. Reliability, robustness and versatility were the reasons for its success." Most important, the car was "acceptable by the customers, which was based on more than a pinch of emotion."

Even Hahn viewed the Beetle as "a real member of the family that just happened to live in the garage or under the streetlamp." The car also served as "an ambassador of Germany throughout the world."

As the Sixties unrolled, even some of those automotive "experts" who had formerly failed to appreciate the Beetle's merits were taking another—more favorable—look. The humble "1200" sedan, said *Car and Driver* magazine in 1963, "doesn't measure up to many of our hallowed standards [and] doesn't embody the virtues we esteem: its grip on the road is less than always secure, its acceleration leaves a flat taste, its braking ability is marginal and its passenger accommodations and comfort have not been well-handled."

Still, they concluded, the VW "is obviously a good car, perhaps in spite of itself." More notably, "it sells.... So it must have something. That 'something' lies as much in Volkswagen the philosophy as in Volkswagen the car."

Before investigating that philosophy further, we need to look at some of those ads.

● Volkswagen Goes Public ●

Through the Fifties, Volkswagen continued to operate without a formal organization—no conventional board of directors, no stockholders. Chancellor Konrad Adenauer's West German government served as trustee for the company, but in the mid-Fifties he was pondering a method of turning the VW organization over to private ownership. "As a part of a program for getting rid of state-controlled industrial properties," *Business Week* reported early in 1957, the Bonn government "wants to convert Volkswagen into a publicly held stock company."

In 1959, Heinz Nordhoff invested $125 million from earnings, boosting output to 3,000 per day. Even at that, the company had back orders, unable to keep pace with the demand for Beetles. By the end of 1960, some 4,000 a day were rolling off the line.

On January 16, 1961, VW finally went public. Employees got first "dibs" on stock. The first share was a gift from the company, and workers were permitted to buy nine more, at 350 Deutschmarks each. Of Volkswagen's 65,000 employees, only a thousand did not participate—mainly, people who earned too much (over $3,100 yearly) to qualify.

Company wages remained higher than the German average as the Sixties began, but still came to just 75 cents an hour. So, most workers would hardly have been likely to become stockholders any other way.

After the offering to workers, remaining shares went to the general public. The 3.6 million shares offered amounted to 60 percent of the total number outstanding. At first, people were permitted to buy up to five, but that limit had to be cut to two, due to strong demand.

Thousands of West Germans flocked to banks to buy "people's shares" in the company. Volkswagenwerk was now a $1 billion per year business, after all, having produced a record million vehicles in 1960 (485,000 of which were shipped to the United States). A 12 percent dividend was anticipated, too. As reported in *Newsweek*, "social rebates" went to low-income groups, workers, and big families.

OWNER COMMENTS: Tina Gibson

A resident of Columbus, Ohio, Tina Gibson inherited her first Volkswagen—a 1976 Beetle sedan—from her father in 1984. She flew to Florida with her husband and son, on People's Express, to drive the car up to Ohio. Tina had "had a stick before but it had been a while since I'd driven one." En route north, they ran into a blinding rainstorm in Tampa and the brakes went out. "Every time I stepped on the brakes," she recalls, the pedal "got lower and lower." So, a brake line had to be installed without delay. "Salt air from Florida wasn't so good for it," she notes.

After driving that car for about 10 years, Gibson took it to Ray Betz's shop for repair, expecting nothing serious. Instead, it turned out to have big rust holes and "wasn't worth fixing."

Fortunately, Betz, well-known in the area for VW work, had a restored 1973 Beetle for sale. So Tina drove home another Volkswagen, painted Porsche red and equipped with Porsche-style wheels. Described as being in "excellent condition," the '73 is driven mainly "to car shows, to church on Sundays, and to cruise-ins." It's "won a few awards" along the way, including a trophy in special class.

Chapter 8

From Strict Transportation to Pop Culture Icon

If your product isn't known, it can't be sold. That's an obvious maxim, which encourages businesses to advertise and engage in public relations pursuits.

In the case of Volkswagen in the late 1950s, they were known—but not quite well enough. Not enough to suit Dr. Carl Hahn, at any rate.

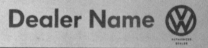

Of all the clever, trend-setting (and successful) VW ads created by Doyle, Dane Bernbach in the late 1950s and 1960s, few matched the "Lemon" for a sophisticated use of self-mockery. Decades after the ads appeared, many Americans still recall them fondly. (Volkswagen)

A protégé of Heinz Nordhoff, Hahn was named head of Volkswagen of America in 1959. At the time, Volkswagen had a six-month backlog of orders. Nevertheless, Hahn decided to hire an advertising agency.

Had he not done so—or had he been satisfied with an ordinary agency—one of the most memorable ad campaigns of all time would never have taken place. Even today, millions of Americans recall those VW print ads with glee, wondering why today's advertisers seldom come up with anything as imaginative—and as honest about their products.

Apart from a brief campaign in 1958 by the J.M. Mathes agency, VW had employed little U.S. advertising. Sales came mainly from word-of-mouth, and indirectly as a result of the jokes—tasteful or nasty—that had sprung up among early Beetle owners. (And among those who *detested* the car.)

Carl Hahn believed that such informal methods and dealer promotion, taken together, could sell no more than 150,000 or so cars per year. To get into the big leagues, and truly rival America's Big Three, he needed to advertise. Big time. That need was immediate, too, because those Detroit manufacturers were about to unveil a group of compact cars, intent on "stealing" sales from the imports.

Hahn Goes Fishing—Hooks DDB

Over a three month period, Hahn interviewed dozens of ad teams and talked with some 4,000 advertising people. He soon grew discouraged. Every agency showed him conventional advertising—just more of the same. As Hahn put it, "all we saw were presentations which showed Volkswagen ads that looked exactly like every other ad.... The only difference was that where the tube of toothpaste had been, they had placed a Volkswagen."

That shouldn't be a surprise. Through the Fifties, advertising agencies had developed a compelling fascination with deep research, with brainstorming, and with the psychological roots of customer motivation.

Ads were tested, retested, and examined yet again, to try and determine their exact impact on readers or viewers. The results were analyzed, and over-analyzed. After all that effort, agencies tended to come up with campaigns that were safe and familiar.

In the world of ad agencies, Doyle Dane Bernbach was different. Truly creative and unique, its ads were unlike those of any rival. DDB ads also did their job well.

Ten years old at the time, DDB had produced impressive results for such clients as Ohrbach's (a New York department store), El Al airlines, and Polaroid cameras. Across the country, far beyond Manhattan, people learned about the products from Levy's bakery. "You don't have to be Jewish to love Levy's," the headline read—a phrase that inspired many imitators, some pale, some amusing.

Arthur Stanton, a Volkswagen distributor and member of VW's ad committee, liked the Ohrbach's ads. After hiring DDB to do ads for his new dealership (Queensboro Motors), he passed the name along to higher-ups at Volkswagen in New Jersey.

In contrast to customary practice, DDB did not turn out samples on speculation. Instead, they simply showed work they'd done for *other* companies. Hahn liked what he saw, and gave the agency an $800,000 budget for starters. For the time being, VW's truck account went to another agency, Fuller & Smith & Ross; but DDB snagged that one, too, a year later.

The creative team—copywriter Julian Koenig and art director Helmut Krone—came up with a "look and tone of voice previously unheard of in car advertising," said the authors of *Is the Bug Dead?* (a recapitulation of the ad campaign). They didn't accomplish such a feat by simply sitting at their desks and drawing boards. No, the folks in charge of the Volkswagen account took off for Wolfsburg, to watch Beetles as they were built.

In the 270 acres of plant space in Germany, the ad men met with engineers, executives, production people, and ordinary assembly-line workers. They learned about the careful production techniques used on each car, and the high ratio of inspectors (beaten only by Rolls-Royce). They also studied the traction advantage of the rear engine, and the bonuses of air cooling. They found out how standardization simplified VW's parts lists and thus made repairs cheaper. They heard about the longer life offered by 15-inch tires.

Germans had long been known for their concern about quality, and for mechanical expertise. Now, they needed to restore that image. Therefore, the only acceptable goal would be to perform their work better than ever.

Back at their New York drawing boards, the ad men got busy. Not only did all the ads share a common theme, but they *looked* the same: a large black-and-white photo at the top, with a modest amount of copy below. Type styles never changed. Neither did the tone or style of the words. Paintings or illustrations never were used, and only occasionally a color photo. Many photos didn't even have people in them. Some lacked a background of any kind—heresy to many an ad man.

In the era of "big is better," Volkswagen's advice to look in the other direction could have ranked as heresy. Instead, it demonstrated a sense of humor that few advertisers could begin to approach—then or later. (Volkswagen)

Most readers probably didn't notice, but the headline always ended with a period. A simple choice, but doing it that way suggested that the statement was absolute fact, not a mere claim. Each paragraph below was written in an easygoing, conversational style, conveying sincerity and trust. If the car itself was supposed to be a simple, easy-to-understand machine, so too were the ads that promoted it.

In truth, the headlines *were* factual. So was the copy. Honesty was a hallmark of all the Volkswagen ads, whether in print or on TV.

Among other differences from customary ads, Volkswagen made no rude comments about competitive vehicles. These ads focused on what was right about the Beetle, not what was wrong with other automobiles.

This overall theme was conveyed in a refreshing, self-disparaging manner. Of all things, Volkswagen was making *fun* of itself. Madness! But a carefully-considered madness, supervised and approved by Paul Lee and Helmut Schmitz, of Volkswagen of America.

Copywriters turned presumed flaws into benefits. Their work was the epitome of the soft sell—a concept that had arisen during the Fifties as a reaction to the pushy, assertive, "anything goes" advertisements that had become the norm.

Advertising Age, a top trade magazine, analyzed one of the first VW ads, late in 1959. Above the headline "Is Volkswagen contemplating a change?," one Beetle was shown alongside another (which was covered up). The copy started off: "Volkswagen is constantly making changes—little changes that improve the car without transforming it in appearance." Even such items as permanent magnets in drain plugs had been introduced, "to keep oil free of tiny metal particles." The ad's final reassurance: "The Volkswagen has changed completely over the past eleven years, but not in its heart or face."

All true—and enormously effective. "This copy is so simple, believable, straightforward," the magazine declared. "No excitement. Just sheer, honest communication."

"No suave, debonair driver" sat behind a Beetle wheel in an ad, the authors of *Is the Bug Dead?* observed. No "admiring female" gazed longingly, either. "The copy treated the reader like an intelligent friend...and it was self-deprecating rather than self-congratulatory. The overall impression was one of friendly straightforwardness and disarming truthfulness."

Both television and the Volkswagen turned into cultural phenomena, despite slow growth in popularity at first. (Volkswagen)

Readers surveyed in 1962 used such terms as excellent, witty, sophisticated, truthful, and delightful to describe the ads. Some owners even collected VW ads in scrapbooks. Another survey revealed that VW ads drew twice the readership of ordinary automotive advertisements.

Advertising Age also liked VW's "Think Small" ad. "Nothing is quite so arresting in an advertising campaign," the magazine noted, "as to take an expression that has long been accepted without any questioning whatsoever and question it."

As for the "admission that these 'strange little cars' have 'beetle shapes,' how more effectively [to] kill off the opprobrium of beetle appearance than to frankly and, with a magnificent sense of humor, admit it?" The analysts praised DDB's use of "shrewd phrases and expressions," adding that the ad "talks candidly and without any exaggeration whatsoever."

Car and Driver noted in 1963 that by means of the "gentle prodding of a clever, consistent and *honest* advertising campaign, the VW became chic as well as practical."

A Few Favorites...

Just about everyone who saw the ads in the Sixties picked out a favorite gem or two—including people who hadn't the least intention of buying a Volkswagen.

"Think small." A tiny Beetle sits alone, forlorn, in the corner of the page, the balance nothing but white space.

"Lemon." Pictured is a Beetle standing by itself. The text notes that it suffered a blemished glovebox chrome strip, thus had to be rejected. That copy also noted that Volkswagen employed no fewer than 3,389 inspectors. Facts and figures were a regular feature.

"A thing like this could happen, even to a Volkswagen. After all, it's only human." This ad showed a VW being towed, alluding to the well-known fact that countless owners viewed their Beetles as virtual family members.

"I don't want an imported car; I want a Volkswagen." One fact of life had been growing painfully obvious to other manufacturers: a person who bought a VW wouldn't necessarily take kindly to any of its foreign rivals.

"It takes this many men to inspect this many Volkswagens." One car appeared with seemingly hundreds of people, standing to its rear.

"After a few years, it starts to look beautiful." Here, the copy elaborated further on a familiar theme, picking out a few phrases that might actually be heard in real life: "Ugly, isn't it?" "No class." "Good for laughs."

"Some shapes are hard to improve on." This ad showed the rear end of a Beetle, next to an egg. Case closed.

"Don't Laugh." Marketers knew that people had indeed laughed at the Beetle—but also that many were no longer dismissing the vehicle so cavalierly from consideration.

Is Volkswagen contemplating a change?

The answer is yes.

Volkswagen changes continually throughout each year. There have been 80 changes in 1959 alone.

But none of these are changes you merely see. We do not believe in planned obsolescence. We don't change a car for the sake of change. Therefore the doughty little Volkswagen shape will still be the same.

The familiar snub nose will still be intact.

Yet, good as our car is, we are constantly finding ways to make it better. For instance, we have put permanent magnets in the drain plugs. This will keep the oil free of tiny metal particles, since the metal adheres to the magnets.

Our shift, we are told, is the best in the world. But we found a way to make it even

smoother. We riveted special steel springs into our clutch plate lining.

The Volkswagen has changed completely over the past eleven years, but not its heart or face.

VW owners keep their cars year after year, secure in the knowledge that their used VW is worth almost as much as a new one.

Think tall.

Our Volkswagen Station Wagon is only nine inches longer than our little VW Sedan. Yet it holds more than the biggest conventional wagon.

How?

Perhaps this picture explains it.

Ideally, in a station wagon, you need maximum room and minimum length. We have answered this with a taller car. (The entire top of the VW wagon is level. This

gives it the shape of a box. There is not a wasted inch in it.)

This is why things that will not fit in any conventional wagon fit easily inside the VW wagon.

An upright piano standing upright. A standard bridge table opened up. Eight adults with all their luggage.

Or, if you open the sun-roof, a huge old-fashioned wooden wardrobe. Even a

horse fifteen hands high.

People are pleased that our VW wagon parks so easily. (If you have ever circled a shopping mart or a commuters' station looking for a big enough space for your big wagon, you can appreciate this.)

When you realize our VW Station Wagon is a good four feet shorter than conventional wagons, you get the picture.

Impossible.

A Volkswagen can't boil over.

It's physically impossible.

The reason is absurdly simple: the VW's rear engine is cooled by air, not water.

Since air can't boil, neither can the car.

If you had to, you could drive a VW all day at top speed through a desert. Or edge along in bumper-to-bumper traffic on the hottest day of the year.

You may get all steamed up, but not your Volkswagen.

Chances are you'll appreciate the air-cooled engine even more in winter. Air can't freeze any more than it can boil. So you don't need anti-freeze. (You couldn't put any in a VW even if you wanted to; there's no radiator. And so no hoses to leak. No draining. No flushing. No rust.)

In the past, a few VW owners have been amused to find a perplexed gas station attendant with a bucket of water and no place to put it.

But we've taken care of that in our '61 model. This year, a windshield washer is standard equipment.

It uses water.

Let the man fill it up.

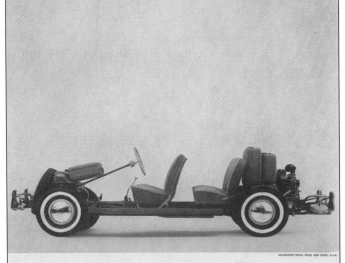

Can you name this car?

Clue: Even on the hottest day, you won't see this car with its hood up. (The engine is cooled by air instead of water. Won't overheat, won't freeze.)

Clue: It cruises at 70 miles an hour all day long without working up a sweat or running up a

repair bill.

Clue: In mud, sand, ice or snow, where other cars skid, this one will go. (The engine in the rear does it.)

Clue: It's put together so air-tight, there have been persistent reports it will even float.

Clue: It's never been changed for the sake of change—and it won't be, either.

Clue: It sells for $1,565,* complete with body. And a used one depreciates less than any other car.

Clue: Its initials are VW.

Our beauty.

Will it spoil the Volkswagen image?

We never thought it would come to this. A beautiful Volkswagen.

All these years we've been telling you about the ugly bug.

And now, the snazzy Fastback sedan.

But don't let its good looks fool you. When you really come down to it, it's still a Volkswagen.

The engine is still in the rear and it's still air-cooled.

It's just as easy to replace parts. It still takes 10 bolts to bolt on a new fender.)

And it's just as easy on gas as any other Volkswagen. The Fastback averages 27 miles on a gallon of gas. Which is pretty good for a car that cruises over 80 miles per hour.)

While we were making this beauty beautiful, we were also making it bigger.

It's got a trunk in the front where most cars have their motors. And a trunk in the back where most Volkswagens have their motors.

And in case you're wondering where we put the motor, well, it's neatly tucked underneath the trunk in the rear.

The Fastback's also got a little more room for passengers than the beetle.

You pay a little more for it, too. ($2,148.)*

Will a Volkswagen like this change our image?

We doubt it.

After all, it's only the world's most beautiful Volkswagen.

Not the world's most beautiful car.

The famous Italian designer suggested one change.

Just because the appearance of the Volkswagen doesn't change from year to year, don't think we take it for granted.

Some time ago, we called in a world-famous Italian body designer and we asked him what changes he would recommend in the design of the Volkswagen.

"That's all?"

"That's all."

We did, starting with the '58 VW.

The Volkswagen is never changed to make it different. Only to make it better.

Changes take place throughout the year. 19 functional improvements have been made in the 1960-1961 car, for example.

wouldn't detect these changes unless we pointed them out. A nice Volkswagen touch is that most of the new parts are interchangeable; they can also be used on previous-year VWs.

We think the Volkswagen approach to automobile design makes sense.

What are you staring at? Haven't you ever seen a station wagon before?

Breaking traditions is a kind of a thing with us.

We once introduced a car that looked like a beetle.

So we felt that a Volkswagen Station Wagon ought to bring something new to the party, too.

This one seats 8 people or a small elephant. And it's only 9 inches longer than a Volkswagen Sedan.

For elephants, say pans and pianos there's a doorway almost 4 feet wide.

And for long things like a tree, you get a hole in the roof. It not only lets the tree out but the sunshine in.

23 windows to look out of. And a sun-roof. (Moon-roof after dark.)

And a walk-thru seat so you can easily seat the children. (This joy is optional.)

And so we come to the price. Ready? $2656.*

Maybe you've never seen a station wagon before, at that.

Never.

We'd no sooner make an over-chromed, two-toned Volkswagen than we'd change the classic beetle shape.

It's not that the chromed version looks so bad; it just doesn't make the car work any better.

That's the rule of thumb we go by: we change the VW only to improve it, not to

make last year's model obsolete.

In 1961, for example, we were able to get more horsepower from our air-cooled engine without making it any bigger or less economical.

(One thing did get bigger this year: the tail lights.)

Everything on the VW happens for a

reason; nothing is for show.

We don't even have a chrome piece that spells out our name.

We do have a little round emblem with our initials on it, though.

After all, we can't let 600,000 Americans go riding around in unidentified cars.

What's a nice-looking car like you doing in a Volkswagen ad?

Nobody made a mistake. That shapely car is the new Volkswagen Fastback.

It's in this VW ad because it's a VW. (We haven't made very many yet, so you probably haven't even seen one yet. That's why we're running this ad in the first place.)

The Fastback isn't a VW in name only; it's a Volkswagen through and through.

The engine is air-cooled so it has no use for water or antifreeze. And it's in the back to make the going easy when the weather isn't.

The Fastback is airtight, like all Volkswagens, because it's made in the same plant by the same people.

Naturally, there are differences, too. The Fastback engine is a little more powerful (the car will cruise at better than 80). It holds 5 nicely. It has disc brakes in front. The upholstery is (for us) kind of jazzy. And it (the Fastback) costs $2128.*

If you've steered clear of a Volkswagen because it wasn't big enough or good-looking enough or expensive enough, you may be forced into thinking it all through again.

Sorry.

©Volkswagen of America, Inc. *Suggested Retail Price, East Coast P.O.E. Local Taxes and Other Dealer Delivery Charges, if Any, Additional. Whitewalls Optional at Extra Cost.

Do you earn too much to afford one?

For many people the Volkswagen would be an ideal car. Except for one thing. It doesn't cost enough.

They're afraid nobody will know they have any money, if it doesn't show in their car. In other words, they buy their car for other people. Not themselves.

Then there are those who earn enough to buy a much better car than the VW. But they don't. Because they can't find one.

For them the best car is one that simply gets them there. Comfortably and economically. One they don't have to worry about. That doesn't make many stops for gas. And rarely needs repairs.

A car where rare repairs don't cost much.

A car where the car doesn't cost much. They feel they can afford to save money with a Volkswagen.

Now next time you see somebody driving a VW don't feel sorry for him.

Who knows? Someday the bank might be using his money to give you a new car loan.

Has the Volkswagen fad died out?

Yes.

But it was an unnerving experience while it lasted.

Because after we introduced our completely sensible car, people ran out and got it for completely frivolous reasons.

The first people bought VWs just so they could be the first people to have one. And a lady in Illinois had one because it looked cute beside her "real" car.

However, the faddists soon found out that the bug wasn't an expensive ($1574) toy, but a cheap ($1574)* car.

As a fad, the car was a flop.

When you drive the latest fad to a party, and find 2 more fads there ahead of you, it catches you off your avant-garde.)

But as a car, the VW was impressive.

If you had to go someplace, it took you. Even when some cars wouldn't. And when you got there, you could park it. In places where other cars couldn't.

Once people took the bug's good points for granted, it became the best-selling car model in history.

And that's when the VW fad ended.

After a few years, it starts to look beautiful.

"Ugly, isn't it?"
"No class."
"Looks like an afterthought."
"Good for laughs."
"Snubby buggy."
"El Pig-O."

New York Magazine said: "And then there is the VW, which retains its value better than anything else. A 1956 VW is worth more today than any American sedan built the same year, with the possible exception of a Cadillac."

Around 27 miles to the gallon. Pints of oil instead of quarts. No radiator.

Rear engine traction. Low insurance. $1799* is the price.

Beautiful, isn't it?

What if it poops out in Paducah?

A thing like that could happen, even to a Volkswagen. After all, it's only human.

And with your luck, it would happen at least 500 miles from home. In Paducah (Ky.) or Brewer (Me.) or Ketchikan (Alas.). Alas.

You may be far from happy, but you'll never be far from a VW dealer. We have one in each of those towns (and in 804 others in 50 states).

So if you want to find out how good VW service is, break down and call us. You won't wait long for parts. All 5,008 are on hand or on tap.

And when we improve a part, we try to make it fit our older cars too. So a '64 clutch, for instance, is right at home in a '53 VW.

And the mechanic won't need all day to install the clutch (the way he would for most cars). Our car is made so the work only takes 2 hours. And many repairs are finished even faster.

Because we designed the Volkswagen as if we expected it to poop out every week. And then we built it so it wouldn't.

Old Volkswagen Station Wagons never die.

The things some people can do with an old box.

But then, he didn't start with any old box. He started with a Volkswagen Station Wagon. Which has about twice the amount of space as an ordinary wagon.

There was room for everything.

A refrigerator, a stove, a table, an in-stant chili dispenser, and of course, the proverbial kitchen sink.

And a way for it all to get in. The two side doors open into a huge 4' by 4' hole.

Also, its roof may be high compared to other wagons, but its overhead is low. Our Standard VW wagon costs only $2,337.*

However, if you're planning to go into the restaurant business, better not buy one new. (The body's been welded into one solid piece of steel, the tires alone will last for 35,000 miles, and on top of everything else, there are four coats of protective paint.)

It'll take too long to get a new one into bad enough shape.

Every new one comes slightly used.

The road to becoming a Volkswagen is a rough one. The obstacles are many.

Some make it.

Some crack.

Those who make it are scrutinized by 8,397 inspectors. 1807 of whom are finicky women.

They're subjected to 16,000 different inspections.

They're driven the equivalent of 3 miles on a special test stand.

Every engine is broken in.

Every transmission.

Many bugs are then plucked from the production line. Their sole function in life is to be tested and not to be sold.

We put them through water to make sure they don't leak.

We put them through mud and salt to make sure they won't rust.

They climb hills to test handbrakes and clutches.

Then comes the dreaded wind tunnel and a trip over 8 different road surfaces to check out the ride.

Torsion bars are twisted 100,000 times to make sure they torsion properly.

Keys are turned on 25,000 times to make sure they don't break off in keylocks.

And so it goes on. 200 Volkswagens are rejected every day.

It's a tough league.

Volkswagen doesn't do it again.

Beautiful. It's not any longer. It's not any lower. And it's not any wider. The 1969 Volkswagen. 15 improvements. Ugly as ever. Beautiful. Just beautiful.

"$1.02 a Pound." Economy was a focal point of many ads—both initial purchase price and operating costs. **"It won't drive you to the poorhouse"** was another example.

"We don't have anything to show you in our new model." The space ordinarily occupied by a photograph was completely blank. Executives in Germany were said to be dubious about this theme for the 1961 model, but it drew a lot of favorable comment. So, it was repeated in slightly different context, in subsequent years.

Karmann Ghia ads came late, emphasizing that the delicious shape concealed a modest Beetle underneath. "Volkswagen Incognito," said one headline. "You'd have to be some kind of a car sleuth to know that concealed beneath the Karmann Ghia's beautiful exterior is the heart of a Volkswagen."

Even when the Beetle began to age, and faced extinction, the clever ads kept coming. "How much longer can we hand you this line?" asked one of them, which used a single drawn line—roughly shaped in Beetle profile—as its illustration.

TV commercials enjoyed a similar response, and focused equally hard on honesty. Though clever, they aren't quite as well remembered as the print ads.

Volkswagen's ongoing program of continuous improvement, without changing the basics, was a focal point of many Beetle advertisements. (Volkswagen)

One video sequence started with outlandish, overblown claims by typical domestic manufacturers. Then, a nerdily-dressed presenter explained calmly: "So Volkswagen will constantly be changing, improving, and refining this car. Not necessarily to keep in style with the times, but to make a better car." A reassuring voiceover concluded: "Of all the promises made at the 1949 Auto Show, we at Volkswagen kept ours."

In another TV sequence, a deceased man's nephew is seen driving a Beetle in a funeral procession dominated by Rolls-Royce. Turns out he gets the old boy's ample inheritance, because his uncle had admired frugality.

Another commercial showed a Karmann Ghia trying to burst through a paper barrier—and failing. "The most economical sports car you can buy," the words intoned. "It's just not the most powerful." One of the best depicted a snowplow driver—heading for work in a VW. Print ads also developed this theme.

Surprisingly, a check of articles during the early 1960s reveals relatively few stories about Volkswagen advertising. While laudatory comments appeared periodically in *Advertising Age*, even that influential publication paid more attention to the conventional ads placed by domestic manufacturers. Ads from certain other foreign cars got more attention, too—in part because Renault was outspending Volkswagen by far.

By 1960, Volkswagen's ad budget topped $1.5 million. But the budgets of Rootes Motors (Hillman/Sunbeam) and Standard-Triumph, whose products never came anywhere close to VW in sales, were in the same league. At the time, Renault was spending $5 million annually to push its Dauphine.

Foreign cars accounted for 10 percent of new car registrations, but were not considered major advertisers. In a readership study, W. Bradford Briggs, publisher of *Sports Cars Illustrated*, said the small car market had expanded tremendously "with only a handful of advertising dollars." He added: "This is one of those rare cases where national advertising cannot take the credit for creating a market of this dimension."

Despite small budgets, *Advertising Age* noted that foreign car accounts were "highly prized [and] sought as prestige business." A lot of import advertising went into "class publications," notably *The New Yorker*, as well as sports car magazines.

A panel for *Printers' Ink*, another trade publication, selected VW ads as best print series, noting their "refreshing off-beat believability and concentration on fact."

VWs in the Movies

Advertising helped Volkswagen boost its sales figures to previously unimagined levels, taking a giant step toward making the car a pop-culture phenomenon. That can't happen, however, until a product begins to appear outside its regular context. VWs wouldn't really become a cultural icon until they were perceived as something more than an automobile. Until they could "go Hollywood," as it were.

That happened in 1969, when Walt Disney Studios released the first of four "Herbie" movies. Classic films these were not, but rather entertaining—and popular—bits of fluff.

One VW ad depicted a car wearing shades, headlined "Our car the movie star." This was a reference to *The Love Bug*, first of a quartet that featured a Beetle named Herbie, wearing number 53 on its doors. Owned by a failed race driver, the seemingly semi-human Herbie managed to spark romantic match-ups, emerge victorious on the track, and lead the action toward a happy ending.

To the surprise of many, *The Love Bug*, produced by Bill Walsh and starring Michelle Lee and Dean Jones, raked in plenty at the box office. A 1974 sequel, *Herbie Rides Again*, starred Ken Berry, Stephanie Powers and Helen Hayes, who called her role "a delightful part." That was followed by *Herbie Goes to Monte Carlo* and 1980's *Herbie Goes Bananas* (in which the car passed through the Panama Canal).

A red Microbus made an appearance in *Alice's Restaurant*, an adaptation of the similarly-named 18 minute talking-blues song by Arlo Guthrie, which captured much of the essence of the peace and counterculture movement.

Not everyone saw the "Herbie" movies, but serious film fans may recall the words of Woody Allen in his 1973 comedy, *Sleeper*. Woody has awakened in a future time, after being frozen for posterity. During his journey toward freedom, he stumbles upon a Beetle inside a dark cave. Naturally, despite having stood idle for a century or two, it fires up at the first crank of the engine. Woody remarks with a knowing nod: "They really built these things, didn't they?"

Other Fictional Volkswagens

Kinsey Millhone is the anti-heroine of Sue Grafton's well-liked mystery series, which began with *A is for Alibi* and has continued through *L is for Lawless* and beyond. Being a nonconformist character, naturally Kinsey drives a Beetle through most of the novels. A well-worn Beetle, at that.

VW fans might enjoy the countless references to Baja Bugs and Cal-retro Beetles, and to actual elements of Volkswagen history, in the 1995 novel *Still Life with Volkswagens*. They might not be quite as appreciative of the fact that Beetles keep blowing up in this quirky British novel, victims of an eco-terrorist group, a troubled VW restorer—or who? If nothing else, this novel by Geoff Nicholson demonstrates the fact that collectible Beetles are just as popular in Britain as they are in the United States.

Much earlier, *The Ultimate Auto*, a children's book by Patrick McGivern used a 1967 Volkswagen as the car that became "one too many" for New York, grinding the city to a halt.

Well into the Nineties, Beetles continue to turn up on TV—not as collector cars, but as regular transportation for a character. Dr. Susan Lewis drove a Beetle in *ER*, the popular medical program of the mid-1990s. Portrayed by Sherry Stringfield, Dr. Lewis continually faced problems at the hospital and at home. Seeing her looking forlorn inside that Beetle helped induce, in the viewing audience, a highly sympathetic reaction to her plight.

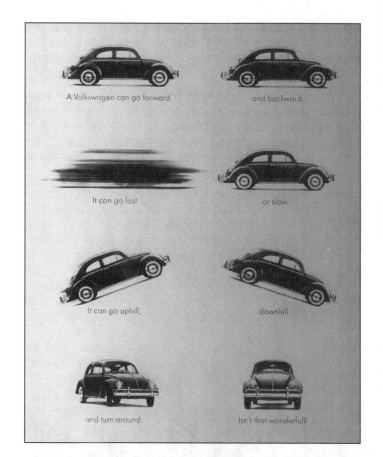

This ad drew criticism from Advertising Age, a trade magazine, on the grounds that the message was overly obvious, saying nothing. (Volkswagen)

More Than Transportation

As owners began to view their Volkswagens as family members or friends, they developed a mystique enjoyed by few automobiles other than the Model T Ford. A Houston newspaper ad trying to sell a used 1962 model called it: "Cheerful, reverent, brave, kind, careful and obedient. Dependable, too." A New Jersey Beetle with a large, rusty dent in its fender wore neatly-lettered paint above, reading "OUCH!" Another dented Bug wore a criss-crossed pair of bandaids at the deepest portion of the damage.

"A policeman who switched to a Volkswagen for use as an unmarked patrol car in a New York town ran into frustrations," a Memphis newspaper noted in the early 1960s. "Motorists didn't take him seriously when he ordered them to pull to the curb."

Celebrities also gave the car a boost into legend. Actor Paul Newman was a longtime VW fan. Leaving a Beverly Hills party for Britain's Princess Margaret and her husband, Newman and wife Joanne Woodward asked the parking attendant to bring their Volkswagen. As described in the *Los Angeles Herald-Examiner*, "the stars drove off in the tiny car amid the cheers of the crowd who saw some 15 Rolls-Royce, three Bentleys and scores of Jaguars and Cadillacs in the jammed parking lot." Back home in England, Princess Margaret herself drove a VW.

Owning a Volkswagen also came to define a certain

type of individual—though in reality, Beetle buyers ran all over the spectrum. Early in the Sixties, Paul Gapp of the *Chicago Daily News* re-examined Park Forest, Illinois, noted some years previous as the archetypical home of the 1950s "organization man." Gapp speculated that "the conformist—the organization man—has four kids, drives a Pontiac station wagon, carries six credit cards, spends a lot of time at home but doesn't understand his children, plays a lot of cards and golf and watches a lot of television." The nonconformist "has two kids, drives a Volkswagen Microbus, carries a paperback book, goes to PTA meetings himself to find out what's happening, and talks, talks, talks to his friends over the hi-fi or the TV show that nobody is watching."

Sydney J. Harris, also a *Daily News* columnist, suggested that VW drivers were "sensible people, with decent values." (Conversely, some insisted that Beetle owners were "intellectual snobs.")

Curious uses for Volkswagens also gave them a distinct image—one that the company's marketers liked to publicize. The massive King Ranch in Texas, for instance, bought VWs for cowboys on fence-riding patrols.

Tales—tall or otherwise—contributed further to the VW mystique. In Salem, Oregon, a group of hunters reportedly left a Volkswagen in the road. Loggers, according to the local paper, later picked up the car and placed it atop a stump. A California woman floated a quarter-mile through flood water, inside a Beetle—which remained dry inside. A South African couple outdid her; their VW was submerged in a flood, yet they emerged nearly unscathed.

No one can say how many counterculture folks owned VWs, but it's safe to assume that most of them carried around a copy of the late John Muir's book, *How To Keep Your Volkswagen Alive.* Suburbanites, too, found Muir's easy-to-understand description of VW maintenance and repair invaluable. Exceptionally clear drawings helped many a novice mechanic repair—and even rebuild—his or her VW. A Volkswagen's "Karma," Muir advised, "depends on your desire to make and keep it—ALIVE!"

Stuffing of college students into Volkswagens was just one of many fads that developed during the Beetle's heyday. This eager group assaulted a 1974 model. (Volkswagen)

VW Fads and Folly

Nothing signifies a product's "specialness" so clearly as when fads sprout spontaneously from its very existence.

The Volkswagen company itself can be said to have started the first fad of sorts, making their vehicle appear to be more than an ordinary automobile. All they did was offer to give a gold watch to owners whose cars passed 100,000 kilometers on the odometer. Who could have predicted that thousands of owners soon would qualify for the honor? By 1961, when the program ended, 160,000 watches, certificates, badges and plaques had been dispensed.

Taking the concept a step further, the company later began to offer Bonds for Babies Born in Beetles. That "contest" was exactly what it sounded like. Starting in 1965, Volkswagen of America awarded a U.S. Savings Bond to families whose latest offspring first saw the light of day inside a Volkswagen. About 20 such bonds per year were issued. "There's always room for one more in a VW," the slogan declared.

In 1969, a total of 31 babies were driven to their birth in a Volkswagen, up from 28 in the previous year. The offer even lasted into the Rabbit era of the 1970s.

Not unlike the college students who'd swallowed goldfish a generation earlier, their Fifties successors took to stuffing themselves into Beetles. An unofficial record was claimed by Bournemouth College of Technology and College of Art, in Britain: 103 bodies in a 1952 Beetle, which was then driven 15 feet. That figure produced considerable skepticism, but American students took it as a challenge. Before long, local TV reportedly documented *113* students at Chicago's Loyola University, squeezing into a VW.

Beetles found their way into artworks and musical performances. Harry Phillips composed a Concerto for Yellow Volkswagen and Orchestra. This wasn't just a VW onstage with the musicians. No, the person playing the English horn occupied the car's roof, while the orchestra performed alongside and the VW's owner sat inside. And if that wasn't enough, the performance at Tuscaloosa, Alabama, included the sound of the engine, horn—even the slamming of its hood—in an ultimate crescendo.

A Volkswagen made of ice was created by art teachers for a festival in Cooperstown, New York. A half-scale Beetle entered the Great Sand Castle Contest of Carmel, California. No wonder analysts began to notice that the Beetle's basic shape was becoming as familiar as that of the hourglass-profiled Coca-Cola bottle.

Then came the floating Beetles. Because the cars were built so tightly, someone observed early on that a VW could actually float for a while. A long while. In addition to a super-snug, relatively airtight interior, the cars had a flat bottom, also tightly sealed to the body. *Sports Illustrated* floated one for nearly half an hour; others went far longer. One 10-year-old Beetle crossed Loch Ness (Scotland) in a half-hour.

A group was formed, called the Waterbugs of America Racing Association. Participants had to enter the water at considerable speed, then traverse a one-mile course before returning to land. How was that possible? Entrants put snorkels on the engine's intake and exhaust ports, stuck a plastic bag over the distributor to keep water away, and greased the door jambs to give an even tighter seal for the duration. Snow tires sometimes were used as primitive paddles, while the steering wheel was sufficient to control the newly-amphibious vehicle's direction.

Beetle Jokes and Cartoons Started Early

Almost as soon as the first Beetles dropped off the boat on the East Coast, wags were making fun of them. One of the most popular cartoons showed an American peering under the front hood of a stalled VW. Says he: "No wonder it won't run. I must have lost my engine." A second motorist, approaching from his own VW, sympathizes: "Don't worry, you're lucky. I just looked in the trunk compartment, and they've given me a spare."

That particular story hung on for years, taking slightly different forms. In the early 1960s, Doyle Dane Bernbach ran ads in such magazines as *Car & Driver*, *Esquire*, *The New Yorker* and *Reader's Digest*, soliciting VW jokes from readers. Most popular: a lady who looked under front hood and thought someone stole the engine. Plenty of readers supplied the familiar punch line: "Don't worry— I've got a spare one in my trunk."

Runner-up in that contest was the definition of a Volkswagen as a "pregnant roller skate." Making the rounds a little later was "pregnant skateboard." In another, a VW owner was annoyed because friends boasted of 50-mpg mileage while he got "only" 30 from his Beetle. A garage attendant sternly advises him: "Lie, like your friends."

Volkswagen itself commissioned a book of cartoons and humor, enlisting the talents of such authors as Jean Shepherd and H. Allen Smith. Oddly, while the cartoons featured VWs, the essays barely mentioned them.

Volkswagens even turned up in political discourse. Describing U.S. Senator Everett Dirksen for the *Chicago Daily News*, critic Edwin A. Lahey noted that the "Illinois senator is leader of the Republican minority whose intellectual giants could be crowded into a Volkswagen." Other forms of comparison, involving technical details and specifications, also were common. "The first stage of the Titan engine," said the *New York World-Telegram & The Sun*, "generates 430,000 pounds of thrust at maximum or the equivalent of the thrust that could be generated by 219,000 Volkswagens." Driving a Volkswagen 2-1/2 times around the world was claimed to consume the same amount of fuel as a Boeing 707 airplane burned in just one hour.

Commentary On the Road

Bumper stickers also added to the VW's charm. Already in the 1950s, impish owners hung stickers declaring that the Beetle was "Made in der Black Forest by der Elves." Said another, in the later years: "Don't hit me. I have a big brother in the garage."

Works of art that featured the Beetle's shape ranged from serious to whimsical. (Volkswagen)

This Beetle crafted of brass rods appeared at the Chicago Auto Show. (Phil Hall)

Beetles were fashioned in oils, in clay, in iron and wood— and even in sand, at a contest in Carmel, California. (Volkswagen)

At Volkswagen car shows today, such as this Ohio event in 1995, Karmann Ghias stand out from the crowd. (Photo: James M. Flammang)

Beetles often were employed as rolling billboards. Even after they'd become commonplace on American streets, VW sedans advertised nationally-marketed products ranging from Busch beer and Dr. Pepper to Jack-in-the-Box fast food, Kools cigarettes, and Levi's. Beetleboards

of America enlisted college students to adorn their Bugs with bold advertising messages.

Local companies also made use of Volkswagen popularity to promote their wares. A VW serving as delivery car for Jim's Rexall Drugs in Reno, Nevada, bore the sign: "Medicine Dropper." A fleet of pizza-delivery Bugs were shaped like ovens. Gamma Photo Labs, a Chicago film-processing service, ran a fleet of orange Beetles for deliveries, through the 1970s. Decorating the company's lobby today is an orange model of that Beetle, company logo prominently displayed.

Ads and fads, then, helped keep VW strong as buying habits changed. The new domestic compacts sent imported car sales skidding fast: from 614,131 in 1960, to 339,160 two years later. But not Volkswagen. VW saw a sales *increase*, to 200,000 in 1962. As we shall see in upcoming chapters, 1968 was the best year, with 423,000 sold. And by the time the Beetle era was over, more than five million had gone to American customers. Without those terrific ads, who can say whether those totals might have been far lower?

● *Small World* Promotes Big Volkswagen World ●

Plenty of automakers have issued magazines and newsletters promoting their products. As a rule, they're sent free to owners of that make of car. Many such publications get tossed into the wastebasket soon after receipt, viewed as little more than "junk mail" and quickly forgotten. Few are kept on file, to be pored through years later.

Small World falls into that latter category of appreciation. From the early 1960s into the '80s, Volkswagen produced this little quarterly magazine. Sent to half a million VW owners in early years, its circulation reached 800,000 in the early 1970s.

A regular "Small Talk" section featured news items dealing with VW ownership, from record-setting achievements and unique uses for the car to tidbits and oddities. Longer stories introduced special VW

owners, described destinations that might inspire a motoring visit, and provided tips for driving and maintenance.

A contest for personalized names for Beetles drew 424 entries. Another contest sought limericks.

Not only did the magazine publish drivers' experiences with Volkswagens, it included occasional complaints. "My Beetle is the worst car I've ever owned," proclaimed one Los Angeles man, daring the publication to print his letter.

Later issues, in particular, contained information on the latest VW models—still presented in a "soft-sell" manner.

A dozen similar magazines went to owners elsewhere in the world—not to mention the independent VW-related publications that sprung up, such as *Foreign Car Guide*.

OWNER COMMENTS: Chuck and Kim Fryer

"It's been everywhere," says Chuck Fryer of their 1969 Westfalia Camper. Purchased in 1994, the Camper isn't the only Volkswagen that has been owned by the Fryers, of Marengo, Illinois. Far from it. In fact, not many VW fans match this young couple in their devotion to the make. They've even made a pilgrimage to Wolfsburg, turning a holiday into a visit to the VW factory.

The Fryers believe their Westfalia was owned by some older people "who traveled in it." They'd seen the rust-free Camper on a dealer lot, but the price was too high. So, they waited a while and wound up making the owner "a really lowball offer," Chuck explains. Soon, the Fryers had another project vehicle.

Interior items were damaged, so they replaced all the seat covers and moldings. Kim herself stained all the cabinets, and sewed the fabric. (She's been sewing since the age of 7.) The Fryers "didn't pay anybody to do anything" on the bus, they recall proudly. "This one's almost too practical to sell," Chuck admits.

Another member of the "family" is a 1959 Beetle, which happens to hold a '67 engine and transmission. Though appreciative of original vehicles, the Fryers are not averse to modifications, to make a good thing even better. Chuck was even contemplating installation of an original 36-horsepower engine in the Beetle—but packing a Judson supercharger. "It's a really neat accessory to have," he says.

Their VWs are for driving, not just show car purposes. Kim drives the Beetle to work: about 100 miles a day. Odometers on both vehicles are approaching the 100,000 mark.

They also have an Air Camper rooftop tent for the Beetle. Made in Indianapolis from green canvas, the accessory tent had never been used when they bought it.

When last heard from, the Fryers also had a 1962 Beetle, recently purchased. But their list of vehicles owned in the past is awesome for such young people: a 1975 Super Beetle convertible, '73 Super Beetle, 1964 and 1973 buses, 1954 and '57 Beetles, a 1975 Beetle, '58 sun roof, 1983 GTI—and that's just a portion of the list.

Kim admits that she'd "always wanted one," and finally had her chance when she spotted a tempting example at a VW dealer's lot in Florida, where her parents lived at the time. She bought that car—but it was "totaled" en route to Iowa. Not a person to give up, she bought the car back from the insurance company, and restored it to workable condition.

"Red ones go faster," Kim suggests with a smile. And "if your horn doesn't work," she advises, "you wave" when you encounter another Volkswagen.

OWNER COMMENTS: Chris McCarthy

Chris McCarthy was a graduate student at the University of Chicago when he bought his first Volkswagen in 1956. A year old at the time, the oval-window blue Beetle—with turn signal semaphores—came from Import Motors on the north side of Chicago. Priced at $1,495 when new, the Beetle brought $1,200 as a secondhand model.

Over the next three decades, McCarthy owned some 20 Volkswagens—bused and Squarebacks as well as Beetles—before finally abandoning the make in the mid-1980s. A number of those cars were mongrels—parts from several cars combined to make one usable machine.

During his VW period, McCarthy and his wife, Betty, owned few other automobiles. "I had a 1950 Chevrolet that I used to push the Volkswagens," he admits.

"They were good snow cars," he recalls. "Driving them was kind of fun. You never spent much money on them. You could always push them to start [and] pop the clutch. Parking was easy" and "steering was sharp," he notes. "They were reasonably comfortable," too, but the heater "was a pathetic thing."

Several of his VWs made long cross-country trips. "We went a long way in Volkswagens [and] tires lasted a long time."

"There was a substantial boost in power" from the 40-horsepower engine, McCarthy remembers, but "I must have burned out six of those engines. I don't know if they were really meant for sustained driving on the high-speed interstates."

"I never took to the Super Beetle," he adds, which "kind of destroyed the symmetry of" the design.

McCarthy also recalls "little tricks" to removing the engine quickly (such as using a guide for a mounting bolt). "You never really took the engine out of the car" to get at the clutch, but just pulled it back.

Even though McCarthy now drives an Asian import from the 1980s, that three decade string of VWs occupies a unique niche in his automotive memory.

Chapter 9

Early VWs On the Road

Except for collectors, even the most ardent Volkswagen fans—those who owned Beetles and Buses in the past—often have forgotten just what they were like to drive. Looking backward, were the Beetles really as pleasing as memory suggests? Conversely, were they as bad as some critics—then and later—insisted? Or does the truth lie somewhere in between?

Rear-Engine and Air-Cooled Traits

For Americans accustomed to six-cylinder Chevrolets and V-8 Cadillacs, to straight-eight Chryslers and flat-head Fords, the early Beetle practically lived in an alternate universe. Chevys and Fords of the Forties weren't totally quiet, for instance, but even when that "stovebolt" six or L-head V-8 wasn't running perfectly, it never sounded remotely like an air-cooled four-cylinder. Compared to American cars, even its staunchest fans admitted that the Volkswagen rear engine sounded a little like a threshing machine. Those flat fours quieted down as the years went by, but never approached silence.

Did it matter? Not really. Such lack of body insulation actually *helped* endear early VWs to their owners.

More serious were the handling differences between a front- and rear-engined automobile. Volkswagen correctly promoted the traction benefits of a rear engine, noting that

As Beetles began to trickle into the United States in greater numbers, some of the primitive technology evaporated. Hydraulic brakes replaced mechanical binders on DeLuxe and Export models, synchronized gears pushed aside the original non-synchro transmission, and the quaint but unsafe turn-signal semaphores gave way to flashing indicators. By the time the final split-windows arrived, the Beetle was a more driveable machine.

placing the powerplant above the drive wheels amounted to elementary logic—just simple common sense. By that measure, conventional vehicles with their engines and drive wheels at opposite ends were the inefficient machines, easily suffering loss of traction when the going got slippery.

What got far less attention was the propensity of a rear-engined car to handle more skittishly. Until its driver learned, and mastered, the niceties of controlling this type of vehicle, the rear end had a tendency to break loose when pushed hard. Volkswagen engineers were well aware of this tendency, but dismissed it because they felt a Beetle couldn't be pushed all that hard anyway. This could be a problem with a Porsche, but not in a VW with only 30 or 40 horsepower at hand.

Most other differences between VWs and American cars were more immediately noticeable, but not necessarily as serious. Like most imports, the Beetle had its gearshift lever on the floor, a decade after nearly all American cars had adopted column-mounted gearshifts. (Not until the 1960s would floorshifts make a comeback, mainly in high-performance machines.) The VW's gearbox had four

forward speeds, too, while three ratios were quite enough to suit most American drivers.

Volkswagen vowed that you couldn't shift into reverse "by mistake." More than one driver slipping behind the wheel of a Beetle alone, for the first time—including the author of this book—learned that lesson the hard way. Who would have thought that you had to push down hard on the gear lever, then pull it toward what Americans had been taught was *first* gear? In the Beetle, that was reverse. After that first embarrassing effort, though, each driver who'd had trouble finding reverse never again forgot the procedure.

The very first Beetles came with unsynchronized transmissions, whereas nearly all American cars had abandoned those nasty "crash boxes" by the mid-Thirties. Pushing on a clutch was bad enough, at a time when automatic transmissions were becoming the rule. Having to "double clutch" regularly—and pay close attention to engine revs—was something few Americans cared to bother with.

Lack of a fuel gauge was really just an oddity, which added to the quirky charm of the Beetle. American cars were

Fitting into snug parking spots was one bonus of owning a Beetle, but that didn't keep the "meter maids" away. (Volkswagen)

turning to automatic chokes, but the VW's manual choke knob—next to the gearshift lever—was no major drawback.

Not every VW owner in the 1950s was aware of the car's fully independent suspension and torsion bar springing. What they noticed was the pleasing ride. Most didn't realize the ramifications of a unitized body, but they noticed the lack of squeaks and rattles. Later on, of course, many of those owners who lived in the snowbelt also noticed the car's likelihood to rust nastily.

Inside a Split-Window Sedan

"Roadability is said to be phenomenal for a light sedan," *Motor Trend* reported in November 1950—evidently before having an opportunity to drive one of the little creatures. Already, the car was said to be rapidly becoming an "outstanding success."

Popular Science magazine had reported on the German minicar a month earlier. "A homely auto to most U.S. eyes," they concluded, "it also has some homely virtues. It gets good mileage [and] burns the cheapest gasoline without pinging. It's rugged. Its body is squeakproof. It's well sprung.... Its articulated rear axle accommodates the back wheels to bumps with little loss of traction."

Not everything was bliss. "A big man has to jackknife to get into the back seat," *Popular Science* warned. "By American standards it is underpowered, even for its size. The pint-sized flat engine must be revved up considerably in third gear before it can take the load in high."

Tom McCahill, the inveterate road tester for *Mechanix Illustrated*, was an early Beetle advocate. "Uncle Tom" drove one of the first VWs, in 1950. He gave the minicar considerable praise, declaring it a great buy. "I became the American godfather of the Volkswagen," he explained a decade later. "Most of the automotive publications and automotive newspapermen thought I'd popped a plug in my foggy little brain."

During his first trial, McCahill drove across fields, "which it took like a Jeep due to its 8-1/2-inch [ground] clearance." Acceleration was deemed "extremely good considering the car's size—zero to 25 took 5.7 seconds, and zero to 50 was 21.2 seconds." McCahill also noted approvingly that the engine could be removed in less than half an hour. No less important, its "extremely small amount of piston travel should mean long engine life."

Did McCahill find fault with the Beetle's ride and rear-engine handling? He did not. Its "steering and cornering qualities are excellent," he reported, "and the four-wheel independent...suspension is the best I have found in the small car field. The car rides well and is extremely quiet."

In its April 1951 issue, *Consumer Reports* marveled that for $1,280, the Volkswagen "contains a lot of engineering." Engine accessibility was deemed "remarkable," and its oil cooler—a rarity on American cars—drew favorable comment. The engine, they reported, was "designed to be able to operate all day at 60 mph which is about the car's top speed." Though "far from quiet...it is better to have the engine noise behind one rather than in front." (Some subsequent road testers took exception to that concept, ada-

mant that the noise emanating from the rear made no difference in its level of annoyance.)

As for the lack of a gas gauge, road testers advised that the driver simply peek into the tank. Or, they could "wait until the engine spits," then turn the reserve tap.

"The car behaves well on ice," the *Consumers Union* magazine advised, "with far more traction than the cars we're used to, and the wheels do not pound into deep holes in the road. The sighting downward over the hood is far better than on any American car."

In later years, *Consumer Reports* would find more flaws in the Beetle. But initially, the little German machine "impressed *CU's* consultants who drove it as a tough, handy little rig that would take four people...most anywhere, including by-roads or no roads."

A year-and-a-half later, in November 1952, *Consumer Reports* still branded its DeLuxe VW "an unorthodox, keenly efficient vehicle." More than one-third of the cars were being exported by this time, and the DeLuxe was selling in the United States for $1,595. "If you're tired of the commonplace in cars," they concluded, "the Volkswagen is a good refresher."

With 56.5 percent of its 1,610-pound weight on the rear wheels, traction was called "superior." *Consumer Reports* testers also praised the solid construction and flawless finish, "from its excellent enamel paint job to the spare fan belt in the tool kit." Accelerating to 60 mph took a painfully sluggish 56 seconds, and a quarter-mile dash demanded no less than 25.9 seconds. "Despite a horizontally narrow windshield and a high cowl," they reported, "driver vision forward is quite good."

The folks at *Consumer Reports* predicted that anyone who piloted a foreign car regularly through traffic would "turn back with regret to the oversized American cars," but on the highway an American auto was "superior by far."

Early Volkswagen interiors looked stark, if not primitive, but the DeLuxe models that arrived on U.S. shores were fitted with extra equipment. Note the separate gloveboxes at each end of the dashboard, and instruments in the center. (Volkswagen)

Of seven cars tested in a 1953 report, *Motor Trend* branded Volkswagen the most fun. Frequent gearshifting was required, but that was no burden because of the lever's positive action, and the fact that it fell naturally to hand. Only a "quick flick" was needed to shift up or down, "thanks to synchromesh like that in the Porsche." Road testers encountered no excessive pitching or body roll, and "no bottoming or tendency to float on rough roads."

Handling was deemed exceptional. "You can break the rear end loose," they admitted, "but only if you work at it. Excellent steering and fine balance give you command of the car and the slight corrective action you may need on the wheel is almost automatic." *Motor Trend* also praised the car's unique features and "really plush" interior, claimed to be as good as in some cars that cost $2,000 more.

Early on, *Road & Track* focused on VW's "alarming" oversteer characteristics, which helped make it fun to drive but could come as an unpleasant surprise to the uninitiated. Road testing a trio of Volkswagens—stock and modified—in 1954, *Road & Track* referred to a "ride that is hard to describe: not soft, not firm. [S]evere bumps give a thumping noise, yet are not felt. It's something that has to be experienced for the car is very comfortable and at the same time free from wallow or roll."

If the Beetle's propensity to oversteer (turn faster than the driver intended) was its biggest flaw, it was also a reason why sports car owners were "so crazy about the VW." Beetles had "a very strong tendency for the rear end to swing outwards, in a fast turn, to the point that the car wants to take the path of an ever tightening spiral." In ordinary driving, however, *Road & Track* declared the car "very safe and controllable," unless some emergency measure became necessary.

A stock Volkswagen took 39.2 seconds to accelerate to 60 mph. This at a time when the American horsepower race was well underway, and some heavyweight V-8 sedans could reach 60 mph in 12 seconds or less. (In contrast, a Microbus took a minute and 15 seconds to reach 60 mph—its absolute, final peak velocity.)

Noise was noticeable—specifically, a "moderate shriek of protest" from the cooling fan at "speeds over the red markings." (Somebody failed to heed the warning against over-revving, evidently.) Furthermore, the engine "fails miserably at lugging below 30 mph in fourth gear."

Certain crosswinds caused the *Road & Track* Beetles to wander a bit, headwinds slowed them appreciably and the lack of luggage space brought grumbles. Faults aside, the magazine's road testers declared Volkswagen "the most amazing and versatile car in its class." Not unlike the Model T Ford, a VW "has its faults but we love them." Perhaps most important, "to say that we had fun on this group road test is an understatement."

Writing in *Popular Mechanics*, veteran auto expert Floyd Clymer noted that a VW's "rear engine gives fine traction, even on rough, sandy roads," and offered "amazing performance." He "found it impossible to overheat a Volkswagen engine under any condition." Clymer did observe "noticeable engine noise," adding that this was common in air-cooled engines, because of their lack of a water jacket around the cylinders. Despite quick steering, Clymer concluded that the Beetle was "well balanced and handle[d] exceptionally well on curves and over rough roads."

In a 1957 *Popular Mechanics* test of suburban commuting, Volkswagen earned a 31.22 mpg average, for a fuel cost of a penny a mile. A Citroën 2CV got 47.78 mpg (0.6 cent/mile). A full-size Ford delivered less than 13 mpg, costing its owner 2.3 cents per mile. Not long afterward, a survey of VW owners by *Foreign Car Guide* found an average of 32 mpg—right at the factory-claimed figure.

An oval-window Beetle, according to *Popular Mechanics*, was "an extremely nimble car...that tempts you to drive at its limit at all times.... It can be driven all day at 65 miles per hour." Work its four-speed properly, and the urban driver could easily "scoot through traffic." Toss in excellent workmanship, and the VW seemed a sure winner.

Wilbur Shaw, then president of the Indianapolis Motor Speedway, drove "Europe's Model A" for *Popular Science* magazine in 1954. "It's well made," Shaw declared. "It's sure-footed. It runs almost indefinitely without repair. It rides well.... With 'fast steering,' requiring little turning of the wheel, the car wound in and out of traffic like a snake."

Fully-independent suspension, said *Mechanix Illustrated* in 1958, gave the VW "a goat-like grip on rough roads" but also that oft-noted tendency to "oversteer and swing its tail when lightly loaded, or on wet or icy roads." Also, their car's cooling fan tended to "howl" at over 50 mph.

Not every road tester bothered to mention the car's driving position, but in 1963 *Car and Driver* observed that a Beetle's windshield seemed "disconcertingly near." Farther ahead, "the hood drops off so abruptly that a [novice's] first VW ride is mostly spent marveling at the proximity of the roadway disappearing below." All true, but owners didn't seem to care much.

Contemporary Owners Deliver Their Own Appraisals

During the 1950s, several magazines surveyed their readers, to seek their views on cars they owned. *Popular Science* and *Popular Mechanics* regularly published the results of their surveys. Volkswagen was one of the subjects in early 1954.

Of the respondents to the *Popular Mechanics* questionnaire, 91 percent rated VW's roadability excellent, 97 percent ranked handling excellent, and 95 percent gave structural rigidity the same ranking. Not surprisingly, only 40 percent declared Beetle acceleration from a standstill to be excellent. Only 21 percent issued that evaluation to its acceleration from 40 mph.

Traction on wet or icy pavement, on the other hand, was called excellent by three-fourths of the respondents. Volkswagen owners reported average gas mileage of 37.4 mpg in country driving, and 32.1 mpg in the city (impressive, yet considerably less economical than, say, a Renault 4CV).

Plenty of readers had specific, favorable comments. "Maneuverable and easy to park," said one Indiana reader, who stood more than six feet tall. "Less tiresome to drive and more comfortable on a trip...than the 'big' cars! Easy to service."

Several readers commented on the lack of antifreeze and radiator concerns, and on the traction benefit of having so much weight in the rear. A student noted that after driving four hours at 65 mph, at temperatures above 100 degrees, the engine could still be touched.

"I have taken roads that only a Jeep could negotiate," said one reader from New York state. A New Jersey owner praised "economy above all," but also the Beetle's "good forward visibility, nice ride, no road shock felt in steering, [and] terrific gearbox." A Connecticut reader liked its "freedom from sidesway due to torsion bar spring[ing]," as well as the "comfort, economy, sure traction on slippery roads [and] easy parking."

"Lower horsepower is no disadvantage," said a New Jersey owner, "since I can maintain a higher constant speed than with my larger U.S. car, which has six times the horsepower." An Ohio physician admitted that he'd bought a VW as an economical second car, but now preferred it to his big American automobile. Another owner in Buffalo, New York, spoke for many, declaring that "the joy of driving has certainly come back to me since I bought my VW."

Not all comments were positive. The Indiana reader who praised a VW's maneuverability bemoaned its "utter lack of quick acceleration above 40 mph [with] no power on steep grades at high speeds." He also faulted interior space, deemed adequate for four only if two of them were children. "Horsepower output is good in the lower ranges," said a Wisconsin owner, "but long hills leave a lot to be desired."

Plenty of owners were unhappy with the poor visibility of the split-window sedans. Some criticized the lack of fuel and oil gauges.

Stepping Up to an Oval-Window Beetle

Improved visibility wasn't the only step forward when the oval-window model hit the market during 1953. Volkswagen was making constant improvements. And considering how favorable many *prior* evaluations had been, the future already was looking rosy.

Sure, plenty of automotive "experts" and industry leaders still laughed at the little car, scoffing at its attempt to carve out a modest share of the American market. They soon would be proved mistaken.

"You can drive a Volkswagen for hours at 65 to 70 mph,"

Oval-window Beetles had a basic dashboard—all instruments in a single round display, with no gas gauge at all. Note the tall gearshift and optional radio. (Photo: James M. Flammang)

An accessory three-gauge panel gave the oval-window driver something extra to study, helping to enhance the motoring experience. Note the parcel shelf below the dashboard—an unusual, but popular, extra-cost item. (Photo: James M. Flammang — Owner: Dale Jensen)

the 1954 sales brochure insisted, "and hardly hear the engine." Even the car's fans considered that statement a stretch.

Already, the company was promoting the fact that its products could be operated reliably just about anywhere, not just in cities and suburbs. "You can drive a Volkswagen in the arctic as well as in the tropics," the brochure boasted. "You could dash up the highest mountains without worrying, or leave it out for days in a snowstorm."

Non-fans might have been forgiven for disputing the claim that a Beetle would "charge up the steepest mountain like a hound on the heels of a jack rabbit." Ambitious owners, on the other hand, were learning that their favorite vehicle could perform nearly-miraculous feats. Slowly, perhaps; but the Beetle managed to get the job done. First gear, for instance, promised to climb a 37 percent grade—steeper than any road in the world.

Consumer Reports took another look at the Volkswagen—and several small-car rivals (Austin A-30, Nash Metropolitan and Ford Anglia) in October 1954. "Considerably improved" at this point, the VW was deemed "more than ever the queen of the small cars, a high-quality car of unique design and surprising all-around abilities." For a

small-car buyer who sought "novelty in design, stamina over the road, and above all quality and good workmanship, the Volkswagen [stood] practically alone at its moderate price."

Despite its recently-enlarged (72.7-cid) engine and 36-horsepower (SAE) rating, the 1954 VW still took 41.1 seconds to reach 60 mph, and 25.4 seconds to wend its way through a quarter-mile run. Acceleration from 35 to 55 mph demanded just over 20 seconds, while overall gas mileage came to a tempting 30.7 mpg.

"The car rides better, and runs more quietly (not very quietly, by American standards)" than prior models, *Consumer Reports* noted. They also praised the car's front vent panes, weight distribution (58 percent on the back wheels), and slow piston travel—a crucial factor in long engine life.

Road testers liked the fold-down rear backrest, the luggage trough and the car's "outstanding" ride on "washboard" surfaces. Rough roads produced "controlled bouncy motion which seldom becomes disagreeable [and] the rear wheels do not skitter or bounce off course." On the other hand, the fact that the turn signal had to be set back after each turn proved to be an annoyance.

Steering easily and cornering well, the VW was classed as fun to drive. Promising low maintenance and running costs, the car was "solidly built...with an excellent paint job, and no cheap details. It has more than its share both of peculiarities and satisfactions," warranting recognition as "the outstanding car in its class." Hard to believe that after such continuous early praise, *Consumer Reports*, like other consumer advocates, would later find considerable fault with the Beetle's handling characteristics.

A few months later, *Business Week* complained that the Volkswagen engine "snuffles noisily." Even so, they admitted that the car enjoyed "a glowing reputation for stamina, simple sound engineering, and gets along with a minimum of maintenance."

In 1956, *Motor Trend* compared the Volkswagen with the Renault—its prime competitor. Both cars were faulted for impaired vision. Both could keep up with traffic, but only by using the gearbox frequently. Most owners enjoyed that duty, but Americans who'd become enamored by automatic transmissions were likelier to find gear-changing onerous.

Steering on both cars was "delightfully responsive and easy," the road testers discovered. Body lean on both cars was found to be "un-sports-car-like," though far less than in typical American vehicles. Each exhibited good ride quality, considered a surprise because of their short wheelbases. The Volkswagen's ride was "more of a compromise between soft and firm, and impart[ed] an odd, insulated feeling to passengers...partly due to the remarkable fit of body panels."

As for performance, Volkswagen was a little quicker in acceleration: 7.5 seconds for 0-30 mph and 23.8 seconds for the quarter-mile vs. 8.2 seconds for 0-30 mph and a 24.6-second quarter-mile for the Renault. More important, the VW dashed from 30 to 50 mph in 12.9 seconds—2.5 seconds quicker than the 4CV. The Beetle reached a higher top speed (68 mph), but lagged well behind the Renault in average city/highway gas mileage: 26.6 mpg vs. 34.2 for the 4CV. At the time, the 4CV was selling for $200 less than a Volkswagen.

Owners Report Again On Their Cars

When *Popular Mechanics* again surveyed Volkswagen owners, in 1956, many of their comments were even more ecstatic than before. Countless owners had virtually fallen in love with their little machines.

"Although not a sports car," the editors admitted, "it be-

An externally-mounted luggage rack helped take care of one common complaint: lack of cargo space. (Photo: James M. Flammang)

An available Volkswagen tool kit fit neatly within the spare tire, during the oval-window generation. When closed, it looked like a hubcap. (Photo: James M. Flammang — Owner: Dale Jensen)

haves like one on the corners." Acceleration still set no records, however, requiring at least 41 seconds to go 60 mph. Top speed came in at 65 mph, and the magazine's test car managed 28 mpg in traffic.

Many owners claimed greater economy. "On a 3,300-mile trip to Florida," a Michigan teacher insisted, "the VW used one-half cup of oil [and] averaged 36.5 miles per gallon." A California cashier described a 4,996-mile highway trip, with a total cost of $51—including a car wash and two grease jobs.

Moving a Beetle by hand always drew crowds and amused comments. A carpenter told *Popular Mechanics* how he and a friend had needed to squeeze into a small parking space. Naturally, they simply "picked up the rear end and moved it into the curb."

Actually, that was a fair amount of weight to lift, considering that the engine sat at the rear. Less-muscular drivers and their friends could shift a Beetle in manual mode, with less risk of hernias, by lifting the *front* end.

The Beetle's "go-anywhere" reputation also was growing. Said a Missouri writer: "I use my VW for exploring river-valley country where there are no roads.... I've climbed earth dams where only 'Cats' and bulldozers have been before." A farmer described climbing "a bunch-grass hillside lined with deep cow trails that has even stumped four-wheel-drive vehicles." Another owner had driven his car for some distance with both exhaust pipes submerged in water.

One Ohio housewife echoed the thoughts of any number of women. The Volkswagen "lets me feel I'm the boss when I'm behind the wheel and not as though I'm driving by remote control." Her concluding comment was even more telling: "As long as VW is made I'll never drive anything else." Already, by the mid-1950s, America had zealous, single-minded fans who refused to get behind the wheel of any other vehicle.

As expected, not all the comments were laudatory. Some drivers didn't like pushing down on the gearshift lever to reach reverse, criticized the slow-moving windshield wipers or faulted the close-together positioning of brake and clutch pedals. Lack of power and performance still drew jeers. So did noisy running.

One reader complained about the difficulty of closing the doors when the windows were shut. Others realized that this demonstrated the tight, virtually leak-free construction of the car.

Complaints also began to come in regarding the fragile rear bumper, which could be pushed in by bigger cars. Quite a few Fifties Beetles suffered the indignity of a sagging back bumper, barely held off the ground by its weakened supports.

On the Road in a Karmann Ghia

One of the first road reports on the new Karmann Ghia appeared in *Motor Trend*, in May 1956. Easy to climb into, the coupe's low driver's seat evoked a decidedly sporty feel. Headroom was described as snug for a tall person, but visibility was "superb all around."

The coupe's interior finish was "flawless and chastely classic," with controls similar—but not identical—to those in the basic Beetle. On the road, installation of a front anti-roll bar and wider frame rails than in the Beetle yielded a rear end that was "less skittish."

Acceleration was only marginally better than the Beetle's at lower speeds. On the highway at 70 mph or more, *Motor Trend* proclaimed, "one realizes most clearly that he is driving no ordinary VW." Traveling one "lonely stretch...the Ghia's high-speed behavior proved impeccable," a result of the car's weight and streamlining.

Floor-level fresh air, delivered through front-end grilles, was another bonus. Summing up, the Karmann Ghia was described as "a custom car in every subtle detail of its lines, every deceptively plain interior feature." This "personal luxury car [served as] a small slice of pure visual and driving delight."

Road Testing the Microbuses

Remember the DKW Karavan? If you don't, you're not alone. That German-built cargo hauler failed to capture much attention in the mid-Fifties American market.

When *Motor Trend* road tested a Volkswagen Microbus in 1956, however, they needed something to compare it

The fortunate soul behind the wheel of a sensuously-contoured Karmann Ghia convertible had to grow used to envious glances. Underneath, however, the Ghia was essentially just a basic Beetle. (Volkswagen)

Volkswagen Campers attracted a different breed of buyer—one who liked the idea of a little "home on wheels." Like all Microbuses and station wagons, the Camper lacked power on the open road, but managed to chug its way up hills that left more potent vehicles struggling behind. (Volkswagen)

against. The sole candidate, it seems, was the little-known DKW. At the time, a Volkswagen Microbus was selling for $2,365, and the Kombi only $2,195.

Whatever its form, the Volkswagen Transporter was "no fury on wheels," the road testers noted right off the bat. Not with a 0-60 mph time of 75 seconds—if it managed to reach that velocity at all. Even making it to 50 mph took more than half a minute. Otherwise, the bus delivered "reasonable and sensible performance with remarkable economy and utility."

"Like the Volkswagen sedan," *Motor Trend* warned, "the larger 'bus' is extremely sensitive to almost imperceptible assists by wind and gradient." That wasn't exactly a startling revelation to most Transporter drivers, who soon realized that the slab-sided body made it susceptible to rockiness from all but the gentlest breezes. Owners also knew that with only 36 horsepower and 56 pound-feet of torque available, climbing a hill tended to turn into a long, drawn-out experience. What some of the critics failed to note, on the other hand, was that the Microbus—with only rare exceptions—always managed to reach the top eventually, courtesy largely of the low gearing within its transmission and final drive.

The Microbus ride was described as undeniably choppy, and road testers advised that "tricky dips must be anticipated to avoid lumps on the head." On the other hand, the buses were deemed "easy to drive, [with] wonderful visibility and easy steering." The bus' "straight-down pedals" were considered "a little awkward for an average foot, but the long gear lever gives typical VW shifts, and the nearly vertical steering wheel provides perfect control with a minimum of fatigue (as on our Greyhound buses)."

At this point, nearly every current or former Microbus owner is probably nodding in agreement. The steering wheel position and pedal placement did indeed seem odd at first, but most Microbus owners quickly grew comfortable in the driver's seat. In fact, they soon felt almost odd when stepping into a conventionally-designed automobile.

Taking the Wheel of a Square-Window Sedan

Through the 1950s, Tom McCahill of *Mechanix Illustrated* had taken periodic spins in Volkswagens. In the May 1961 issue, he declared that the improved Beetle still ranked as "the greatest dollar-for-dollar buy in the automotive world today." Since the beginning, more than a thousand changes—large and small—had been made. Among other improvements, McCahill's '61 had a new front passenger grab handle, a standard windshield washer and an automatic choke.

The latest 40-horsepower engine, he noted, was a development of VW's truck powerplant, with a new camshaft and more advanced ignition timing, running on 7:1 compression. Transmission ratios had changed, and first gear

In 1967, its final year, the first-generation Campmobile continued to attract outdoor-oriented families who embraced the vehicle's versatility. Most of them cared not a whit about its lack of a muscular engine. (Volkswagen)

was now synchronized. McCahill's 1961 VW took 20.2 seconds to reach 60 mph—more than six seconds quicker than a '59 model. Acceleration to 30 mph took 8.0 seconds.

In contrast, the first Beetle McCahill had driven, in 1950, required a leisurely 42.1 seconds to hit 60 mph—and wouldn't go much beyond that figure. Now, the factory claimed a 72 mph top speed, and some drivers were able to eke out a few more.

McCahill admitted that a Beetle tended to roll easily, but only if it was "over-driven." Although the car could "corner amazingly well up to a point," the quick steering and unfamiliar handling might get an uninitiated driver into trouble. "Quite a few people," McCahill believed, "just never knew exactly where that point was until they went over because when a VW flips it doesn't give you the slightest warning."

By 1963, when Car and Driver magazine presented a road test of the "1200" Beetle, Volkswagen had made even more changes to its car—including, finally, a gas gauge. The magazine's testers found a lot to like, including finish work that was "beyond reproach," inside and out. They appreciated the fact that it was "easy to get a full

arm's length away from the wheel without seriously impinging upon the rear seat passengers' area."

Sticking with 15-inch tires, on the other hand, helped push the wheel wells inward, leaving less room for the driver's feet. Drivers also found "a distinct resistance, even at rest, to engaging first gear," though the gear ratios themselves were described as "perfect for the car."

Most notably, they pointed out that the gearshift lever demanded quite a reach to get into third gear. "The sight of a driver swaying fore and aft as he goes from gear to gear," they explained, "is practically a VW trademark." As for noise, with their car's sun roof fully open at speeds over 30 mph, "the drumming was almost unendurable." Obviously, everyone has a different tolerance for noise or gear-reaching, as many owners didn't find these failings quite so irksome.

Not everyone—expert or ordinary driver—praised the Beetle to the skies. Nevertheless, the sales charts continued to soar—even when sales of foreign cars as a whole dropped off sharply in the late Fifties. In the next chapter, we'll look at some reasons why.

OWNER COMMENTS: Conrad Holcomb

Conrad Holcomb of Watertown, Wisconsin, started to work on Volkswagens in January 1961. After working for dealers for almost 11 years—initially in La-Crosse, Wisconsin—he started his own shop: Connie's Import Repair Service.

"My first love is still the German cars," Holcomb reports. Early in 1996, he owned 1952, 1953 and 1954 Beetles, and also a '56, which was for sale. His son Brian owned a 1960 single-cab pickup in showroom condition.

"We run all over with the '54," Holcomb says. It's a sun roof model, and he'd put 10,000 miles on it the previous summer. After restoration is completed, his '53 "will be for special occasions." He also has a '71 Super Beetle, in the process of being fixed up for sale.

"I said several years ago, Volkswagen was going to be the collector car of the Nineties," Holcomb asserts, despite such failings as their lack of heat. "Nobody in their right mind would drive one in the winter anymore."

Conrad Holcomb bought his first VW in September 1959—a spanking new '60 model. After completing military service in England, he brought it back to the United States. Soon, he traded that Beetle in for a '61, which suffered big problems. That was the first year of the 40-horsepower engine, which endured bad pis-

tons, soft cams and followers, soft valves and plastic speedometer cable woes. "That '61 soured people on Volkswagens," Holcomb reports.

His '62 also had troubles. "Carbon spark plug wires swelled," he recalls, and "fuel pump flanges swelled up and stuck the plunger." Because his '66 had bad valves, Holcomb recalls that Volkswagen "called them all back from dealers. J. C. Whitney wound up with all the engines that were known to cause trouble.... There were a lot of recalls like that, years back. In 1965 they finally got the 40-horse to be a better engine."

Holcomb says he'd "always underestimated" the 1300 engine, believing "it was a lame-brained engine."

Volkswagens aren't Holcomb's only automotive pastime. He has two Morris Minor convertibles, a 1928 Ford Model A coupe, a 1935 Ford slantback Tudor (which his father bought new), a 1928 Whippet and a 1919 Willys-Overland touring car. Though he speaks of "pride of accomplishment," he believes it's no longer possible to make much money in old cars.

"They're so simple," Holcomb says, "that you sometimes overlook the problem." People tend to assume it's something more serious. Service customers "only hear what their pocketbook lets them hear." Holcomb advocates changing to hardened valve seats, but doesn't worry much about reformulated and no-lead gas for old cars.

Chapter 10

Why Was the Beetle So Popular?

Any number of reasons might be cited for the intense popularity of the Beetle. Of course, many of those factors also applied to other cars, whether imported or domestic—at least in some degree. The question to be studied is why Volkswagen, out of the dozens of European-built small cars introduced to the U.S. market in the 1950s, was one of the few that survived. Not only that, but why was it the *only* one to turn into a sales sensation?

Almost from the beginning, Volkswagens became known for possessing such alluring traits as:

• **Simplicity** — At a time when American cars were growing more powerful and more complex, the Beetle and several of its competitors made a virtue out of straightforward, no-frills, common-sense engineering and design. Said Heinz Nordhoff of American cars in the mid-1950s: "The longer and sleeker they build them in the U.S., the better we like it."

• **Craftsmanship** — Here Volkswagen excelled, at least in people's perceptions, as evidenced by the fact that no other German subcompacts came close to VW's sales totals.

• **Frugality** — Sure, fuel economy was a Volkswagen "plus." But in the real world, dozens of small imports got gas mileage at least as good as a VW—and often better. Why did VW garner the reputation, if it was never number one in fuel economy?

• **Compact size** — True enough, but many of the rival imports—the ones that failed—were roughly comparable in dimensions.

• **Uniqueness** — Nothing ever looked like, or was constructed like, a Beetle. Renault may have come closest in distinct design and rear-engine handling with its 4CV, but the French reputation for less-than-ideal assembly quality hindered sales. Psychologists may have debated whether a Beetle's egg-like shape brought out maternal impulses, or had some sort of sexual overtone. (They tended to unearth hidden meanings in *many* common objects.) Owners simply liked it, and felt affectionate toward it, whether or not there was any deep, hidden dimension to their adoration.

• **Fun** — That's not a term that everyone applied to the typical small car of the 1950s and '60s, but Beetles actually were—and still are—fun to drive. In fact, a surprising number of sports car fans took to them. *Road & Track* wondered in 1954 why, of all imported cars, the Volkswagen appeared to have "such a strong appeal to the sports car owner—the ex-owner with family."

• **Ease of repair** — VW built its reputation partly on this factor, but not everyone who worked on Beetles agrees that they were quite that easy. Sure, pulling an engine was a snap. Yet back when the cars were new, some independent mechanics tried to *avoid* working on them—especially on the transmissions and suspensions. At the other end of the spectrum, many a non-mechanically-inclined owner was able to learn a host of repair methods, from replacing a broken accelerator cable to adjusting engine valves—a vital periodic-maintenance task.

• **Dealer network** — Volkswagen stood hands-down at the head of the pack in this area. As early as 1954, Volkswagen had an enviable network of 14 regional distributors and more than 300 dealers, staffed with knowledgeable service technicians. "No Volkswagen," said *U.S. News & World Report* in 1956, "was permitted to be shipped to a foreign country until a complete system for servicing and repair had been set up in that country."

• **Non-finicky behavior** — Foreign cars in the 1950s were widely regarded as unreliable, complicated, touchy, and subject to bizarre failures. Volkswagen quickly gained a reputation for dependability and predictable operation.

• **Lack of planned obsolescence** — Even before the ads touted VW's never-changing shape and familiar technical details, people got to know that every Beetle looked and behaved just about the same. "Can you imagine a Volkswagen with tailfins?" the company asked rhetorically in 1957.

• **Continuous improvement** — The phrase didn't enter the auto trade as an industry buzzword until the 1990s, but VW adopted this laudable concept from the start.

• **High resale value** — Unlike the vast majority of imported cars, Beetles held their value amazingly well. A secondhand VW commanded previously unheard-of sums—not so far removed from their selling price when new. Who wouldn't want a car that would still be worth plenty when the time came to trade it in, or sell it off?

If sales totals are the measure of popularity, Volkswagen beat all of its rivals by a mile. Here, at a VW test track, a batch of Beetles symbolically pass a Model T Ford, holder of the world record as most-produced automobile. Until February 17, 1972, that is, when the 15,007,034th Beetle rolled off the line at Wolfsburg to grab the title. By then, 5,625 were leaving the factories each working day.

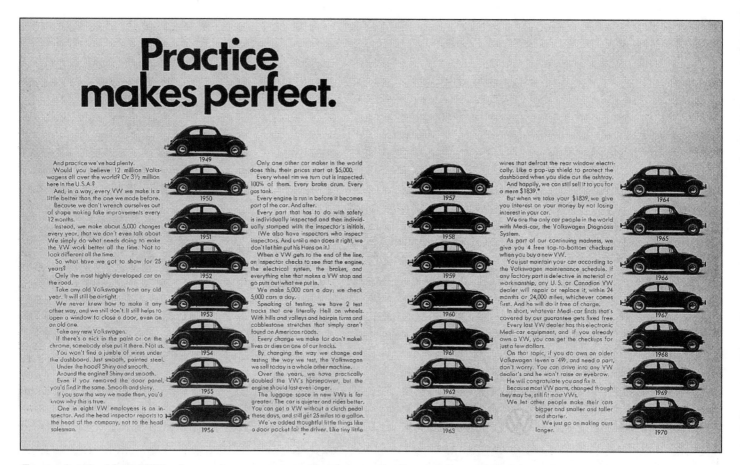

Except for the Model T Ford, no other car came even close to the Beetle's legendary life—constantly improved, but otherwise little-changed from the 1940s into the '70s. (Volkswagen)

• **Charm** — Critics might have branded the Beetle an "ugly duckling," one of the homeliest cars on earth, but that didn't prevent millions of owners from falling in love with the shape and its function. Charm isn't easy to define in a person, much less a machine, but the VW possessed it in quantity. Even the distinctive sound of its engine and exhaust, and the subdued whine of its gearbox, added to the Beetle's charm—not unlike those same characteristics in the Model T Ford.

Life magazine wasn't alone in dubbing the Volkswagen "a member of the family that just happens to live in the garage." Later, in the 1970s, Volkswagen of America called the Beetle "one of the few mechanical things that brings out a person's sense of whimsy and even affection."

• **Cachet** — Ordinary imported sedans were typically driven by comparatively ordinary people. Academics and intellectuals came to the VW fold early. So did celebrities. What other low-priced vehicle, imported or domestic, could boast an owner roster ranging from pundit William F. Buckley to actor Paul Newman? VWs were popular in the Kennedy administration, for their lack of ostentation.

• **Camaraderie and shared experience** — "When you buy a Volkswagen," wrote Dr. Jean Rosenbaum in *Is Your Volkswagen a Sex Symbol?*, "you don't just get a car; you also acquire a lot of friends—other Volkswagen owners. The Volkswagen is a way of life."

One *Popular Mechanics* reader referred to the "spirit of friendship between VW owners." Apart from Beetle fans, only sports car owners earned a serious reputation for hand waving at fellow enthusiasts whom they encountered on the road.

When it first appeared in the United States, seen in New York and at Chicago's International Trade Fair, the Volkswagen suffered such unsavory nicknames as "Hitler's Flivver." That monicker was applied by *Popular Science*, which further noted that the VW's price differed little from "more commodious imported cars such as the Hillman Minx." What it offered, in their view, was "high novelty value."

The first Beetles "seemed to be the antithesis of American drivers' dreams," wrote the authors of *Vintage Volkswagens*. How could a strictly functional, no-frills machine *ever* hope to capture the attention—and dollars—of Americans, who seemingly adored their chrome trim, brawny engines and lush new hardtop coupes? A typical European automobile, wrote Herbert Brean in 1958, for *Life* magazine, "caters to its less opulent owner's thrift and individualism, the typical American car to its fortunate owner's pride and love of luxury."

Few would ever admit it, or understand it, but Americans also had grown accustomed to the concept of "planned obsolescence," as introduced by General Motors back in the 1920s. Car shoppers—and tirekickers—

eagerly looked forward to seeing what each season's crop of cars looked like. They wondered what new marvels lurked under the hood and ahead of the driver's seat. How, then, could *any* automobile survive if it had no intention of delivering dramatic changes on a regular schedule?

"Through the years," *Business Week* declared in 1964, "Volkswagen became a byword for cheap, reliable transportation." The original design was even deemed "invincible." By then, millions of Americans had learned to *applaud*, not deplore, what writer/historian Peter Vack later called Volkswagen's "stubborn resistance to change."

Eventually, wrote Louis Steinwedel in *The Beetle Book*, VW became "the benchmark by which other small cars are judged."

True enough, but few predicted such a monumental outcome in the car's developmental years. "In Detroit," *Business Week* had reported in 1955, "there are yawns. Auto men still don't believe (or at least won't say) that there is a big market here for European-style small cars."

One reason Americans bought foreign cars, *Business Week* continued, was that they didn't go out of style every two years. On the down side, the magazine insisted that "wives generally don't like [the] VW's proletarian look." Such a comment might draw fire today, but in the Fifties there was no shortage of statements suggesting that women were influenced by looks, while men viewed automobiles with a more critical eye.

"The move to suburbia and to two cars, increasingly crowded highways and limited parking space," *Business Week* added, "might carry Volkswagen to as high as 50,000 annual sales." Even so, that figure was deemed "a spit in the ocean," considering that 710,000 cars a month were rolling out of Detroit.

Wolfsburg saw things differently. "Our only problem," Heinz Nordhoff had exclaimed in 1953, "is to make all we can sell." As early as that, close to half of Volkswagens were being exported.

Owners Fall Hard for the Mid-1950s Beetle

"What is there about this small, ugly, low-powered import," *Popular Mechanics* asked itself in 1956, "that excites people all over the world and makes every owner talk like a salesman?" The magazine also asked hundreds of owners.

"Unbelievable" was the word used to assess their responses. "These owners actually have fallen in love with a car," the report stated with amazement. Not one surveyed owner had rated his or her VW as poor. On the contrary, almost 96 percent branded the car excellent. Many even tacked a "plus" sign onto their commentary. Overall, this was considered the most enthusiastic group of owners ever to have taken part in a *Popular Mechanics* Owners Report.

Volkswagens were nothing if not practical. Beetle owners found ways to stuff startling amounts of merchandise inside—though a sun roof on this 1964 sedan made it easier to load garden gear. Sun roofs could be retracted even when traveling at highway speed, fitting flush with the rest of the roof. (Volkswagen)

Many traditionalists mourned the loss of the Beetle's original ample fabric sun roof, but the smaller steel unit was better than nothing. By 1965, nearly one-fifth of the VW sedans sold in America had a sun roof. (Volkswagen)

"This is the first major love affair of my life," a Florida businesswoman admitted. She was not alone in declaring her Beetle virtually on a par with a human boyfriend or girlfriend—one who regularly proved to be a lot more dependable than some living counterparts.

"The VW is an engineering masterpiece," a Texas engineer insisted. "I have spent 10 or 12 hours behind the wheel and arrived in better shape than when I drove a Detroit car—and I had a much better time driving."

"I want to beam every time I look at the VW," a California homemaker explained, "and have noticed the same expression on most VW owners when they wave or toot their horn as we pass each other." A Californian liked "the peace of mind I have knowing I am driving the finest engineered automobile in the world." To a Florida student, the Beetle was "a car with its own personality."

Such gushing praise never seemed to end. "Words can hardly describe my elation over having come in contact with the VW," said another reader of *Popular Mechanics.* "It's the most wonderful thing that has happened to me since I've been driving automobiles."

How many owners of a Buick or Dodge or Studebaker could bring themselves to pen words of that magnitude? Even when laden with chrome and packing a mighty V-8, those were machines, after all. Yet VW owners took their cars personally, endowing them with human qualities.

Readers of other magazines also were impressed by Volkswagens—and by foreign cars in general. Responding to a 1958 article in *Life,* one reader applauded the "actual involvement" a driver got when motoring in an imported car. More important than fuel economy, he insisted, was the fact that "the driver of the import can get close to his machinery and feels that he owns it rather than the other way around." Said another: "We never agreed to 'love, honor and obey' Detroit."

By the end of 1957, America had 11,088 import dealerships—triple the number at the start of that year. Only 1,920, however, were import-only. During that year, 206,827 imported automobiles were registered (less than 3.5 percent of the total). Volkswagen tallied 64,242 of those registrations, for a 31 percent share of import sales (down from over 50 percent in 1956). Renault was second, with 22,586 registered; English Ford third. All told, 1.07 percent of cars sold in the United States that year were VWs.

As VW sales rose, other imports began to falter. "Volkswagen successes have come out of the hide of British automakers," *Business Week* accurately reported in 1955. According to *New Yorker* magazine's studies of the foreign car market, "sales of the British MG—once queen of the imports with 7,499 sales in 1952—dropped 47 percent last year." British Fords and Austins fell 55 percent and 50 percent, respectively. The British had "pioneered the U.S. market for imports [and] popularized the economy sedan and the sports car," but already by the mid-1950s they were losing ground. Quickly.

Target Buyers for the Beetle

Locating the likely buyer, and dealing appropriately with him or her, was a Volkswagen priority from the beginning. Early sales manuals identified 41 varieties of potential customers in the German market, including "absent-minded professors."

"You can sell even a bully a Volkswagen," the manual continued, "but above all, don't incite him." Most American customers were a bit easier to deal with—more likely to be casually puffing a pipe than throwing their weight around the showroom.

Early distribution was carefully orchestrated. "Cars went only to those customers who were likely to attract the most attention," *U.S. News & World Report* explained in 1956; specifically, to "movie stars, politicians and others in public life. The idea that it was a privilege to drive a Volkswagen was encouraged."

In the American market of the early 1950s, Volkswagen's ambitious leader, Heinz Nordhoff, aimed the Beetle at two-car families—then a rather small part of the U.S. picture. "If an American can afford only one car," Nordhoff told *Newsweek*, "he'll pay a couple of hundred dollars more and buy an American vehicle." Or pay about the same as the VW price and get a fairly new, but second-hand American machine. "That's a real automobile, while your people still regard ours as a toy." Nordhoff looked forward to a day when Volkswagen might be able to lower its price, to capture a greater share of the market.

. Of those owners who reported to *Popular Mechanics* in 1956, for 56 percent their Volkswagen was the sole family automobile. And 73 percent of two car families used their VW the most.

Volkswagens, like other small cars, generally were easier to sell in the east or west—though plenty of midwesterners found themselves in VW showrooms, ready to drive home a Beetle. Chicago, for one, was a major market.

In 1955, some 54 percent of sales were west of the Mississippi. California led the list of small car buyers in a 1958 survey, with nearly one-fourth of owners. New York got more than eight percent, followed by Florida, New Jersey, Texas and Pennsylvania.

Shoppers could expect a different sort of buying experience at the VW dealership, once the sales/service network was in place. As described by *Business Week*, Volkswagens were "bought" rather than "sold." National advertising had not yet begun and little dealer advertising was employed. Free publicity, on the other hand, was plentiful from the start.

U.S. News & World Report noted that VW "dealers were given detailed advice on how to operate. Used cars, for example, were not to be displayed alongside new cars."

Changing Times advised in 1956 that Volkswagen dealers used none of the shady methods that had become commonplace in the auto trade—and which were bringing about Congressional investigation, following gross excesses in 1953-54.

Word-of-mouth remained VW's foremost marketing tool through the 1950s. "A commuter parking at the station interests his mates," *Business Week* explained; and "a factory hand who buys one can be counted on to 'sell' a couple more at the plant where he works." *Changing Times* speculated that "solid citizens who have never before looked twice at anything less than a standard-size American model, are even talking of getting one. Revolutionary? Yes." Volkswagen seemed to be "the first car to convince Americans that a really small automobile is not, somehow, funny."

Buying a car in the Sixties could be a pain, but most shoppers found the experience at a VW dealership to be more refreshing. Dealers generally steered clear of the high-pressure tactics used to market domestic automobiles. (Volkswagen)

Porsches dominated the front rows at this dealership, but Volkswagens were the realistic choices for most shoppers. (Volkswagen)

Those who bought a Beetle could expect top-notch service when anything went wrong. Teaching mechanics toured the country, imparting their knowledge and factory-taught skills to counterparts at local dealerships. The vast network of parts made it likely that necessary replacement components were available nearby. Service delays were a big sore point among imported car owners who quickly learned that an axle, a brake drum, even a set of ignition wires, might take weeks to arrive from a distant warehouse—if not from across the ocean.

Practical Temptations—or Secret Yearnings?

Life magazine in 1958 attributed import popularity in part to a "switch in the public attitude toward the *owner* of the small foreign car. Once he was held in the good-natured mixture of envy and contempt accorded every village sport. Today he is widely regarded as a sensible fellow with the courage of his convictions."

Motivation researchers were busy in the Fifties, trying to dissect peoples' true reasons for buying foreign cars. Owners might insist that they liked the frugal gas mileage of an import, its ease of parking and other sensible virtues. In one 1958 survey, in fact, more than 40 percent of owners cited lower operating cost as a reason to buy, one-third spoke of overall economy, and nearly 20 percent cited lower initial cost.

The deep-motivation, psychology-oriented crowd distrusted reasons as logical as that. Instead, these hard-probing researchers were convinced that Americans invariably sought change. Therefore, they searched for ways to spend their surplus money in fresh ways, all to attain new forms of prestige. *Life* magazine noted that "for many people, a small car is evidence of taste, since it is foreign and perhaps exotic, [and] demonstrates one's disregard for convention."

Even if imported cars eventually grasped one-tenth of the U.S. market, the experts consulted by *Life* predicted that they would be popular mainly in congested urban areas. Despite that limitation, the trend toward imports was considered "no more a fad than is the growing U.S. taste for foreign foods, clothes and decor."

U.S. News & World Report asked "Why People Buy Small Cars" in late 1958. For starters, the typical monthly payment was $47 for a small import vs. $73 for a domestic car. The total price for an import was 37 percent less: $1,800 vs. $2,870. Imports were likely to have fewer gadgets and a simple engine—thus, fewer items to go bad.

Hanging Onto Its Value

In their first few years, Volkswagens didn't necessarily retain their value better than other imported automobiles. Not until it became better known could the car command strong secondhand prices. By the end of the Fifties, on the other hand, it was common knowledge that the buyer of a Beetle could sell it a year or two later, without losing many dollars at all. Full-size American cars lost a bundle the moment they were driven away from the showroom.

Not only did the Beetle earn a reputation for long life and dependability, but it never looked out-of-date. Any used car that looked similar to those that were sitting in new car showrooms naturally commanded a higher price. Those that appeared antiquated brought far lower prices on the used car lot.

A legal confrontation helped prove the Volkswagen's high level of retained value. When a 12-year-old Beetle owned by a Connecticut woman was hit by a truck, her insurance company refused to pay for the loss. The company claimed her car had no value. She won in court. In an ironic aside, reported in *The Beetle Book*, one person involved in that very case was allegedly trying to sell *his own* older Beetle for far more than its "book" value.

High demand for new cars also helped keep used car values high. If a person faced a waiting period to grab a spanking new Beetle, he or she just might opt for a secondhand one instead. A Washington, D.C. dealer, for instance—one of the top import stores—ordered 800 VWs per month in the 1956 period, but could count on receiving only 300 or 400. Some dealers simply stopped taking orders, at least temporarily.

Accessories Add to VW Charm

Adding extra cost goodies to one's car was a popular American pastime, whether that car was a Cadillac, a Ford V-8 or a Beetle. Whether those accessories came from a factory catalog or an aftermarket supplier, they let owners transform their vehicles into personalized objects.

Not since the 1920s, though, had factory option lists included such items as flower vases. Made of porcelain, cut

A surfboard fit the suntanned lifestyle of many VW convertible owners. This '66 had a real glass rear window. (Volkswagen)

● **Volkswagen Accessories** ●

In 1955, Volkswagen dealers offered items such as these to dress up and "improve" the Beetle:

Fuel gauge
Electric clock
Ashtray (pull-out, or on gearshift)
Rear ashtray
Flower vase (Rosenthal, tinted glass or chrome)
Horn ring
Ivory-colored steering wheel
Cigarette lighter
Reclining seats
Floor mats (five colors)
Door grip
Passenger hand-hold
Reading light (with mirror)
Outside sun visor
Anti-dazzle sun visor (passenger)
Seat covers
Telefunken Auto-Super radio
Roof net (above inside mirror)
Outside mirror (door hinge or door frame mounting)

Windshield washer
Luggage set (three suitcases for rear compartment, one for front)
Roof rack for luggage
Wheel trim rings (plain, fan-shaped or ornamental)
Rear-fender protector
Rear-window blind
Hinged rear windows
Hanging strap
Coat hook
Exhaust extension
Tire chains
License plate mounting
Spotlight
Foglight
Backup light
Curb finder
Spare wheel hubcap (with tools)
Chrome-vanadium tool kit

Aftermarket vendors entered the business early, too, offering a broad range of items for Beetles and Buses. Catalogs and ads listed hundreds of items, from engine compartment silencer pads and chromed air cleaners, to flared tailpipes and rubber fender flaps, to headlight visors and backup light kits.

It wasn't necessary to own a Campmobile to go camping with a Volkswagen. Aftermarket suppliers produced tents that fit onto the top of Beetles. This one was produced by Carbak Camper of Tampa, Florida. The current Ohio owner bought the unit from a dealer in 1975. (Photo: James M. Flammang — Owner: Mike Young)

glass or ceramic, offered in a selection of shapes, these fancy holders found their way into many a Volkswagen.

Most accessories were somewhat more prosaic. A grab handle and sun visor for the front passenger, for instance. Or a special dashboard panel, including a clock and trio of real gauges. Because radios weren't yet standard equipment, install-it-later Telefunken units proved popular.

Before long, the aftermarket firms developed a host of performance add-ons, as well as body "improvement" kits. By the mid-1950s, for example, a Beetle owner could order a custom fiberglass hood and Continental spare tire kit. While some deplored such gross revisions of the Beetle's body lines, other people liked the idea of driving a distinctive variant of what was *already* something different—thus, two steps removed from the mainstream.

David Turns Into Goliath

"Will Success Spoil VW?" was the title of an article in *Popular Mechanics* by Arthur R. Railton, who'd visited the Wolfsburg plant in 1957. "Defying most of the rules," Railton marveled, "a maverick all the way, the Volkswagen has become the world's first international car—a machine 'at home' in 100 countries with customers in most of them waiting months for delivery." Here was "a machine so unpretentious that the American auto industry laughed when it first began to sell in this country."

Some still laughed, but in his view, "an empire [was] being created." Railton noted that some experts were tying the future economy of Germany, if not of Western Europe itself, to the success of Volkswagen.

To grab an ever-greater share of the U.S. market, Volkswagen was not above making certain "condescensions" to American tastes. Railton pointed out, for instance, that the latest dashboard wore a useless strip of chrome, "something Dr. Porsche would probably have ripped off with his own hands." He also advised that the newly-installed, flat gas pedal had been redesigned to satisfy women drivers.

Detroit's Compacts Arrive—Imports Decline

In recession year 1958, for the first time ever, the United States imported more cars than it exported. Half a million foreign vehicles dotted American roads (out of 56 million in all). Imports accounted for 7.3 percent of new car sales. Volkswagen alone beat both Chrysler and Studebaker in the American marketplace.

Youthful customers may have liked the "fun" qualities of a Beetle, but families bought them for their practical virtues. Automatic Stick Shift made this '69 appealing to more consumers, but the unit soon proved troublesome. (Volkswagen)

Importers of European cars were worried as the Big Three unveiled their compacts late in 1959. Studebaker already had its Lark on sale, showing a healthy response. Naturally, Ford's Falcon and Chrysler's Valiant were expected to draw even greater numbers of customers who liked the idea of a smaller-than-usual vehicle.

The relatively radical, rear-engined Chevrolet Corvair was a wild card. No one could say for sure how Americans would accept its unconventional engineering and out-of-the-mainstream design. Having a fully independent suspension and air-cooled rear engine put the Corvair far afield from all the other new American compacts, which were essentially scaled-down versions of full-size automobiles.

During the Fourth International Automobile Show at New York's Coliseum, in April 1960, a total of 86 manufacturers from 10 countries exhibited their wares. More than 300 models went on display. Quite a few featured quad headlights, following a trend unleashed on domestic cars a couple of years earlier. Tailfins were seeing their final days on American automobiles, but more than a few imports flaunted those appendages.

Small-scale station wagons drew attention at the show. So did a crop of true minicars. Toyota brought its Toyopet Tiara, planning to put the car on sale in August. Datsun displayed the new Bluebird. New Morris and Austin 850 models from British Motor Corporation vied for attention. So did the NSU Prinz, Peugeots, Isettas, Saabs and many more—all the way to Bentleys and Benzes. Said one exhibitor: "It's the suburbanite we want to sell."

There seemed to be no end of ways to personalize one's Beetle. (Volkswagen)

Volkswagen had skipped the prior year's show, because it stood so far ahead of the competition. Now VW was back—perhaps a sign of concern about the growing rivalry for small car buyers?

"Few observers think even the U.S. market can support such a broad array of cars," *Business Week* noted. As things turned out, imported sales did begin to shrink—badly. For 1960, U.S. sales of British makes fell 30 percent. Volkswagen, on the other hand, was one of the few imports to show sales *growth*: up 39 percent. Of the 10 top imports, all except VW declined.

What could be a finer driver on a spring day in 1969 than a VW convertible? Whether on campus, at the beach, or out on the road, the distinctive and diminutive Beetle ragtop exuded a cheery disposition. (Phil Hall)

After peaking at 10.2 percent of the market in 1959, foreign cars as a whole dropped to little more than seven percent—of a shrunken total, at that. The percentage dipped below five percent a year later. The import "boom," pundits quickly reported, appeared to be turning into a "bust."

Dealers "stress that the novelty has worn off imports," *U.S. News & World Reports* claimed early in 1961, "and with it any prestige that came from owning one. Instead, dealers were turning away from imports, to focus full attention on the new domestic compacts.

And why not? That's where the profits were, after all—especially because Americans soon were leaning toward fancy, high dollar versions of those new compacts, not the no-frills "entry level" editions. The cars might have been smaller, but their selections of extra cost goodies began to rival those ordered on full-size automobiles.

Three years later, Volkswagen was still going strong, and import sales showed a modest rise. Still, predictions of VW's decline were more frequently heard. "The Volkswagen mystique is fast becoming a thing of the past," a spokesman for a rival automaker reported to *Business Week*. "I think the company has reached its summit in sales and from now on can only go down."

In 1963, Volkswagen captured a 3.2 percent share of total new car sales in the United States and 62.3 percent of the import market. In the first eight months of 1964, Volkswagen was still the top seller in the United States, taking 63 percent of the import total. After VW came MG, Triumph, Renault, Volvo, Opel, Mercedes-Benz, Fiat, Austin-Healey and Simca. In 1965, too, more VWs were sold in America than all other imports combined.

Eventually, many of the comforts that were commonplace in conventional cars found their way into Beetles—including air conditioning by the time this 1973 Super Beetle was built. (Volkswagen)

Car and Driver noted in 1963 that "owning an import in the early 1950s was a gamble. Volkswagen took the chance out of owning a foreign car by providing absolutely reliable transportation." Because the original Beetle had been "overdesigned, overstressed and enduring beyond belief...even the most inept or malicious flogger [could not easily] break it."

Tempting as the Beetles were, nothing is perfect. And nothing lasts forever. Or does it?

OWNER COMMENTS: E.C. (Erv) Smith

"At the time I bought my first one," Erv Smith says of his series of Volkswagens, "I was teaching." He had a DeSoto hemi and Dodge hemi. "My gas bills, even with cheap gas, were too high." So, he bought an Arctic White 1960 sun roof, for $1,818. Although his wife—also a teacher—didn't care for the car at first, she quickly grew fond of driving it. Then, he "had to fight to get it."

With a growing family, they needed a plain-Jane sedan. Instead, his next car was a 1964 VW convertible. "You're going to buy that convertible," his wife said, or nothing at all. It had dealer-installed Porsche 356 chromed wheels and caps, halogen H4 headlights and an AM/FM radio. In Poppy Red with gray leather interior, it cost $2,154.

Next came a Squareback; then a 1985 GTI. At one point, Erv and his son drove the convertible to a Seattle car show (200-plus miles away). The attendant determined that the ragtop was a "show car," despite the bugs it had accumulated on the trip. It won an award. "We cleaned it up and showed it for about three years," Smith says, in shows from Los Angeles to British Columbia. It took about 51 awards. "So I retired it."

Smith had been searching for an oval-window. The Jungle Green '56 he finally found "looks like it just came out of the showroom." It had been painted 30 years earlier, at the Oregon State Penitentiary.

Next came a 1969 Karmann Ghia coupe, Chrome Blue, with 47,000 miles. It won three class awards in three outings.

His sun roof car eventually was totaled. He'd once driven it from New York to Oregon, carrying three adults and nine full-size suitcases and averaging "700 miles a day in the little thing."

Now that he's retired from duties as a school principal and vice-principal, Erv has time to "play with my Volkswagens" at home in Salem, Oregon. His opinion of VWs is simple: "I just love them."

Chapter 11

The Beetle Compared—How Good (Or Bad) Were They?

In 1949, a group of German automobiles went on exhibit at Berlin's first auto show since the war. More than 80 companies participated in the event, which marked the 50th anniversary of the Automobile Club of Germany.

Popular Mechanics noticed American influence in several of the new cars, including the Hansa 1500 (built by Borgward) and Ford Taunus. Not so the Volkswagens, led by a dramatically two-toned convertible. Any resemblance to American cars of the 1940s was difficult to discern in the VW's bulbous, nearly symmetrical profile—not to mention its technical configuration.

Not many people outside of Germany knew about the Volkswagen's development, during Hitler's regime. Those who did were aware that the 1949 model hadn't changed all that much from Dr. Porsche's original designs. Most of the car's basic elements had been selected early, and remained in place for the postwar version. Those included:

• **Rear-mounted engine** (thus, no need for a long driveshaft).

• **Lightweight engine components** (helped by extensive use of aluminum and magnesium).

• **Air cooling** (no radiator or coolant needed). Each of the "long-ribbed" airplane-type cylinders was cooled by a constant stream of fresh air. As described in a 1960s brochure, the engine's "fan driven by the crankshaft sucks in air through the louvers under the back window and blasts it over a series of cooling fins that surround the cylinders."

• **Horizontally-opposed cylinders.** Volkswagen's sales brochure noted that the flat design not only saved space but permitted a short four-bearing crankshaft.

• **Low-speed engine operation** (thus, low-wear). The oversquare design (larger bore than stroke) resulted in low piston speeds—a principle also adopted by developers of modern, overhead-valve American V-8 engines, starting with the 1949 Cadillac and Oldsmobile.

• **Platform-type chassis** with central backbone (tubular spine) and integral floorpan.

• **Four-wheel independent suspension**, described as "ingenious" in the VW brochure. Of course, most owners didn't realize the significance of an independent rear suspension—or even that it differed from domestic vehicles.

• **Torsion bar springing** at all four corners, with twin swinging half-axles at the rear and eight-leaf torsion bars up front, instead of conventional front coil springs and rear leaf springs. Volkswagen called the suspension setup "Torsi-O-Matic," insisting that it delivered a neat blend of comfort and handling, "years ahead of its time." Considering that Chrysler products adopted torsion bars in 1957, that claim is not without validity.

• **Low unsprung weight**—a concept more often spoken of regarding performance cars, than ordinary passenger carriers.

Nothing in the above list remotely resembles the configuration of any American car. Neither do these qualities suggest other European makes.

Beetles had many other distinctive features, some seldom found even on cars that cost far more:

• **Jacking pads** for easier tire changing.

• **Engine oil cooler**—an item more commonly found in expensive sport and racing engines. Because of automatic oil cooling, the brochure explained, "the engine does not fatigue even if it is driven at maximum speed hour after hour on a turnpike."

• **Warning lights** for low oil pressure and the electrical system—which, because the fan belt ran the generator, served also to indicate a broken belt. This was part of what *Motor Trend* described as "VW's inspiredly parsimonious instrument panel."

• **Built-in hot-air heater**. As described more or less accurately by *Consumer Reports*, "heat dissipated from the cylinders is blown through pipes to warm the car interior, which it does fairly well, and to defrost the windshield." As many a real-life owner quickly came to realize, the amount of warm air delivered from the Volkswagen's "heater" outlets on a chilly morning ranged from meager to virtually none. Owners in the northern regions soon took a compelling interest in aftermarket gasoline-fired heaters.

Few engines looked anything like the Beetle's, with its shrouded fan blowing air toward a quartet of finned cylinders. To an onlooker accustomed to inline sixes and burly V-8s, the flat four tucked into the rear of a Volkswagen barely resembled an engine at all.

Only a handful of other automobiles in the 1940s and '50s used rear-mounted engines. Porsche took the lead in this area, and continues to offer an air-cooled, rear-engined 911 into the 1990s. In America, the ill-fated 1947 Tucker contained a six-cylinder rear engine. Among the small car set, Renault used a rear engine, but water-cooled.

Air-cooling had been experimented with by many automakers, but the only one that lasted for an appreciable time was the American-built Franklin, produced into the early 1930s.

Not everything about the Beetle was flawless, of course—especially near the beginning. "When Nordhoff took over," *Popular Mechanics* reported in 1958, "cylinder

Collectors favor VWs from the split-window generation, as demonstrated by these two 1951 sedans.

Oval-window Beetles rank second-best in desirability, as collector cars. These are 1956 models.

walls were good for about 10,000 miles. Today, he says, they will go 100,000 miles without reboring. VW officials estimate the useful life of a VW at about 125,000 miles."

Director Nordhoff vowed in 1954 that he would not "make Henry Ford's mistake with the Model T. We will keep altering and improving the present model, making it better and more attractive."

Nordhoff explained in 1958 that "the only decision I am really proud of is that I have refused to change Porsche's design. It's hard to remain the same. You can always sell cars by being new. But we chose a different course.

"We are striving for perfection," he continued, "to make our cars run forever, if possible." A prime problem was "to keep the spirit and the productivity of the engineers at a high level despite the fact their work is almost entirely destined to be put aside, not to be translated into reality at this time."

Why did Renault—the most logical rival to Volkswagen—fail to succeed, despite a heavy advertising budget? A large part of the reason had to be the reputation for German craftsmanship. That contrasted sharply with the French reputation—at least partially well-deserved—for unreliable products. French cars were consistently among the most distinctive on the global market, but never known for longevity or trouble-free operation.

What about the German also-rans? Why did the DKW, the Goliath, the Borgward not come close to Volkswagen in the sales race? Weren't they well-crafted machines, too?

For one thing, those imports—like most imports other than Volkswagen—lacked a strong dealer/service network. Buy almost any European car other than a Volkswagen, and you couldn't be certain that parts would be immediately available in case of breakdown, that the car would be serviced expertly and that the job wouldn't cost a fortune.

Volkswagen's mid-1960s sales brochure vowed quicker service, because VW mechanics didn't "have to start from scratch each year relearning the car.... Improvements have been gradual and as the VW has evolved, our mechanics have kept pace with it."

Each dealership had to meet certain standards before hanging out the blue-and-white VW shingle. All tools had to be VW-approved, machined to fit VW parts perfectly. Dealers had to have at least a 2,272-item parts inventory to start (growing to 3,500 when business was well underway). That selection was augmented by stocks at 14 parts depots around the country. "When we make an improvement in the Volkswagen," the company explained, "we try to make the new part fit older model VWs as well."

Were Beetles As Great As They Say?

Wander around a Volkswagen show today, and you're sure to see row after row of handsome, well-maintained, sweet-running Beetles and Buses. As with other collectible makes, it might be said that only the strongest survive. Most of the others fell victim to the crusher, years ago.

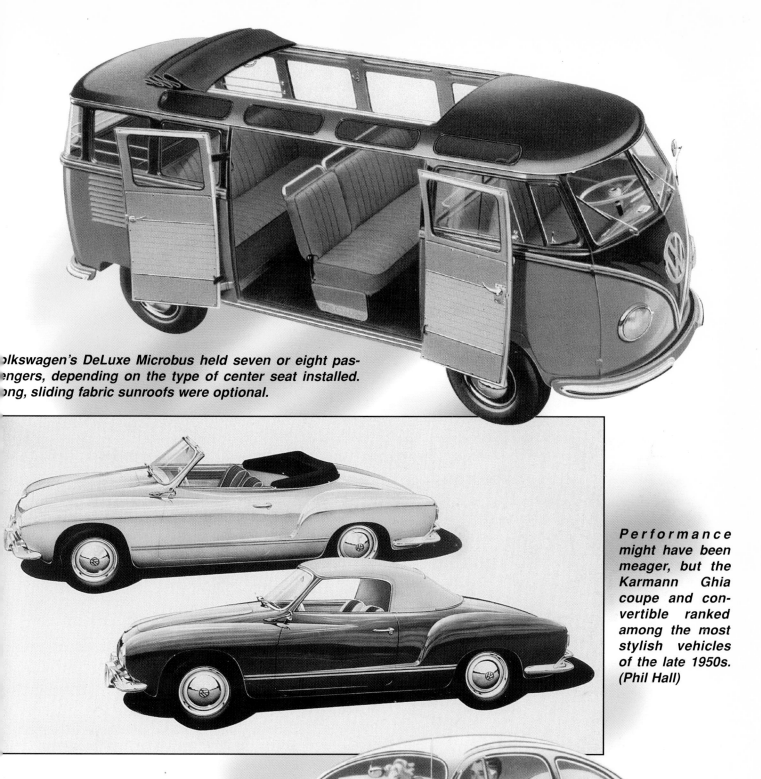

Volkswagen's DeLuxe Microbus held seven or eight passengers, depending on the type of center seat installed. Long, sliding fabric sunroofs were optional.

Performance might have been meager, but the Karmann Ghia coupe and convertible ranked among the most stylish vehicles of the late 1950s. (Phil Hall)

Dramatically styled artwork in early Volkswagen brochures helped capture the attention of people who knew little about the "people's car" when it first arrived in the U.S. market. (Phil Hall)

1 Spare wheel
2 Fuel tank
3 Steering gear
4 Hydraulic, double-acting long-stroke telescopic shock absorbers
5 Longitudinal torsion arms acting on front wheels with independent suspension
6 Cross-tubes with two 8-leaf torsion bar springs
7 Divided tie rod

8 Super balloon tires
9 Master cylinder for hydraulic foot brake
10 Pedal assembly
11 Steering column lever operating direction signals
12 Heater outlet

13 Defroster vent
14 Vent wings with inside ca
15 Rotary knob for close reg
16 Battery isolated from eng
17 Cross-tube with circular se
    suspension of rear wheels
18 Spring plates

...omesh transmission

...uretor with accelerator pump

26 Ignition distributor with vacuum-adv
27 Fuel pump
28 Generator with voltage regulator
29 Stop lamps combined with tail lamps
30 License plate lamp
31 Adjustable sun visor

Cutaway shows basic elements of the Beetle design, including rear-mounted, air-cooled engine; torsion-bar suspension all around; and spare tire and fuel tank up front. (Phil Hall)

Volkswagen of America launched Small World, *a quarterly magazine for VW owners, early in the 1960s. Many owners kept every issue, which contained details on current models, history, technical advice, do-it-yourself tips, stories about special Beetles and their owners – plus articles on places to travel with one's VW.*

SMALL WORLD
FOR VOLKSWAGEN OWNERS
IN THE UNITED STATES

INTRODUCTORY ISSUE

For close to three decades, convertibles served as the glamorous members of the Beetle family. (Owner/Photographer: Phil Hall)

19 D 59

Not quite everything is original or authentic in this 1959 Beetle—including the engine, which started life in a later model. Many Volkswagen enthusiasts like to tailor their cars to their own tastes, mechanically and aesthetically. (Photo: James M. Flammang — Owner: Kim and Chuck Fryer)

Beetle dashboards were basic, as demonstrated by this 1960 model, photographed when it was nearly new. (Owner/Photographer: Phil Hall)

Split-window (pre-1954) sedans are among the most-wanted Volkswagens by today's collectors and enthusiasts. (Photo: James M. Flammang)

"The Thing" was built for fun, but also for commercial applications. Made in Mexico, it was sold in the United States for only two seasons. (Owner/Photographer: Phil Hall)

Not everyone narrows their Volkswagen interest to full-size automobiles. Toys and models are also popular. Mark Garrett, of Ohio, has transformed his entire basement into "a VW heaven," containing some 1,200 Volkswagen toys.

Is the VW Fastback a completely new Volkswagen?

The Type 3 came in both sedan and Fastback form. Both models had air-cooled engines—not unlike the Beetle's but flatter, mounted low at the rear, out of sight. (Phil Hall)

Whether in the hazy tones penned by a graphic artist, or in the metallic flesh, a top-down Volkswagen easily inspired visions of joy on the road. Long after the Beetle's heyday, its shape remained among the most recognizable images in the world.

Sales brochures also featured ordinary owners, who told of their experiences with the car—and their love for the little machine. This Connecticut woman liked the way it parked. (Phil Hall)

891·943
CONNECTICUT

Not only is this 196[?] Westfalia Camper a "dai[?] driver," it goes campin[?] often. The young owner drove it 30,000 miles in [?] single year. Origina[?] equipment includes [?] child's cot, jump sea[?] rear screen, and side ten[?] Seats were recovere[?] and new curtains sew[?] for the windows. (Photo [?] James M. Flammang – Owner: Kim and Chuc[?] Fryer)

Introduced for 1995, the latest Cabrio blends a cute body with a spirited personality. The previous Rabbit-based convertible lasted for 15 years in the VW lineup.

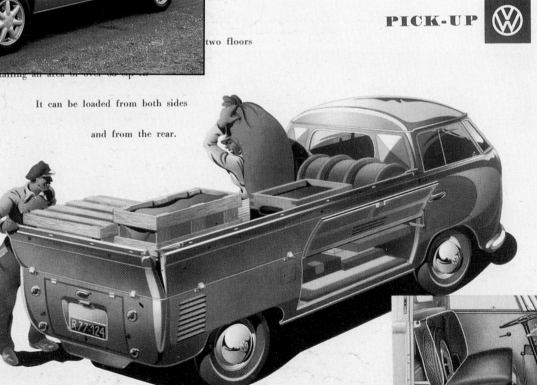

PICK-UP VW

two floors

totaling an area of over 35 sq. ft.

It can be loaded from both sides

and from the rear.

Commercial vehicles came in various forms. Note the auxiliary enclosed storage compartment in the lower section of this pick-up truck. (Phil Hall)

Beetle convertibles always had a youthful personality. Like many Volkswagen fans, its owner has had a succession of VWs over the years. (Owner/Photographer: E.C. Smith)

For 1996, Volkswagen offered two versions of the GTI: with a four-cylinder, or the innovative VR6 narrow-angle V-6.

Beetle engines looked about the same through the years, but escalated periodically in displacement and horsepower. (Photo: James M. Flammang)

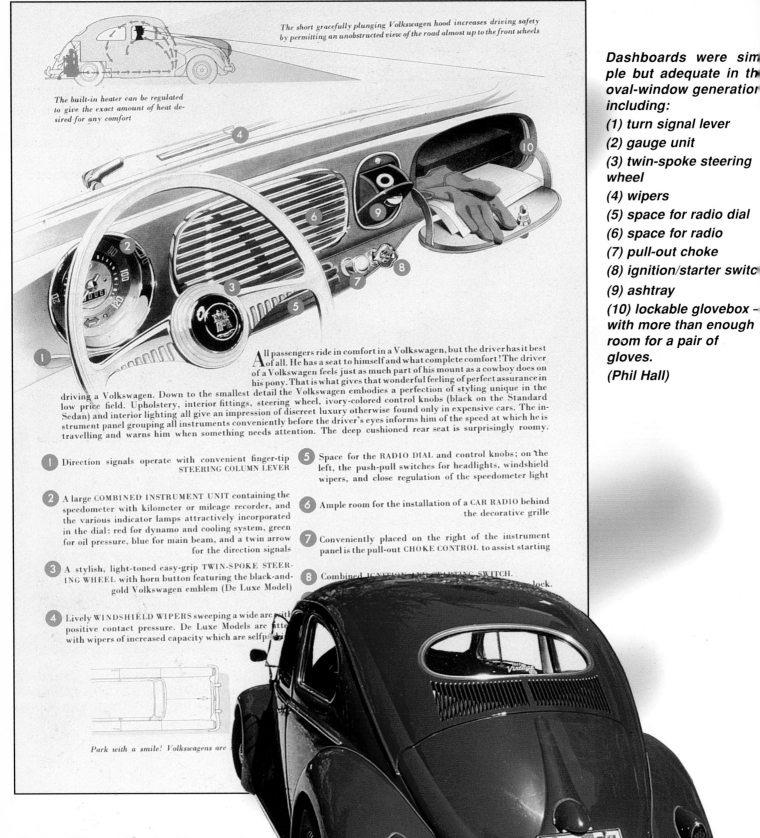

The short gracefully plunging Volkswagen hood increases driving safety by permitting an unobstructed view of the road almost up to the front wheels

The built-in heater can be regulated to give the exact amount of heat desired for any comfort

Dashboards were simple but adequate in the oval-window generation including:

(1) turn signal lever
(2) gauge unit
(3) twin-spoke steering wheel
(4) wipers
(5) space for radio dial
(6) space for radio
(7) pull-out choke
(8) ignition/starter switch
(9) ashtray
(10) lockable glovebox – with more than enough room for a pair of gloves.
(Phil Hall)

All passengers ride in comfort in a Volkswagen, but the driver has it best of all. He has a seat to himself and what complete comfort! The driver of a Volkswagen feels just as much part of his mount as a cowboy does on his pony. That is what gives that wonderful feeling of perfect assurance in driving a Volkswagen. Down to the smallest detail the Volkswagen embodies a perfection of styling unique in the low price field. Upholstery, interior fittings, steering wheel, ivory-colored control knobs (black on the Standard Sedan) and interior lighting all give an impression of discreet luxury otherwise found only in expensive cars. The instrument panel grouping all instruments conveniently before the driver's eyes informs him of the speed at which he is travelling and warns him when something needs attention. The deep cushioned rear seat is surprisingly roomy.

1 Direction signals operate with convenient finger-tip STEERING COLUMN LEVER

2 A large COMBINED INSTRUMENT UNIT containing the speedometer with kilometer or mileage recorder, and the various indicator lamps attractively incorporated in the dial: red for dynamo and cooling system, green for oil pressure, blue for main beam, and a twin arrow for the direction signals

3 A stylish, light-toned easy-grip TWIN-SPOKE STEERING WHEEL with horn button featuring the black-and-gold Volkswagen emblem (De Luxe Model)

4 Lively WINDSHIELD WIPERS sweeping a wide arc with positive contact pressure. De Luxe Models are fitted with wipers of increased capacity which are selfparking

5 Space for the RADIO DIAL and control knobs; on the left, the push-pull switches for headlights, windshield wipers, and close regulation of the speedometer light

6 Ample room for the installation of a CAR RADIO behind the decorative grille

7 Conveniently placed on the right of the instrument panel is the pull-out CHOKE CONTROL to assist starting

8 Combined IGNITION AND STARTING SWITCH. ... lock.

Park with a smile! Volkswagens are ...

Some VWs are kept 100-percent stock; others are modified either a little or a lot. The owner of this fine '57 oval-window sedan learned to drive in a Volkswagen. Its maroon paint is the same color as a 1950 split-window he'd owned years earlier. Euro-type bumpers have been installed. (Owner: René Rondeau)

Volkswagen artwork takes a variety of forms. This postcard, using early brochure graphics, was sold in Britain in the mid-1990s, by Mayfair Cards of London.

Ads for the Rabbit could be clever, but weren't in the same league as the Doyle, Dane Bernbach print ads for the Beetle. (Kurt Wendt)

To drivers accustomed to American cars, the steering column of a Transporter seemed almost vertical—like a Greyhound bus. Apart from truckers, Americans weren't used to such an upright driving position. (Phil Hall)

The owner of this much-modified, vividly-hued '63 grew up in a family that favored unusual imported cars—including a Goggomobil. Restoration from a solid California-desert bodyshell took 2-1/2 years. The low stance was accomplished by turning the rear torsion bars down a notch, and by welding select-a-drop adjusters into the front axle beam. Providing the power is a Jim Corman-built 1775-cc engine. (Mike Fornataro)

Dune-buggy owners are nothing if not individualistic. (Photo: James M. Flammang)

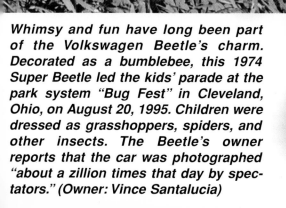

Whimsy and fun have long been part of the Volkswagen Beetle's charm. Decorated as a bumblebee, this 1974 Super Beetle led the kids' parade at the park system "Bug Fest" in Cleveland, Ohio, on August 20, 1995. Children were dressed as grasshoppers, spiders, and other insects. The Beetle's owner reports that the car was photographed "about a zillion times that day by spectators." (Owner: Vince Santalucia)

Most Americans never heard of the VWs sold elsewhere in the world. This Karmann Ghia TC was a Brazilian product. (Phil Hall)

Truly an open-air vehicle, "The Thing" had a fold-down windshield, and its doors and windows were removable. (Phil Hall)

GTI editions of the Rabbit (and its Golf successor) attracted performance-oriented Volkswagen fans in the 1980s. (Kurt Wendt)

Sunroof sedans and convertibles joined the basic Beetle sedan early in its history, adding a touch of sport and glamour to the economy-car experience. (Phil Hall)

After getting much publicity from the Concept 1 coupe, Volkswagen designers got to work on a Cabrio version.

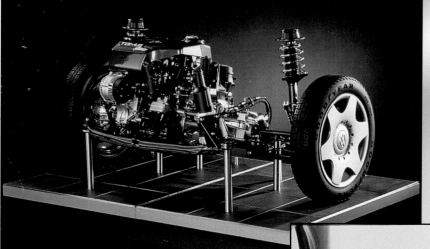

Finally, at the Geneva (Switzerland) Motor Show in March 1996, Volkswagen announced that the production car—likely to debut in 1998—will be called "The New Beetle." Dimensions are larger than the prior Concept 1 version, and the glass roof isn't likely to remain when production begins.

At the January 1994 debut, three possible powertrains for the Concept 1 were displayed: diesel, electric, and hybrid-electric. The actual production car probably will have a conventional front-mounted gasoline engine with front-wheel drive.

Volkswagen is no exception. Despite their admittedly advanced engineering, regardless of the careful craftsmanship exhibited by VW's assembly workers, they weren't perfect automobiles. Millions of them provided reliable transportation year after year for their owners. Still, they were hardly immune to failure. At the same time, many of the warnings and admonitions heaped upon the car by friends and neighbors of those owners—and by a flurry of alleged experts—proved to be false or exaggerated.

Critics early in VW's heyday, for example, fretted about the longevity of the air-cooled engine. In hot weather, they insisted, the finned cylinders of that flat four would fail to deliver enough cooling power to the inner workings. And if that happened, you'd have a seized engine. The end.

Seized engines weren't exactly unheard of through the Beetle's lifespan. Counteracting that prediction of doom, however, countless owners began to report that they'd taken their cars through treacherous desert heat, driving hard, without mishap. And that the little air-cooled engines would come back again and again, virtually begging for additional mistreatment.

The rear-engine configuration also drew its share of criticism: some valid, but much of it overblown. Early road

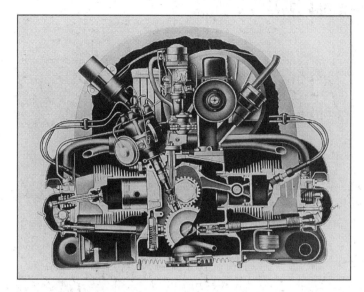

Though familiar at a glance to aficionados, Volkswagen's horizontally-opposed engine differed dramatically from conventional powerplants of its time, whether in domestic or imported automobiles. By 1962, the flat four developed 40 horsepower and had a crankcase ventilation system. (Volkswagen)

A plastic breather tube in the 1962 engine sent crankcase fumes back into the carburetor's air cleaner—an early form of emission control. Few engines have ever been as easy to remove for serious servicing as the Beetle's. (Volkswagen)

Engineers worked constantly on refinements to improve ride and handling qualities. A modified rear suspension for 1969 kept rear wheels virtually vertical, even under extreme conditions—quite an improvement over early Beetles, whose wheels could tilt frightfully inward if they left the ground. (Phil Hall)

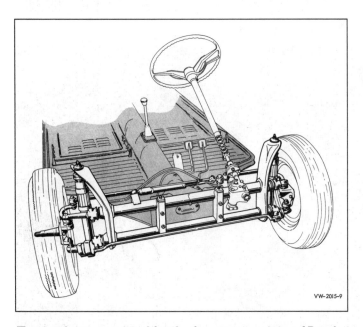

Torsion bars were used for the front suspensions of Beetles from the beginning—until the Super Beetle of 1971. Shown is the 1969 version. (Phil Hall)

testers delivered dire warnings of what would happen if an inexperienced driver got into trouble with a Volkswagen. The rear end would break away in an instant, they predicted, with severe consequences lying in wait. If cars were meant to have rear-mounted engines, some people insisted, American engineers would have done so long before. And when they did, with the Corvair, plenty of American car buyers steered clear, wary of trying something so radical.

Ads insisted that the Corvair's powerplant, "America's only airplane-type horizontal engine," was "in the rear where it belongs." They also foolishly branded the car "revolutionary," a trait that does not easily translate into sales in the U.S. market.

Observers such as Tom McCahill took a different approach. While acknowledging the theoretical safety hazard of a rear-engine design, they felt a Volkswagen could not travel fast enough to get its driver into much trouble anyway.

Common sense, on the other hand, suggests that the combination of a rear engine and swing axles could be asking for trouble in hard driving. All a person had to do was look at a Beetle or Microbus up on a grease rack. When not pressing upon the pavement, the tires (and wheels) angled dramatically inward. What if that happened when going around a fast corner? This looked like a disaster waiting to happen.

After consumer advocate Ralph Nader attacked the rear-engined Corvair's alleged propensity to become similarly skittish, at least under demanding conditions, he and others issued comparable warnings about the Volkswagen. Nader even warned that it was "hard to find a more dangerous car than the Volkswagen." Otherwise, imports had not received much safety criticism.

While the Corvair-based cautions got loads of adverse publicity, VW managed to escape the brunt of the attack. A lengthy 1970 critique by the Center for Auto Safety called for recall of 3.2 million Beetles, but yielded no such result. Only VW's "The Thing" (Chapter 17) earned the full wrath of safety advocates.

In 1966, however, VW earned an unwanted distinction: it became the first imported make to be recalled. Worldwide, 480,000 Beetles and Karmann Ghias were affected, including 175,000 in the United States. New, permanently-lubricated ball joints had inadequate plastic sealing rings. Corrosion in those joints could lead to loose wheels and front-end shimmy.

Quick steering and a rear engine are what made the VW fun. While some drivers endured all the handling deficiencies inherent in rear-engined cars, which are balanced far differently than conventional front-engine designs, others enjoyed their Beetles for that very same reason.

Dependable and Unique Machines

Among the many items of interest in *Small World*, the Volkswagen owners' magazine, were occasional reports of long-lived Beetles. A British owner, for instance, had driven his 1950 model more than 600,000 miles, going through three engines. Long before, the company had realized that its cars were hanging on longer than expected. They practically ran out of those gold watches issued to owners whose Beetles ran 100,000 kilometers (60,000 miles).

Business Week in 1953 noted that Volkswagenwerk was "so cocksure of the quality and dependability of their production that finished cars undergo no exhaustive tests before being shipped." They had no test grounds at all.

Popular Mechanics in 1958 described VW's Research and Development building in Germany, where the author "saw engines tested by running them under full load at wide-open throttle for 100 continuous hours.... When torn down," he exclaimed, "they show no appreciable wear." Because VWs were sold in a hundred countries by then, they had to be reliable under all conditions: "Dust conditions in the Sahara, extreme cold in northern Sweden, destructive humidity in the jungles, long, hard pulls in the mountains of Switzerland."

Before leaving the factory, said a mid-1960s sales brochure, "every engine is given a final instrument check. At all speeds. That's why you can run your new Volkswagen at top speed the first time you drive it. We've already broken it in for you at the factory."

Not only did no other car on the road look like a Beetle, none sounded like a Volkswagen. Quite like the Model T Ford, the Beetle had its own distinctive resonance—a sound that, once heard, never was forgotten.

Plenty of people who knew how to pick a vehicle of excellence had turned to Volkswagen. A high percentage (nearly 28 percent) of owners reporting to *Popular Mechanics* in 1956 were engineers, craftsmen and technicians.

A substantial number of women worked in the Wolfsburg plant, but most were assigned to trim work. (Volkswagen)

Quality control and craftsmanship helped make the Volkswagen a global leader, while so many other imported automobiles failed. Body shells were originally assembled piece by piece, then welded together. By 1958, all three main body sections were produced on automatic lines, then welded together in setups such as this one. In 1963, a fully-automated line replaced 14 separate assembly jigs. (Volkswagen)

A broad network of dealership service centers contributed to the success of Volkswagen in the late 1950s and '60s. (Volkswagen)

Trouble Spots

Certain design considerations drew unfavorable comment early on. "The battery is in the open," *Motor Trend* warned in 1953, "just under the right-hand edge of the rear seat. We view this with some alarm. Acid can spill in a collision, and all lead-acid batteries emit smelly fumes."

Actually, the result could be worse than that. One Chicago owner described what happened when his overweight sister-in-law took a ride in the back seat of an early 1960s Beetle—at a time when the car had seen better days. Her bulk caused the seat springs to sag and short out the battery, resulting in a small fire. Fortunately for all parties, the fire was put out quickly, and no one suffered anything other than embarrassment.

Not as risky to life or limb, but a conspicuous defect nonetheless, was the dreaded rust. Not only was it unsightly, but rust could impair structural integrity. Spots to watch—then and now—include:

• Rocker sills
• Suspension attachment points
• Front luggage compartment
• Heat exchange boxes
• Battery containers

Starting in 1970, dealerships offered a comprehensive Diagnosis/Maintenance program. Here, a technician checks engine timing—not a difficult task with the Beetle engine. (Volkswagen)

The most likely rust spot may be the Beetle's rear end, where the back bumper is mounted. Starting in the 1950s, a sagging bumper became almost a "trademark" of Volkswagens. Some Beetles—including a 1957 oval-window once owned by the author of this book—ran around with their rear bumpers barely attached at all.

That same '57 suffered another malady that was far from uncommon in pre-1962 models: a leaky fuel tap. Lack of funds and initiative at the time deterred the owner from bothering to fix the leak, so occupants simply got used to an aroma of gasoline wafting regularly into the passenger compartment.

Convertibles had their own set of possible problems, due mainly to the fact that their tops were complicated—thus hard to repair. The mechanism consisted of hundreds of parts. The side frame girders used in convertibles also were rust-prone and difficult to fix.

Fading paint was another problem. Some VWs, *Mechanix Illustrated* reported in 1961, had paint that "deteriorated quite rapidly" (especially some gray shades).

Creature Comforts

To an American family accustomed to a six-passenger Ford or Chevrolet, not to mention a block-long Cadillac or Lincoln, a VW was little. Tiny. Miniature.

Sure, four passengers might fit neatly inside, but they wouldn't like it there. Would they?

In fact, those four folks had an easier time of it than do the occupants of most of today's subcompacts—or even compacts. Climbing into the back seat of a Beetle wasn't so easy for a person of advanced years and scant agility, but at least it could be done. And once ensconced therein, the two rear seat riders weren't exactly cramped for space.

Heat was another story. VW owners in the northern regions learned to dread chilly mornings, because they knew that the Beetle's interior would remain frigid through the whole commute. Or through the whole vacation trip. That air-cooled engine simply could not deliver the kind of cozy warmth that Americans were used to—or anything close. No wonder those gas-fired auxiliary heaters became such a popular accessory item—a prime selling point when secondhand Beetles were advertised in the snowbelt.

Was a VW easy to drive? Absolutely, provided that one didn't insist upon an American car experience. Steering was quick and responsive. The sharp steering wheel angle that seemed strange at first, soon began to feel friendly and right. *Motor Trend* warned (correctly) that brake and clutch pedals were a bit too close together, but most drivers quickly got accustomed to that oddity. And if only all of today's five-speed manual gearboxes shifted as neatly and smoothly as the four-speed in a Beetle, this would be a wonderful automotive world indeed.

Were the Beetles slow? Of course they were—but they never seemed nearly as sluggish as the 0-60 mph times suggested. A VW could keep up with traffic on the highway, and whip around town quicker than many big sedans. What more could a reasonable person ask?

Considering the attractive dashboard and handy gearshift lever, Karmann Ghia drivers could easily convince themselves they were piloting a true sports car—until they tromped hard on the gas, that is. Acceleration was not a strong point. (Volkswagen)

A Boon for the Do-It-Yourselfer

Ease of repair is another way in which the Volkswagen shared a kinship with the Model T Ford. Both vehicles were known to be easy to analyze, and easy to fix. Even the mechanically inept could learn to do a few basic tasks on the Beetle engine. A broken throttle cable, for instance—one common failing—was easy enough to replace. Accomplishing that task also gave the car's owner a greater sense of "oneness" with his or her machine.

A batch of "simple" do-it-yourself repair books burst upon the scene, encouraging even the neophytes to pick up a wrench and try their hand at changing spark plugs, replacing a belt or adjusting the carburetor.

Most-used of the group may have been John Muir's *How To Keep Your Volkswagen Alive*, which was issued and re-issued repeatedly. Muir's "hippie-style" tone, with

Despite the similar profiles, hundreds of changes had taken place between the split-window generation and the 1968 model (left), with a "1500" engine. (Phil Hall)

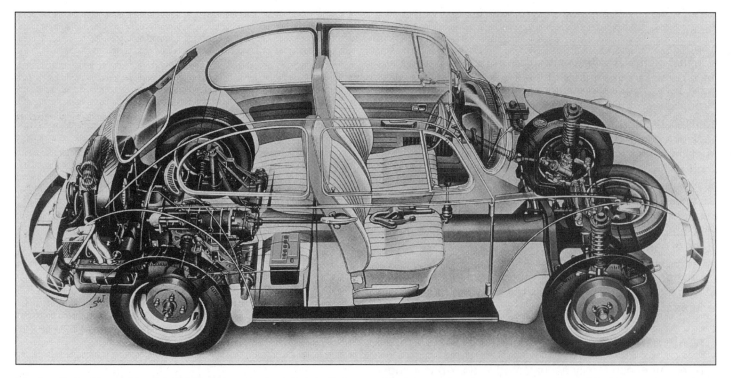

Not until the Super Beetle did Volkswagen veer away from torsion bars, adopting a more modern MacPherson strut front suspension. By 1973, the windshield was deeply curved, and seats were redesigned for added interior space. VWs came with a 24-month, 24,000-mile warranty, purchased from 1,200 dealers. (Phil Hall)

talk of the Beetle's "karma," naturally made the book most popular among the counterculture VW owners. Its crystal-clear drawings of engines and suspensions also attracted a mainstream audience of readers who simply wanted to learn to fix their vehicles.

Removing an engine was an arduous task when working on an American automobile, or even on most imports. But a Beetle or a Bus? Nothing to it. Detach a few wires and hoses, take out a few bolts, and out it came.

Once extracted, however, the engine wasn't necessarily easier to repair than a conventional six-cylinder or V-8. And many a mechanic refused to work on a Volkswagen's gearbox or suspension, fearing it involved too many hours of effort.

The fact that engines and transmissions could be removed by the do-it-yourselfer meant it was easy to stuff in a new one—perhaps not an original. When buying any VW today, then, it's important to check and see whether the engine is the same kind that powered the vehicle when it was new. So many parts are interchangeable, and one engine slips in just as easily as its older or newer companion, that conversions have become commonplace.

No Stopping the Beetle—Unless...

Motor Trend noted in the Fifties that the Beetle was "a car that breaks sharply with tradition, and does so with undeniable competence." It was also created with "limousine craftsmanship" and "built to appeal to discriminating world drivers." *Motor Trend* applauded the car's "almost electric smoothness, its faithful service, and above all the feeling it gives that all is well in the engine room and that there is near-complete rapport between it and the driver." Can't ask for a loftier appraisal than that.

At home in Germany, however, Volkswagen was facing fresh competition by 1963-64, especially in the form of a new Opel Kadett and the Ford Taunus 12M. *DM*, Germany's controversial consumer magazine, ranked the Kadett ahead of the VW, calling the latter "old-fashioned" and deficient in comfort, visibility and speed. In a single season, VW's share of the West German market fell from 33 to 28 percent, while GM's rose from 18 to 23.5 percent and Ford went from 14 to 16 percent.

Volkswagen's name and reputation popped up repeatedly in all sorts of contexts—typically, totally unrelated to automobiles. "Volkswagen and Hershey Chocolate follow the...sound practice of sticking permanently with a proven product," declared economist John Kenneth Galbraith in a book review for the *New York Herald Tribune*.

"If I could only have one car," initial importer Max Hoffman had told Tom McCahill in 1950, "it would be a Volkswagen." Millions of Americans had affirmed Hoffman's statement. How long could the Beetle keep going?

Chapter 12

Rising Toward a Fall: Improved Beetles (1965-1970)

"Offering people an honest value" said VW chief Heinz Nordhoff before his death in 1968, "appealed to me more than being driven around by a bunch of hysterical stylists trying to sell people something they really don't want to have."

Volkswagen continued to offer its customers "value" through the 1960s, but the car's phenomenal popularity inevitably began to wane. Nothing lasts forever—even the Beetle. Especially not in the hard driving U.S. automotive market, increasingly subject to influences from the government and from global forces. In its home market, too, Volkswagen faced what *Time* magazine in 1967 called "serious competition."

"Will we ever kill the bug?" one U.S. advertisement asked. "Never," was the simple, straightforward retort. "As long as I'm general director," Nordhoff insisted in the mid-1960s, "the basic VW will continue to be built."

Despite protestations that the Beetle would live virtually forever, executives knew that a more modern vehicle was necessary in order to remain competitive. Meanwhile, they retained the policy of continuous improvements with the Beetles and their basic offshoots. After all, despite the dire warnings that the Beetle's days were numbered, VW in the mid-1960s ranked fourth in world production. Beetle sales finally began to decline after 1968, while the Buses (and Fastback/Squareback) peaked in 1970.

Beetles in the Mid-Sixties

Visibility got the nod for 1965. Beetles gained 15 percent greater glass area, making for a more roomy feeling interior, as well as slightly curved front windows. Door windows were 6 percent larger; rear quarter windows grew by 17.5 percent; back glass by 19.5 percent. Door pillars slimmed down, and the windshield stood an inch higher and slightly wider. Windshields could be demisted more rapidly, via four thermostatically-operated flaps at the fan housing, which let air flow as soon as the engine started.

Longer windshield wiper blades, operating by a more powerful electric motor, now "parked" themselves on the driver's side, not the passenger's. Simpler heater control levers near the parking brake handle replaced the familiar old knobs.

A modern push button now opened the engine lid. VW's chassis numbering system also was new, supplanting the former consecutive numbering scheme.

Volkswagen insisted that its sedan had more changes than ever, but cautioned that "even an expert will have to look closely to tell it from a 1964." Modifications, the automaker warned, were "more apparent in the driving than in the looking." Bucket seats were claimed to be more comfortable, while thinning and re-contouring the front seatbacks added some rear legroom. Pivoting sun visors were installed. Rear luggage space was more convenient to access, past a new rear backrest that folded nearly flat. Brakes were alleged to be more responsive and longer-lasting, demanding less pedal pressure.

A Beetle sedan started at $1,563 in 1965, and weighed 1,609 pounds. A sun roof added $90 to the tariff, while the convertible went for $2,053 and weighed an extra 111 pounds.

For 1965, Beetle sedans got increased visibility, greater leg room, and a new rear backrest that folded down to convert the passenger area into a utility compartment. (Volkswagen)

J. Stuart Perkins served as president of Volkswagen of America, Inc. during the Sixties. (Phil Hall)

In June 1965, Stuart Perkins was named Volkswagen of America's vice-president and general manager. Six months later, he attained the presidency, succeeding Carl Hahn. Born in 1928, in London, Perkins had been one of VW's first three U.S. employees in 1955, rising to the post of general sales manager in 1960. By the end of 1965, Volkswagen had 909 dealerships in the United States.

Time magazine reported that the 1966 revisions were "some of the most fundamental changes in years." Output

New "skirts" partially enclosed the base of bucket seats on the 1966 Beetle. Volkswagen even encouraged owners with small children to fold down the back seat, to create a "play pen" for use on trips. (Phil Hall)

ratings of the Volkswagen air-cooled engine sounded pretty puny during the American "muscle car" era. So, VW responded by enlarging the flat four to a mighty 1285 cubic centimeters (78.4 cubic inches) of displacement, capable of whipping out 50 thunderous horses.

That extra 10 horsepower made a noticeable difference in acceleration—especially on the highway in third and fourth gears. Despite a compression boost to 7.3:1, the "pancake" four-cylinder engine still used regular gasoline. VWs with this peppier powerplant flaunted "1300" script on the engine lid.

New wheels for 1966 had a conventional bolt pattern but 10 ventilating slots (for greater fade resistance), and wore flatter hubcaps. Headlight dimmers no longer sat on the floorboard, but were built into the turn signal lever. The electrical system added a four-way emergency flasher, and the half horn ring that had been deleted two years earlier was reinstated.

Adding a third warm air outlet for the windshield resulted in quicker defrosting. To improve rearward visibility, the inside mirror was enlarged. New safety latches securely locked the front backrests into fixed position, and a "progressive" gas pedal yielded smoother accelerator control.

Fancier interiors and axles that needed less greasing were among the 22 other improvements. The new front axle assembly adopted ball joints, cutting the frequency of lubrication by half. The 1966 Beetles weighed slightly more, but prices rose only by a few dollars, to $1,585 for the sedan and $2,075 for the convertible.

Engines aimed at the U.S. market grew further yet a year later, to a whopping 1493-cc displacement, pumping out three more horsepower. Torque output increased by 14 percent. (Other countries kept the "1300" powerplant.) On the engine lid, the word "Volkswagen" replaced the engine size designation, and the license plate sat more vertically than before. The lid also offered greater clearance between the rear bumper, when opening the engine compartment.

A new third-gear transmission ratio also helped deliver quicker acceleration on level ground, plus better performance on hills (with less need for downshifting). Rear axle ratios were lowered, reducing engine speed in each gear for the most frugal gas mileage. Top speed rose from 50 to 56 mph in third gear, and to 78 in fourth.

These and other modifications, from a softer ride to new dual braking, were deemed "American-inspired."

For 1967, President Perkins noted, the American Beetle was "different in appearance from the 'bug' built for other parts of the world. This shows up on the front fenders, which have been slightly reshaped to provide a new headlight mounting." Glass shields that formerly covered recessed sealed beam headlights were eliminated, and the lights moved outward. Parking lights, formerly resting in headlight recesses, moved into the front turn signal units.

A decade after most American cars had adopted 12-volt electrical systems, VW finally made the move. The switch to a 12-volt, spill-proof battery promised quicker cold weather starts and brighter lighting. To reduce the risk of a dead battery, the new alternator began to charge at idle speed.

New safety door locks had push-button locking controls on window frames, and interior door handles were recessed. Volkswagens destined for the U.S. market also added retractable, self-adjusting lap-type seatbelts in front, lap-belt anchorages in the rear. Soft plastic knobs were used for controls and window cranks.

Rear track width was two inches greater, and rear torsion bars were softened, to ease the ride. An auxiliary spring over the rear axle produced a progressive effect, coming into play when the load increased or the car was driven over rough ground.

Backup lights now were standard, and two-speed windshield wipers installed. Dual tandem-type master cylinders ensured safer and more efficient braking. If the front or rear half became inoperative, the other half still functioned.

Prices and weights for U.S. models again rose, but not by much. The 1,698-pound 1967 sedan started at $1,639 ($90 more for a sun roof), while the convertible tipped the scales at 1,786 pounds and commanded the same $2,075 as before.

Like other manufacturers, Volkswagen was subject to increasingly stringent requirements—regarding safety and emissions—by the U.S. government. New safety features for 1968 included higher, stronger one-piece bumpers (no more bumper guards), padded dashboards,

Except for newly-slotted wheels and flattened hubcaps, nearly all the changes for 1966 were beneath the skin, including a new front-axle assembly and a peppier engine. (Volkswagen)

brake warning lights and collapsible steering columns. Engines adopted new exhaust emission controls.

Volkswagen of America called the 1968 models the "Most-Improved of All Time," claiming that "Performance, Convenience, Safety All [were] Increased." New built-in headrests added about 10 inches to the height of the contoured bucket seats. Some called the new seatbacks "Sarcophagus" setups.

Volkswagen claimed that the 1967 model had more major improvements than ever before. Technical changes included progressive springing, a dual brake system, and 12-volt electrical system—years after American cars had abandoned six-volt batteries. Front fenders were slightly reshaped, for better headlight mounting. (Volkswagen)

By 1967, about one out of five Beetles had a sun roof. This year's modified rear suspension promised a smoother ride, while the bigger engine delivered better performance. Dual backup lights were installed, and the new alternator charged even at idle speed. Retractable front lap belts also were new. (Volkswagen)

Beetle sedans got safety rim wheels to help hold tires on their wheels in the event of a blowout. Overall length dropped by an inch-and-a-half, and the rear decklid now bulged slightly. A certification sticker on the door post advised that the car met federal safety standards.

Backup lights went within new, larger taillights. A spring-loaded door in the right front fender now covered the gas filler, so the tank could be filled without opening the trunk. Cowl-type fresh air intake vents were incorporated into the hood, which opened via a push button in its handle. Trigger-type, flatter door handles replaced the prior push buttons. Improved windshield wipers included a pneumatic washer system. The Beetle's gearshift lever moved rearward, to permit sports-type gear changes.

Prices and weights continued to edge upward, but serious inflation had not yet arrived. A 1968 sedan could be driven home for $1,699, and the convertible cost just $400 more.

Beetles Go Automatic

Finally, Volkswagen had to give in to the clamor for automatic shifting. Many of its econocar rivals already were offering some form of automatic transmission. So in 1968, VWs could be ordered with a new Automatic Stick Shift.

Dual exhaust outlets were a Beetle hallmark for most of its life in the U.S. market. By 1968, taillights were vastly larger than on early models, and engines considerably zippier.

A 1493-cc engine went into the 1967 Beetles, developing 53 horsepower. Two hoses now channeled preheated air into the carburetor, whereas prior pre-heaters drew warm air from only one side. The engine compartment lid was reshaped to provide greater lid-to-bumper clearance with the bumper. (Phil Hall)

As the name suggests, the transmission wasn't quite fully automatic. Instead, the semi-automatic unit could be shifted from Low (recommended for starting out on steep hills) to either of two driving ranges, simply by moving the gearshift lever. No clutch pedal was provided. Drive 1 was for driving around town. Drive 2 performed like an over-drive, for use at speeds above 55 mph.

Automatic Stick Shift drew considerable attention, but soon proved troublesome. Volkswagen called the unit "just about automatic," noting later that it resulted in a 50 percent increase in female drivers.

Nordhoff Era Ends

Few heads of companies were as closely tied to the success of their organizations, for as long a period, as Heinz Nordhoff, who announced in 1967—at age 68—that he expected to retire at the end of the next year. His chosen successor was Dr. Kurt Lotz, appointed deputy chairman on June 1. Later in June, Lotz addressed the corporate board, wielding the reins temporarily because Nordhoff had taken ill, with heart failure.

Nordhoff returned that October, but his health had suffered. He died on Good Friday, in April 1968, at age 69.

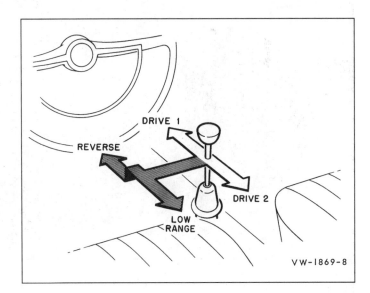

Automatic Stick Shift debuted on 1968 models, with a shift pattern similar to that used on three-speed manual transmissions. "Drive 2" permitted no-shift driving, but "Drive 1," usable up to 55 mph, yielded better acceleration for startups and passing. Running through the gears—Low to Drive 1 to Drive 2—also was permissible. (Phil Hall)

● Porsche and Audi Join the VW Parade ●

Late in the Sixties, Volkswagen underwent a corporate expansion program, forming ties with several major automakers. Early in 1965, for starters, VW bought a half-interest in Auto Union (which had been a subsidiary of Mercedes-Benz since 1956). That produced an initial connection with Audi—an offshoot of the Auto Union group. Eventually, Audi models went on sale at Volkswagen dealers around the world.

Four years later, in 1969, Volkswagen acquired the assets of the NSU organization. Then, in August, VW merged it with Audi to form Audi NSU Auto Union AG. That maneuver brought about another new model: the K70 (built at Salzgitter). The NSU K70 was a conventional evolution of the Wankel-engined Ro80—a new breed of VW, featuring a water-cooled front-engine.

Early in 1969, Volkswagen and Porsche joined forces, forming VW Porsche (Volkswagen-Porsche Vertriebgesellschaft). At the Chicago Auto Show that year, Herbert W. Anderson Sr., of Norwood, Massachusetts, was named the first franchisee for the new Porsche Audi Division. Another 250 such dealerships were expected to open in 1969, bringing Audi into the U.S. market for the first time.

A Volkswagen-based Porsche, the 914, arrived in 1970, with an air-cooled rear engine. The 914 was dropped in 1974 when Porsche launched a new 2+2.

After Volkswagen bought Porsche in 1969, the new company issued a two-seat Porsche 914 sports car, with its 85-horsepower engine ahead of the rear axle. Features included a Targa-style roll bar and all-disc brakes. This is a Canadian edition. (Phil Hall)

Meanwhile, the 1969 Beetles had debuted, under the theme: "Greater comfort and increased convenience" in a "year of refinement." New features included an electrical rear window defroster, and a day/night inside mirror to reduce headlight glare. The steering column held an ignition switch lock. Outside, a locking gas flap opened using a lever under the right side of the dashboard. The Beetle's hood release was concealed within the glovebox—after moving outside a year earlier.

Far more significant was the new double-jointed rear axle—a truly independent rear suspension, which VW of America President Stuart Perkins claimed would deliver "greatly improved ride and better handling qualities." Incorporating semi-trailing arms instead of the long-familiar swing axles, the double-jointed setup had debuted a year before on the VW buses.

Floor-level heater outlets in front were repositioned, and new warm air outlets speeded defrosting. Front backrests sported a greater adjustment range. Later in the year, the odometer added readings in tenths of a mile.

The 1969 Beetle sales brochure asked a simple and continuing question: "Why do so many people buy Volks-wagens?" Typical owners who responded, and whose comments were printed, included Ed Coady, who'd driven VWs on his 175-mile newspaper route since 1959 and liked the car's economy. Ray McMahon, a member of the research expedition at Rumdoodle Depot, Antarctica, didn't "think we had any choice but a Volkswagen" for the frigid temperatures his group encountered. They wanted a car "that any member of the expedition could hop into and drive off without a moment's hesitation."

Actor Paul Newman had purchased his first Volkswagen in 1953. The company noted in 1969 that he was on his fifth, printing a picture of the performer with his 1963 Beetle convertible in the sales brochure. "I started buying them when I started as an actor," Newman was quoted as saying. "Today, I drive them out of loyalty." By 1969, of course, the once-canvas convertible top was made of vinyl, with leatherette inside and an inch-thick blanket of insulation in between. Volkswagen had more than a thousand dealers in the United States, as well as in 139 other countries.

Like other vehicles sold in the United States, the 1970 Volkswagen had its Vehicle Identification Number (VIN)

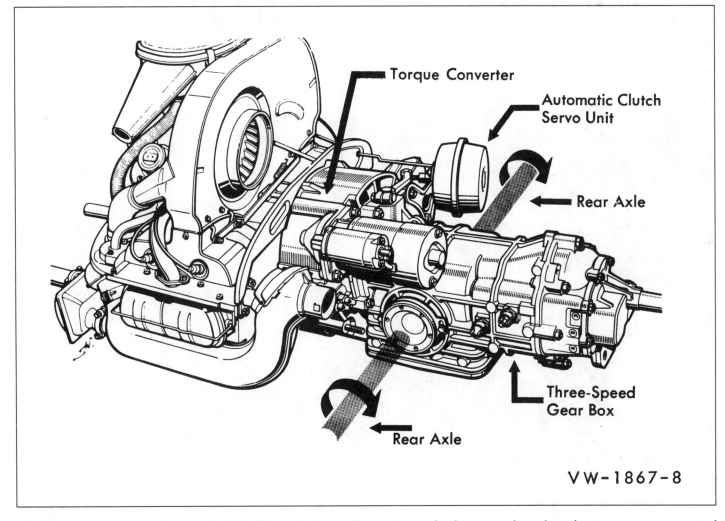

The torque converter for Automatic Stick Shift sat between the engine and a three-speed gearbox. A vacuum servo operated the clutch automatically, whenever the driver moved the gearshift lever. (Phil Hall)

Though small in size, the optional sun roof on a 1969 Beetle gave at least a hint of open-to-the-sun driving. (Volkswagen)

Convertibles continued to draw attention in 1969, and could have most of the same options as Beetle sedans—including the Automatic Stick Shift transmission. Unfortunately, that unit soon proved troublesome. (Phil Hall)

Viewed from the side, Beetles of the late 1960s didn't appear to have changed much in two decades. Underneath the surface, it was a different story.

A slightly larger engine gave 1970 Beetles extra response, and swifter acceleration in lower gear ratios. Note the rear-window decal, indicating presence of the semi-automatic, clutchless transmission. (Phil Hall)

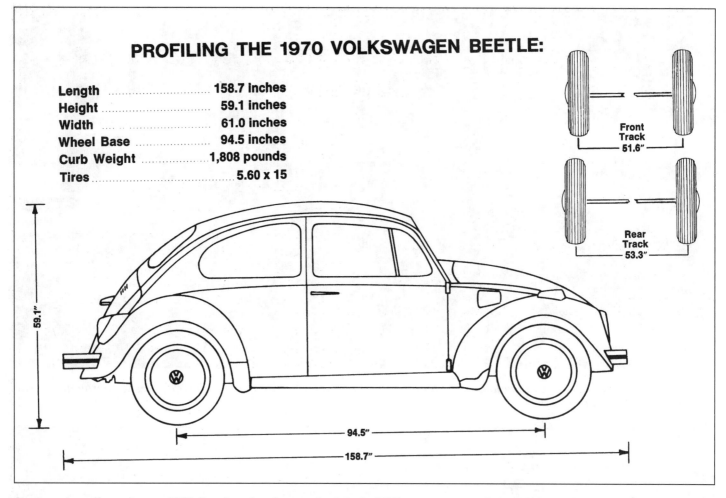

PROFILING THE 1970 VOLKSWAGEN BEETLE:

Length	158.7 inches
Height	59.1 inches
Width	61.0 inches
Wheel Base	94.5 inches
Curb Weight	1,808 pounds
Tires	5.60 x 15

Front Track 51.6"

Rear Track 53.3"

59.1"

94.5"

158.7"

In size as well as shape, 1970 Beetles closely matched their 1950 counterparts; but weight had edged upward over the years. (Phil Hall)

displayed on the left front of the instrument panel, visible through the windshield. Good thing, too, as nearly all the improvements that year were hidden.

Taillights grew and added side reflectors, as did the enlarged front signal lights, now combined with side marker lamps. The engine lid added two horizontal air slots (first seen on convertibles).

As for the engine itself, it now displaced 1585 cubic centimeters, ostensibly earning a "1600" designation but still commonly referred to as a "1500" sedan. Its 57-horsepower output beat the previous powerplant by four horses. A Beetle could now reach a claimed top speed of 81 mph, while the Karmann Ghia coupe was good for about three more.

Head restraints were smaller, and the glovebox added a lock. All VW models got buzzers to warn if the driver's door was opened before the key was removed from the ignition. Bumpers added rubber inserts and sat higher. Reflectors went on the rear bumper and taillight housings.

Volkswagen's 1970 sales brochure called the Beetle "the car of the future," despite its aging design. Although it "may not be very adventurous looking compared to the other 1970 cars," the text admitted, "when you take the

Bug out for an adventure, there probably won't be any other 1970 cars around to compare it to."

By now, the company unflinchingly used the term "Bug" as well as "Beetle" in its promotional material. Frugality remained a strong selling point, both in terms of gas mileage and resale value. At trade-in time, Volkswagen predicted, "you can count on getting back more of your initial investment on a VW than you could on almost any other car."

Sales literature also promoted the fact that Volkswagens were subjected to 16,000 different inspections, conducted by 1,000 inspectors. About 200 cars a day were rejected. Marketers also noted that the Beetle had enjoyed some 2,200 changes in its 21-year lifespan, from wiper blades and gas caps to the suspension and brake systems. Beetles came with a 2-year/24,000-mile warranty.

Volkswagen's diagnosis and maintenance program was introduced this year. Dealerships received diagnostic centers, an industry "first," that made up to 96 different checks. Buyers of new VWs got coupons good for four free diagnostic services, at 6,000-mile intervals.

Meanwhile, quite another brand of Beetle was waiting in the wings. A *Super* Beetle.

● Year-by-Year Changes, 1965-1970 ●
Beetles

1965:

More window area—front windows slightly curved
Side quarter and rear windows grow
Door pillars are thinner
Larger wipers park on driver's side
Luggage space grows, via new fold-down rear seat
Two new heater control levers replace old knobs
Push button replaces T-handle on engine lid
New chassis numbering system used
Improved braking efficiency
Maintenance-free sealed steering system
Pivoting sun visors installed
More back seat knee room
Fold-down rear backrest added

1966:

Engine grows to 1285-cc displacement and 50 horsepower—pickup improves in third and fourth gear
New slotted wheels use conventional bolt pattern
Hubcaps are flatter
Headlight dimmer no longer on floor
Four-way emergency flasher added
Engine lid adds "1300" script

1967:

Engine grows again, to 1493-cc
Horsepower up by three (to 53); torque up 14 percent
Other countries keep "1300" engine
12-volt electrical system installed
"Volkswagen" replaces "1300" script
Engine lid holds license plate more vertically

Backup lights now are standard
Sealed-beam headlights no longer are covered
Dual master cylinders installed

1968:

New safety features include one-piece bumpers, front headrests, collapsible steering column
Bumper guards are gone
Backup lights incorporated into new tail-lights
Emission controls installed on U.S. engines
Gas filler is covered by opening behind right front fender
Fresh air intake vent incorporated into hood, which opens via push button
Automatic Stick Shift introduced; soon proves troublesome
New double-jointed rear suspension installed
Trigger-type door handles replace push buttons

1969:

Electrical rear defroster installed
Ignition lock added to steering column
Day/night mirror installed
Locking gas flap opens using lever under dashboard
Hood release is concealed in glovebox

1970:

Speedometer shows tenths of a mile
VIN is on left front of dash
Taillights add side reflectors, as do enlarged front signal lights
Engine lid gains two vents
Engine is now 1585-cc; makes 57 horsepower

Chapter 13

Super or Regular: Super Beetles and Special Editions in the 1970s

Volkswagens had been on sale in the United States for two decades. Fans and foes alike commonly referred to the critters as Beetles or Bugs. Company literature occasionally used those nicknames, too, but neither moniker had officially designated a VW model

Not until 1971, that is, when the Super Beetle debuted. What was "super" about it? Mainly, an all-new coil spring front suspension and, in turn, a bigger trunk. Yes, the torsion bars that had been installed on Beetles from the beginning, finally were abandoned. They were edged aside by—of all things—MacPherson struts.

Well, not completely. Volkswagen continued to market standard Beetles, with traditional front/rear suspensions,

for customers who liked the way the originals rode and handled. They even dropped the price of standard models.

"We've made so many improvements," the Super Beetle sales brochure proclaimed, that "they're beginning to show."

Why a Super Beetle? For one thing, Volkswagen needed a serious rival to the new Ford Pinto and Chevrolet Vega—first of the domestically-built subcompacts—as well as to the growing number of imports from Japan. VW's other models, the Type 3 and 411 (Chapter 15), weren't exactly firing up the sales charts. So, why not try to turn the familiar old Beetle into a more modern piece of machinery?

A bulging front end made the 1971 Super Beetle easy to spot. Traditionalists disliked not only the change in profile, but the new front suspension underneath. (Phil Hall)

Switching to coil springs not only added trunk space to the Super Beetle, and altered its handling, but reduced the car's turning circle by more than four feet. (Phil Hall)

One big bonus in the Super Beetle was increased storage capacity. The front trunk held nearly twice as much as a standard model's. Super Beetles measured three inches longer, too. (Phil Hall)

In addition to the Super Beetle (foreground), Volkswagen continued to market the standard version (rear) in the United States. Both used the same 60-horsepower engine, but handling characteristics differed sharply. (Phil Hall)

The Super Beetle's new front suspension was deemed modern, up-to-date, sophisticated. Many an early 1970s shopper preferred its softer qualities, as exhibited during a test drive. The wheelbase changed slightly, and Super Beetles measured three inches longer than regular sedans. Rear ends sported the recently-initiated double-jointed halfshafts, again aimed at keeping the drive wheels flat against the pavement, but handling was far different from standard models. Among other bonuses, the car's turning circle proved to be a lot better than any Volkswagen ordinarily could manage—tighter by an impressive 4-1/2 feet.

Toss in nearly twice the usual amount of front luggage space—a failing about which owners had been complaining for two decades—and it sounds like quite an alluring package. That extra 4.3 cubic feet just might turn a previously-limited Volkswagen into a practical luggage hauler for a family on vacation.

Despite the addition of 155 pounds to the car, Volkswagen insisted a Super Beetle had added "not one single ounce of fat." Why? Because they'd made "90 meaningful improvements."

Included among that number was a boost to 60 horsepower from the Beetle's enlarged, 1585-cc (96.6-cid) engine. One way to cope with increasingly stringent emission standards, it seemed, was to add horsepower to an engine. "Any automobile engineer will tell you," Volkswagen insisted, that adding horsepower "will make it last even longer." Why? Because the engine "doesn't have to

work as hard to get from one place to the other." So, all 1971 Beetles—standard and Super—had three more horses than '70 models.

Well, purists were horrified. They wouldn't go near a Super Beetle, as long as a regular model could be found. Or even if it couldn't. Why, this news was almost as bad as the notion of a water-cooled Volkswagen, or one with a front-mounted engine. Surely *that* sort of heresy would never happen!

Partly because of the Super Beetle's increased weight, performance was less than stimulating. After all, the Super Beetle held the very same 60-horsepower engine as the regular model. Yes, a Beetle of the early Seventies, with its considerably-enlarged engine, was quicker than its predecessors. But a speedster—something super—it was not.

Accelerating a Super Beetle to 60 mph took nearly 18 seconds. Running the quarter-mile meant 21 seconds, reaching a modest 64 mph. When *Road & Track* tested a Super Beetle and four other cars, they complained: "No car has ever come in more resoundingly last in a car to car evaluation." In that magazine's eyes, the Super Beetle was a "last-ditch attempt to hold onto what was left of the traditional Beetle market." Adding insult to injury, only drum brakes were offered, at a time when many modest automobiles had turned to front discs.

So, what kept the sales totals at a steady—if not furious—pace? The answer has to be VW's continued reputation for quality. That and a realistic price. The 1971

Super Beetle cost just $1,985 ($140 more than a regular sedan). Air conditioning added $267, and the semi-automatic transmission demanded $139 more. In contrast, a new Vega listed for $2,090; the Pinto, $1,919.

Spotting a Super Beetle was a snap. Not only did it have chrome trim around its side windows, but the front lid displayed a noticeable bulge. In fact, the whole car looked plump and bulbous. Not much time passed before more than a few wags referred to this chubby new model as a "pregnant" or "overweight" Volkswagen, if not by nastier epithets. On the other hand, the Super Beetle captured quite a few sales, despite the protests of traditionalists who wanted their Beetles to look—and act—the same as they always had.

With its lumpier nose, the Super Beetle further abandoned the original car's basic shape. Not by much, but enough to turn off those earlier-day fans. Sure, that bulged front end was needed to contain the new front suspension, and yielded some welcome extra luggage space. All told, the Super Beetle had 9.2 cubic feet of cargo volume up front, plus 4.9 cubic feet behind the rear seat. That wasn't enough to suit those who preferred their Beetles straight and regular, thank you.

New flow-through exit vent ports went behind the rear side windows. Headlights now turned off with the ignition, courtesy of a "memory" switch. The front track dimension grew wider, as the turning radius got smaller—a possible "plus" for nimble handling around town.

Regular Beetles lacked some of the Super's interior appointments, but did get flow-through ventilation and

MacPherson struts with progressive coil springs made up the front suspension of Super Beetles, replacing the traditional torsion bars. (Phil Hall)

"memory" headlights. A two-speed blower vowed to keep fresh air moving through the passenger compartment "even when in stand-still traffic."

Computer-analysis plugs were installed in models built during the second half of the 1971 model year, for diagnostic troubleshooting at the dealership. That didn't help

Super Beetles also came in convertible form. When folded, the tall-stacked fabric top looked as if it were about to tip the car backward. (Phil Hall)

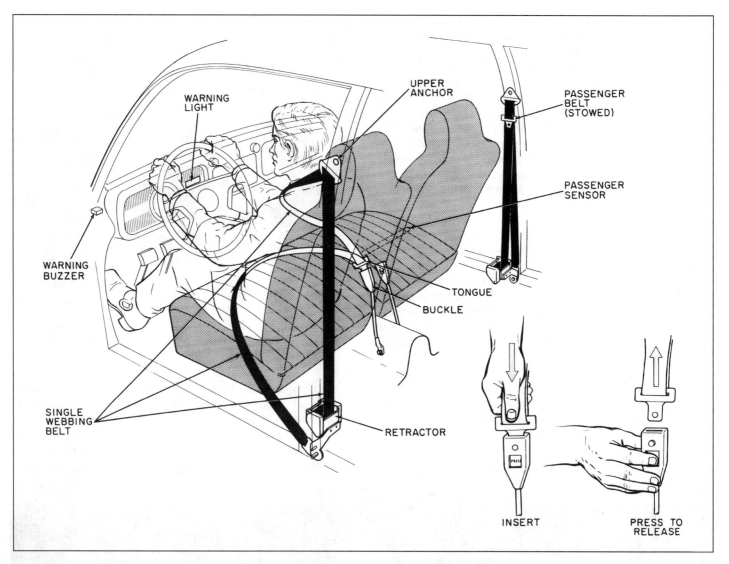

New lap/shoulder safety belts for 1972 included a dashboard warning light and buzzer, as well as an emergency-locking retractor. The system was supposed to let occupants move freely, but provide immediate restraint in the event of an impact—or when braking or cornering hard. (Phil Hall)

do-it-yourselfers much, but could shave considerable time from a visit to the service bay.

Marketers again pushed the intense inspections that VWs went through at the Wolfsburg factory. "If they so much as find a nick in the bumper, or a scratch on the inside of the glove compartment, it doesn't make it." Each of the 5,115 parts in a Beetle was inspected three times, the sales literature insisted.

Going a giant step further, random cars were plucked from the assembly line for test driving at a test track referred to as "Hell on Wheels." Each one journeyed through eight road surfaces ranked "from good to awful." They went through mud, water and salt to be sure no leakage or rusting began. (Readers were assured that none of these heavily-tested cars ever went on sale, of course.)

On October 27, 1971, the five-millionth VW was shipped to the United States. Then, on February 12, 1972, Volkswagenwerk released its 15,007,034th Beetle, breaking the record long held by the Model T Ford, for production

of a single model. That record-breaking Beetle was painted silver-blue. By then, more than five million Beetles had been sold in Germany, a million in Brazil—plus six lonely Bugs in China and three in Antarctica.

After turning out a Super model, what could any company do for an encore? Not much, it turned out. Changes for 1972 were modest, including installation of a four-spoke, energy-absorbing safety steering wheel with a four-inch collapsible hub. Standard Beetles and other Volkswagens used collapsible steering columns, while the Super Beetle adopted a double-jointed, elbow-action column.

Inertia-reel seat belts were new. The rear window grew larger (except in convertibles), and a hinged parcel shelf covered the luggage well behind the rear seat. Four groups of horizontal intake vents were installed on the engine lid (formerly two), and extra body insulation helped reduce road noise. Drivers could now control the windshield washer/wiper without lifting a hand from the steering wheel, using a control on the right-hand stalk.

Beetle engines ran on no-lead gasoline, as the compression ratio dropped to 7.3:1. The intake system gained more precisely-controlled air preheating. Towing capacity was increased—and yes, quite a few VW owners did tow moderately-sized trailers or boats behind their automobiles.

Taillights had grown, and grown—and grown some more—over the Beetle's lifespan. They got larger yet for 1973, a circular lamp complex vastly removed from the tiny twinklers that had dotted the rear ends of the old oval-window sedans. Like other passenger vehicles marketed in the United States, Volkswagens were compelled to adopt crash-resistant bumpers—able to absorb a 5-mph impact in front, and 2-1/2-mph in the rear.

VW clutches never had demanded a terribly heavy foot, but the 1973 version required even less pressure. The still-optional Automatic Stick Shift added a "park" position. Heater levers were redesigned.

Super Beetles and convertibles gained a deeply-curved wraparound windshield, aiming to deliver a more roomy interior personality. If the bulging body of a Super Beetle turned off purists a year or two earlier, the concept of a panoramic windshield now finished the job, sending traditional-minded VW fans scurrying back to their pre-1958 favorites. Revised fender sheet metal added to the fresh look of the sedan.

Volkswagen actually touted the Super Beetle's revised body, with its curved windshield, as "the most dramatic styling changes since the familiar Bug first came to America."

Volkswagen's safety steering wheel for 1972 incorporated a four-inch collapsible hub, to help absorb "second collision" forces during a front-end impact. (Phil Hall)

Standard Beetles remained available in 1972, for customers who didn't need the extra luggage space—or preferred the handling qualities of front torsion bars.

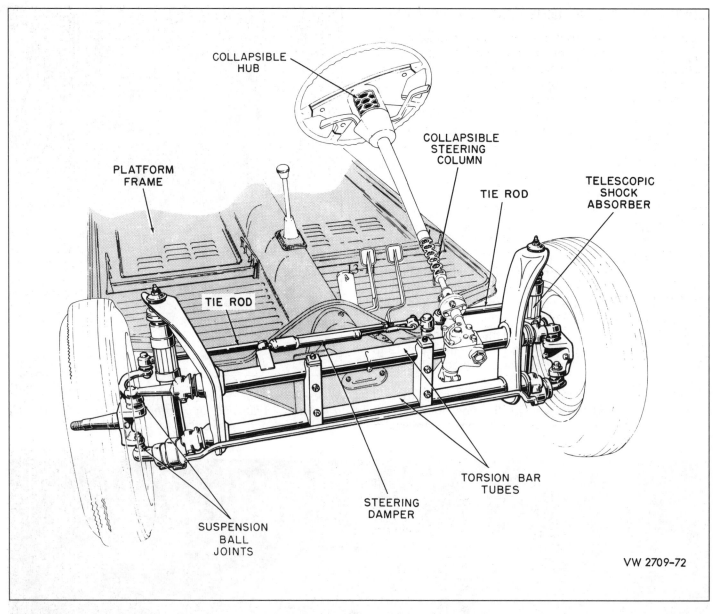

COLLAPSIBLE
HUB

COLLAPSIBLE
STEERING
COLUMN

PLATFORM
FRAME

TIE ROD

TELESCOPIC
SHOCK
ABSORBER

TIE ROD

SUSPENSION
BALL
JOINTS

STEERING
DAMPER

TORSION BAR
TUBES

VW 2709-72

Volkswagens still had a platform frame, but much of the front end had changed by 1972—especially in the Super Beetle. (Phil Hall)

Volkswagen Products Corporation offered air conditioners for the Super Beetle, as well as for other cars sold by VW— now including the Audi and Porsche. (Phil Hall)

A redesigned dashboard, heavily padded, held improved vent outlets. Defroster outlets now ran the full windshield width. Rocker switches replaced knobs, and the glove compartment offered bi-level storage. The familiar perforated headliner cloth was gone—another loss of a traditional component.

All Beetles had sporty black windshield wiper arms. Redesigned front seats could be adjusted 77 ways to make anyone comfortable—if anyone were so inclined to tinker, that is. Improved intake air preheating was installed, to deliver quicker starts in cold weather.

After years of mild price hikes, inflation was beginning to raise its ugly head a little further. A Standard Beetle sedan now started at $2,299. The Super Beetle (which weighed 169 pounds more than a regular model) went for $2,499. Convertibles could not be found for less than $3,050, and were heavier yet.

Love, Sports and Sun Bugs

Not everyone realized it, but the Beetle was slowly dying in the U.S. market. Protestations of never dropping the design aside, most analysts knew that the original VW model could no longer compete favorably, much less lead the import pack. Beetles failed to draw the attention they once had, against a far different breed of competition.

Something new was in the air, being readied for market in the hope that it would bring Volkswagen some sales totals to boast about.

Meanwhile, what could be done about the Beetle—which wasn't quite ready to expire? How about a series of special editions, to spark interest in the make and eke out a few more sales than the ordinary models might be able to elicit? None was quite so special as the sales brochures suggested—more cosmetic than pragmatic. They were a bit like the "spring specials" that Detroit automakers trotted out during the high-push selling season. Cute but hardly earthshaking, they helped to keep the Beetle badge alive a while longer.

Special edition Number One was the Sports Bug, launched during the 1973 model year. Beneath the surface, except for 170/70x15 radial tires on wide (5-1/2 J15) rims, it was just another Beetle. But it sure looked the part of something special: beltline striping and black bumpers/trim outside, plus racing-style bucket seats and an Indy-type steering wheel (small-diameter, with thick padded

Super Beetles again attracted a new breed of buyer in 1973—folks who weren't fazed by the car's bulbous proportions. Impact-absorbing bumpers and greatly-enlarged taillights went on 1973 models, and revised front seats adjusted to 77 positions. Several built-in sensors let service people take advantage of VW's exclusive computer diagnostics. (Volkswagen)

rim) inside. Those seats had contoured sides to "hold you when you're cornering," plus a "firm bottom that communicates a real seat-of-the-pants feel of the road." Sounds like a promotion for an Alfa Romeo or a Corvette of the time, rather than a spiffed-up Beetle.

To mark Volkswagen's success at road racing in Mexico, the company issued a Baja Champion SE in 1972. (Volkswagen)

Volkswagen launched a series of special editions in 1973-74. Riding on 170/70x15 radial tires, this Sports Bug featured special beltline striping and black bumpers/trim, as well as race-style bucket seats and an Indy-type steering wheel. (Volkswagen)

Only two body colors were offered: Saturn Yellow or Marathon Metallic Blue. "On rare occasions," the Sports Bug's sales brochure explained, Volkswagen "put out a limited production run of a real fun car." Marketers promised that its short-throw transmission, of "stop-synchro" design, handled "some really heavy driving." In fact, they insisted, "the harder you shift, the faster the action." Quick steering (2.7 turns, lock-to-lock) promised to help the car's nimble handling, but in fact, most of the technical details weren't greatly different from those of a conventional Beetle, even if the body was sprayed in "scintillating" Marathon or "pulsating" yellow.

For quite some time, Volkswagen had been promoting the "sunny" personality of its Beetles. So, why not a special Sun Bug? Introduced for 1974, this was to be "The VW that will Let a Little Sunshine Into Your Life!" Behind the wheel of this Bug, you'd be ready to "Smile your way through problems and strife."

So read the sales literature, at any rate. One brochure even included sheet music for "Let a Little Sunshine Into Your Life" (with words modified to suit the Sun Bug, naturally).

Offered in two "romantic colors," the 1974 Love Bug borrowed its name from the earlier Walt Disney movie—featuring "Herbie." Special editions held racing-style wheels. (Phil Hall)

Available as a convertible, sun roof Beetle, or Super Beetle, the Sun Bug "puts the simple joys back into driving," the literature alleged. Each one "comes on bright and strong in a gold metallic sun color." Piloting one "makes a holiday out of a shopping trip [and] even makes commuting a picnic." A tall order, but VW owners were inclined to be optimistic souls, so why not?

Drivers faced a padded sports steering wheel "with the feel of leather," complemented by a special gearshift knob on the tunnel console. Special sports wheels were installed, too. Super Beetle Sun Bugs included an automatic pop-up wind deflector.

Contoured seats vowed to "embrace your body," and some models featured plush inserts. Color-coordinated mocha carpeting cradled your feet. A rosewood-grained dashboard inlay went into the convertible and Super Beetle. All this and the promise of 25 mpg fuel economy? For 1974, not a bad deal! Environmentally-conscious consumers could drive a Sun Bug, Volkswagen promised, and "enjoy the world without wasting its resources."

Borrowing its name from the Disney movie series (see Chapter 8), the Love Bug arrived in mid-season of 1974. "At $2,524," the sales brochure proclaimed, "it's a sweetheart of a deal." This one came in a choice of "two romantic colors. Red-hot red. And luscious lime green." Racing-type wheels and "cute" black trim rounded out the details. "A love like this doesn't come along every day," VW reminded the brochure's readers. Not at "a price that will steal your heart away."

One more special edition went on sale for 1975: the La Grande Bug, with metallic paint, sport wheels and fancy upholstery. Promotional literature made customers feel they were practically getting a luxury limousine, complete with chauffeur. "You don't drive in it," the brochure advised, "you *arrive* in it."

La Grande amenities included special leather-grained seating with plush corduroy inserts, a leather-grained steering wheel, rosewood dashboard applique and matching rosewood on the optional tunnel console. Body colors were special, too: Ancona Blue or Lime Green metallic, not found on other Beetles. Driving a La Grande, the brochure concluded, "tells the world that you are a motoring Bug who has arrived." This was the "Ultimate Bug," but with the same promise of 33 mpg highway fuel economy as its less posh companions. (The EPA city mileage rating was a less-frugal 22 mpg.)

Last Gasps of the Beetle

Those who failed to fall for the temptations of a Sun Bug or Love Bug didn't see much that was new in 1974. New self-restoring, energy-absorbing bumpers weighed more than the previous units. Engine output failed to change—still rated at 46 horsepower, under the SAE rating system that had been used since 1972. Super Beetles and convertibles had new front suspension geometry. A self-centering steering system helped the car track straight when braking. Headrests were smaller.

A plush La Grande Bug (bottom) arrived for 1975, wearing metallic paint, special upholstery, and special wheels. Even the ordinary Bug (top) got electronic fuel injection and other engine improvements, plus reduced clutch-pedal pressure and a better heater. (Volkswagen)

The Beetle's familiar dual exhaust outlet pipes (right) disappeared in the 1975 models (left), as a catalytic converter was installed. A slotted, "bustled" skirt beneath the rear bumper covered and ventilated the new catalytic converter, installed to control emissions. Volkswagen tested its converters in 30,000-mile road trials in Southern California. (Phil Hall)

Following the lead of prior special editions, the 1976 Beetle got metallic paint and sports-style wheels. Standard features included a heated rear defroster and full carpeting. The fuel-injected engine earned a 22/34-miles per gallon EPA fuel mileage rating. (Phil Hall)

End of the line. The final Beetle sedans went on sale in the United States in 1977, but the convertible continued for two more seasons.

Except for a new handbrake-seat belt light and seat belt-ignition interlock system, that was about it for 1974. Prices, on the other hand, continued their upward trend, reaching $2,625 for the sedan, $2,849 for the Super Beetle, and $3,475 for a convertible.

"There are no plans to stop Beetle production," insisted a 1974 article in *Small World*," Volkswagen's popular owners' magazine. "You don't scrap a winner." Even though "auto writers predicted the end of the Beetle as early as 1957," the article continued, VW wasn't about to let it die. Or was it?

Electronic fuel injection became standard in Beetles for 1975, base-priced just a buck below $3,000. Convertibles cost no less than $3,595. Engine lids displayed a "Fuel Injection" emblem, but hoods no longer held a VW insignia. Fuel injection had been around for several years on other Volkswagen models, but some owners complained of troublesome operation.

"Unleaded Fuel Only" dashboard stickers went on U.S. models. After so many years with twin exhaust outlets, the 1975 Beetle dropped back to a single tailpipe. Why? Because of the engine's new catalytic converter—an emission control device installed on most automobiles that year.

New louvers helped ventilation, but otherwise not much was different. Rack-and-pinion steering replaced the worm-and-roller setup. Seats now reclined completely.

Sporty wheels went on the 1976 Beetles, and a rear window defogger was made standard. This sedan started at $3,499—twice the price of a 1968 model. Speedometers now were calibrated in both miles and kilometers per hour. The license plate light was slightly modified. The 1976 models added several former "luxury" extras as standard equipment, including full carpeting, front vent windows and metallic paint. Prices rose again, to $3,699 for the sedan and $4,799 for a convertible.

The last Beetle sedans went on sale in the United States in 1977. No more Super Beetles were marketed, but a broader range of colors was available, and seats got separate adjustable front headrests. By then, the Environmental Protection Agency rated the Beetle at 23 mpg city, 33 mpg highway. Convertibles added an electrically heated rear window.

As the 1978 model year opened, Volkswagen still was turning out 1,000 Beetle sedans daily. But not for America. Not anymore. Only the Beetle convertible remained in the U.S. market after 1977. Of the 19.1 million Beetles produced by then, close to 5 million had been sold in the United States.

On July 1, 1974, the last Beetle had emerged from the Wolfsburg plant. The last one made in Germany rolled out the door on January 19, 1978. Volkswagen had promoted the fact that of the 5,115 components in a Beetle, only one remained into its final years: the clamping strip for the hood seal.

Nevertheless, Beetles remained in production around the globe. No matter. In the eyes of its American fans, the real thing was gone. (See Chapter 20 for details on final convertibles.)

Meanwhile, the Karmann Ghia Dies

Without much fanfare, the final Karmann Ghia coupes and convertibles rolled into dealerships in 1974. For close to two decades, these shapely 2+2s had continued to attract a modest but loyal following—folks who didn't demand that the car's performance match its luscious body lines.

Though unhesitatingly calling it a sports car, Volkswagen never had pretended that the Karmann Ghias were anything other than good-lookers. Promotional materials concentrated on appearance and panache, and on the car's relatively limited availability.

In the car's final season, Volkswagen literature noted that the Karmann Ghia was "a sports car that looks like a Maserati or De Tomaso" but "acts like a Volkswagen." To the end, a Ghia took more than 18 seconds to accelerate to 60 mph—slower than some economy sedans of the early 1970s.

Through the years, Karmann Ghias had benefited from most of the technical improvements that hit regular Beetles, including engine enlargements and power boosts, but stuck with their basic road personality. No equivalent to the Super Beetle went on sale. Karmann Ghias kept their original torsion bar suspensions all the way to the end, but did gain the virtues of front disc brakes—unlike the Beetles.

"Our sports car was almost too beautiful," VW admitted in 1974, referring to the original design. "It had too many subtle curves. Intricate lines.... It just wasn't suitable for mass production.... That's why the Karmann Ghia you see today looks just about the same as when Ghia first designed it." But not for long. VW had another breed of sporty coupe waiting in the wings—one that *would* deliver performance to match its shapely contours: the Scirocco. (See Chapter 18 for details on that sporty VW for the late 1970s.)

The last German-built Beetle left the Emden plant on January 19, 1978. Of course, the sedans remained in production in Latin America through the 1980s and into the '90s. (Volkswagen)

● Year-by-Year Changes, 1971-1979 ●
Beetles

1971:
Super Beetle debuts
1585-cc engine now develops 60 horse-power
New flow-through vent system uses exit vents on each side of rear window
Headlights turn off with ignition

1972:
Four-spoke safety steering wheel installed
Rear window increases in size
Four groups of horizontal intake vents now used (formerly two)
Engines now rated in SAE net (46 horse-power)
Dealerships use new diagnostics socket for troubleshooting

1973:
Taillights grow larger yet
Clutch is improved
Heater levers are redesigned
Wraparound windshield installed
Restyled dashboard has additional padding
Internal airflow is improved

1974:
New handbrake-safety belt light is installed
New "self-restoring," shock-absorbing bumpers add to car weight
Track width is increased
Special editions available: Sports Bug and Love Bug
Last Beetle leaves Wolfsburg plant on July 1
Self-centering steering installed on Super Beetles

1975:
Beetles get fuel injection, with designation on engine lid
Hoods no longer show VW emblem
"Unleaded Fuel Only" stickers go in U.S. models
Plush La Grande Bug marketed as "ultimate" Beetle
Improved rear camber geometry
Rack-and-pinion steering replaces worm-and-roller
Fully-reclining seats installed

1976:
Speedometers now calibrated in mph and kph
License plate light is slightly modified

1977:
Seats get separate headrests
Broader range of colors is available
Final year for Beetle sedan in U.S. market

1978:
Last Beetle made in Germany on January 19, 1978

1979:
Final Beetle convertibles go on sale in United States

Chapter 14

Transforming the Beetle

Not much time passed before a handful of Volkswagen owners—and a few auxiliary manufacturers—took a close look at the little Beetle and determined that they could go the factory one better. Even in the early postwar years, in fact, Germans had converted Kübelwagens and Schwimmwagens to sport machines.

Like the hot rodders who transformed Ford V-8s and small-block 1955 Chevrolets into eye-catching custom machines, American Volkswagen fans sought ways to turn their favorite vehicles into a new breed of little road warrior. Rooted largely in Southern California, their creations ranged from mild to wild, in appearance as well as performance.

Why the trend toward modification? Mainly, because Volkswagens were so easy to work on. When an engine can be pulled in minutes, and a body extracted without much more effort, why not turn that everyday Beetle into a personalized object of beauty—perhaps one that also happens to travel faster than Heinz Nordhoff or Dr. Porsche might have envisioned.

Like restorers of domestic makes today, Volkswagen purists prefer their Beetles and Ghias bone-stock. Of the estimated million-plus VWs that still prowl American roads, however, quite a number are modified—whether as "Cal-look" customs, Baja Bugs, dune buggies or in ways that defy such categorization.

Note: Modified Volkswagens are an intriguing subject unto themselves, discussed only briefly in this chapter. For a detailed story of the "Cal-look," in particular, consult *California Look VW* by British author Keith Seume, and check recent issues of such magazines as *VW Trends*.

Incarnations of the original Beetle ranged from desert riders to cargo/passenger haulers. Though intended for off-road adventures, dune buggies also were used for transportation in regions with mild climates. (Phil Hall)

Bill Devin earned credit for the idea, but dozens of companies marketed kits to turn an old, ordinary Bug into a dune buggy bent on fun. (Phil Hall)

Dune Buggies Take To The Off-Road

Even before the first Beetles lost their body shells and were converted into off-roaders, dune buggies could be found in the southwestern deserts.

In 1954, *Life* magazine presented a picture report on "desert dune bugs" in the Imperial Valley near Yuma, Arizona. Made from old hot rods with bald tires, these machines typically rode shortened (six-foot) wheelbases. Drivers sat over the rear axle.

Bill Devin earns credit for the idea of using the Beetle as a basis for desert-bound vehicles. Around 1954, Devin employed a mold from an Italian Ermini, to create fiberglass bodies that fit neatly atop the VW chassis. *Voilà*— the dune buggy was invented.

Dune buggy success over the subsequent years led to the development of such off-road events as the Baja 1000 race. By autumn 1968, more than a hundred VW-powered dune buggies, in four classes, signed up to participate in that year's 1,000-mile Baja trial. A Meyers Manx "fun bug" had won the previous year's Baja race, from Ensenada to La Paz on the Baja California peninsula in Mexico.

Dozens of companies produced dune buggies in the Sixties, either completely assembled or in kit form. Most were powered by VW engines. Most also used the Beetle's platform frame, transmission, axles, and dozens of other standard VW components. The company itself advised that "the best starting point for a spanking new dune buggy is a slightly beat-up VW 'beetle.'"

Some dune buggies were homemade; others professionally constructed. Conversion began by removing the body shell from the chassis, and discarding it. Then, it was necessary to cut out about a foot of the platform frame's center section (and discard that as well). The two larger pieces then were welded back into a platform frame—typically shortened about 15 inches. Top it off with a colorful, lightweight, bathtub-shaped fiberglass body, add oversize low-pressure tires, and another dune buggy was born— fully open to the sun and the elements, and to all-terrain desert and mountain fun.

In the early Sixties, a Devin do-it-yourself kit went for $1,295, its fiberglass body shell featuring a hand-rubbed acrylic finish. The kit included a steel frame, on which major VW parts (engine, transmission, front axle, etc.) bolted into place. Devin claimed the whole process took less than a day.

At modern-day Volkswagen shows, dune buggies continue to draw attention. Engine modifications could be mild or extreme. (Photo: James M. Flammang — Owner: Ben Smith)

Not many dune buggy exhaust systems were quite as blatant as this one, which turned up at a 1995 VW show. (Photo: James M. Flammang)

Cheryl Lee, named Playboy magazine's "Bunny of the Year" in 1971, drove home an Arabian Dune Buggy, created by Performance Designers of Daytona Beach, Florida. (Phil Hall)

OKRASA: High-Performance Bugs

Although hot rodding was commonly considered an American hobby in the Fifties, the first serious hop-up equipment for Volkswagens hailed from Europe. By 1956, Oettinger's Kraftfahrtechnische Spezial-Anstalt (OKRASA, or Okrasa) was turning out a high-performance tuning kit for early Beetles and Karmann Ghias.

Run by G. Oettinger at Friedrichsdorf, Okrasa quickly gained a reputation for results. In its April 1957 road test of a VW-Okrasa Karmann Ghia, *Road & Track* magazine noted that there were four ways to get higher performance:

1. Install high-compression pistons, a reground cam and similar components, which could yield 0-60 mph times of 24-25 seconds and 77 mph top speed.

2. Install the Okrasa tuning kit.

3. Add a supercharger, which "offers the most performance gain per dollar spent." This could reduce 0-60 mph acceleration time to 16-17 seconds, with a top speed approaching 90 mph. On the down side, the air/fuel ratio had to be "checked out carefully, as too lean a mixture will produce overheating." Also, the "driver must use his extra performance with proper respect for an air-cooled engine."

4. Install a Porsche engine—the expensive route.

Manufactured in Germany, the Okrasa kit cost $249.50 (plus installation) at the time. Top speed went from 76 to 86.5 mph. As for acceleration, 0-60 mph times dropped from 28.8 to 18.4 seconds, 0-30 dipped from 6.9 to 5.5 seconds, and the Okrasa car could reach 70 mph in 30 seconds rather than the usual 49.2 seconds. Improvement in quarter-mile times was less impressive, dropping from 23.6 to 20.0 seconds.

The Okrasa installation put out 46 horsepower at 4200 rpm vs. 36 bhp at 3700 rpm for a stock engine. Torque rose 18 percent, from 56 to 66 pound-feet. "There is absolutely nothing about this kit which will give any outward clue as to the modifications," *Road & Track* commented. The engine "idles the same, sounds the same, feels the same." Unfortunately, that also made it "much too easy and too tempting to over-rev."

The Okrasa kit contained special cylinder heads and related parts, boosting compression to 7.5:1 (without using high-compression pistons). Cooling was improved, by use of more fins. Additional room was provided for a much larger intake valve, and enlarged ports were not "siamesed" as in standard heads. Such lack of siamesed intake ports also made installation of twin carburetors more practical.

Speaking of superchargers, Judson Research and Mfg. Co. offered a positive displacement-type blower with six pound boost, guaranteed to increase rear wheel horsepower by 45 percent and cut 0-60 mph time to 15.5 seconds. Judson promised "big car performance" from its superchargers, based on testimonials from owners and road tests by top auto magazines.

Do-it-yourself books began to appear, such as Floyd Clymer's *Souping the Volkswagen*. Before long, dozens of other aftermarket suppliers had hop-up parts for VWs. A 1962 ad, for instance, offered everything from venturis, counterbalanced hoods and special intake manifolds to tuned exhaust pipes and carburetor conversions. Heat boosters, rear-end stabilizers and bumper reinforcements also sought customers. But only one of those firms became a virtual legend.

The EMPI Connection

Restorers and original-Beetle enthusiasts might never have heard of Joe Vittone. But those who like their air-cooled VWs to have distinct personalities—with performance to match—consider Vittone a virtual godfather of the breed.

In 1954, Vittone formed Economotors, a Volkswagen agency in Riverside, California. In addition to selling Beetles off the showroom floor, Vittone took an interest in improving the inner workings. He started small, developing a set of valve guides for the flat four engine—guides that would be less likely to wear down quickly (a failing in the original design).

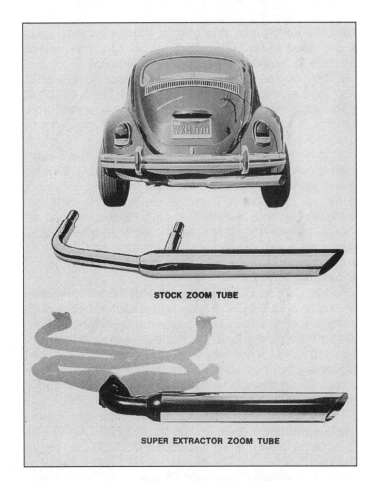

Hundreds of aftermarket performance components went on sale in the late 1950s and '60s. A Zoom Tube, from Per-Spec Industries in Alhambra, California, aimed to "dominate the rear" of a Beetle. The Super Extractor model, complete with glass-pack muffler, attached to exhaust headers. (Phil Hall)

Dune buggies held specially molded fiberglass bodies, in a variety of shapes, typically without a top. Quality varied considerably. This is a 1969 EMPI IMP, one of the better versions. (Photo: James M. Flammang — Owner: Jon Knoll)

Two years later, in 1956, Vittone opened European Motor Products Inc., soon known across the country as EMPI, a supplier of high-quality aftermarket accessories for VWs. By then, the hot rodders who'd formerly hopped up flathead Fords had a slew of small-block, overhead valve V-8 engines to hold their attention. So, why not a similar pastime for lovers of the humble Volkswagen?

EMPI soon became an agent for Okrasa components, and supplied the test car used by *Road & Track*. By 1958, EMPI also was selling high-performance imported from Denzel, in Austria—including engines with aluminum rods and dual-port heads.

Vittone designed a front anti-sway bar for the Beetle, shortly before it became a standard item at the factory. He also began to market a rear stabilizer (known as a camber compensator) to remedy the tucked-in back wheels that were a worrisome feature of swing-axle cars. Vittone arranged to import such temptations as BRM wheels (specially made by Speedwell, in Britain) and Shorrock superchargers (purchased from Sidney Allard of Allard automobile fame).

In 1962, a new EMPI dual-carb kit for the 36-horsepower engine cost $69.50. It gave a horsepower boost of up to 15 percent, without switching to higher-octane fuel. Included was a precision-built throttle linkage for smooth action and identical control of each carburetor. EMPI issued plenty of other hop-up gear, including a $149.50 Ram induction manifold kit, $42 glass-packed mufflers and a $29.50 cylinder head temperature gauge.

By 1966, customers could get a complete car, loaded with performance gear, known as the EMPI GTV. The GTV came in four versions, priced $437 to $1,239 higher than a stock Beetle. The entry level Mk I had a sport exhaust, E-Z-R gearshift, chrome wheels, camber compensator and selection of dress-up items. The top-dog Mk IV included such goodies as a ram-induction carburetor, Boge shocks and reclining seats.

EMPI also issued a dune buggy, named Imp, and campaigned a series of rail dragsters—Volkswagen-powered, of course. Across the country, many conventional VW

dealers also became EMPI agents—a dual operation that Volkswagen of America did not fully appreciate, perhaps unaware at the time of the potential in hopped-up Beetles.

Unfortunately, EMPI bit the dust in 1971, sold to Filter Dynamics (makers of Lee filters). By then, however, dozens of other aftermarket companies for Volkswagens had sprouted up—though not all delivered the kind of quality for which EMPI had been noted.

The "Cal-look" Arrives

As the name suggests, the "Cal-look," like so many automotive trends, started in California. Southern California, to be exact; specifically, in Orange County.

According to modified-VW expert and author Keith Seume, a photographer named Jere Alhadeff coined the term "Cal-look" in the mid-1970s, but the theme had been around for a while. The first car to warrant that designation, he believes, was a 1963 sun roof Beetle with a modified engine and mag wheels, built by Greg Aronson. Later owned by Jim Holmes, that Beetle appeared on the cover of the February 1975 issue of *Hot VWs* magazine.

Plenty of Beetles already were prowling the western states with super-wide tires, bulging fenders, bizarre metallic paint jobs and bodacious powertrains. As the "Cal-look" term took hold, it referred to a specific style of customization. These were quick, street legal Beetles, subtly modified—tasteful but powerful—typically sprayed in a vivid single hue.

Seume credits Volkswagens Limited, a California VW club formed in 1964, for setting the stage for the "Cal-look." Later renamed Der Kleiner Panzers, the Orange County group gradually adopted a particular style in which to keep their Beetles—a style related to certain drag racing VWs of the day.

At first, the cars kept their chrome trim, lights—even the "factory" paint schemes. They also sat at stock ride height. Interiors were mildly revised, perhaps with a speed shifter and tachometer added. Engines enjoyed only modest modifications.

Bumpers began to disappear from these cars late in the 1960s. Paint jobs and interior work got more attention, including special seats and installation of Stewart-Warner or VDO gauges. As the Seventies began, what would become known as the "Cal" style was changing—starting with lowered front suspensions. Lowered rear ends came later, and the cars started to lose their chrome trim. Some Beetles sported such extras as smoked Lexan quarter windows, and alloy back wheels borrowed from Porsches.

Engines grew hotter than ever, and equal-length headers gave way to wilder-yet exhaust systems. Naturally, a potent stereo setup became part of the "Cal" picture, as cassettes and CD players edged aside the old 8-track units.

At a glance, from afar, even the more outrageous "Cal-look" Beetles don't look all that different from stock Volkswagens. But up close, the details tell a story of their own; a tale that veers far afield from what Ferdinand Porsche had in mind for the "people's car."

Baja Bugs and Super-Performance

During the Sixties, Volkswagens had won both the Baja 500 and Mexican 1000 races. In 1971, Volkswagen offered the Baja Champion SE, a special-edition Super Beetle to commemorate "the ruggedness, dependability and victories of VWs in tough Mexican off-road races."

Painted metallic silver-blue, the Baja Champion SE wore wide-spoke sports wheels with black center sections. Black leatherette upholstery decorated the interior. At $2,224, this Baja edition cost just $65 more than a regular Super Beetle.

Personalized Volkswagens that went a step beyond the subtle "Cal-look" adopted the designation Baja Bug. Instead of the usual lid at the rear, these assertive machines kept their flat-four engines exposed. Wicked "stinger" exhaust systems were typical, not only emitting raucous sounds but dominating the rear end.

To build a Baja, enthusiasts took a stock sedan and shortened it by a foot, mainly by eliminating bumpers and chopping off nose and tail metal. Add a fiberglass front hood, high-cut fenders, perhaps a roll bar and tubular bumpers, and the car was ready for show—and "go."

High-performance modifications didn't stop with exhaust headers and cylinder heads. A number of owners squeezed Porsche engines into the backs of their Beetles, taking advantage of the escalated output but retaining the air-cooled qualities.

Naturally, that wasn't enough for the handful who needed to have the utmost in go-power. So, a few Beetles wound up with seemingly-impossible powertrains, such as Chevrolet V-8s. At least one such installation went into an otherwise stock-looking Volkswagen sedan, which might have been the ultimate "sleeper." Even a small-block V-8 was a lot larger than VW's flat four, of course, so this Chevrolet engine occupied nearly all the back-seat space. A set of fake luggage covered the forward end of the engine, so passersby had no clue as to the supreme motivational force concealed therein.

New Noses and Customized Bodies

Sticking a different grille onto the front end of a car was an old idea. Thousands of custom and semi-custom American hot rods wore a grille that had started life on a completely different automobile. Aftermarket suppliers must have been strangely offended by the sloped nose of the Beetle, however, because they came out with so many bolt-on units to alter its shape.

Prominent snouts appeared in a variety of forms, becoming surprisingly popular. Among the favorite choices were grilles styled like that of a 1939 Ford, or a Rolls-Royce or a Mercedes-Benz.

Plastic Pacesetter Industries, for instance, marketed a chromed stainless steel "Rolls-Royce Classic grille," complete with hood and all hardware for installation. Not only

Beetle-based off-road machines weren't limited to the United States. This "Country Buggy" with a 9.2-inch road clearance went on sale in Australia. Hard and soft canopies were available. (Volkswagen)

Beetles also hit the nation's dragstrips, packing all sorts of powertrain combinations, from much-modified flat fours all the way to V-8 engines. (Volkswagen)

did it produce a completely different front end appearance, it promised to increase luggage compartment space by almost 50 percent. A steel mounting was laminated into the fiberglass or ABS plastic hood, in order to use the stock hinges and latch. The high-luster finish needed only light wet sanding before painting, according to the company's literature.

Aftermarket firms often came up with a modification before the factory got around to it. Carrosserie Zund, for instance—a shop near Berne, Switzerland—offered a large custom rear window before VW launched the square-window model for 1958.

Individuals, of course, had their own ideas about customized Volkswagens. An Arizona woman, for one, covered her VW with acrylic leopard skin. A rug salesman coated his Bug with indoor-outdoor carpeting, while a Wisconsin dealer transformed a Beetle into a dual-cowl phaeton.

Racing and Rallying

Volkswagen's involvement in racing started early, and took many forms. A Mexican dealer, Prince Alfonso de Hohenlohe financed a *Carrera Panamericana* racing team in 1954. Seven cars started, and all finished the rugged 1,800-mile course, with no repairs or tire changes.

By the 1960s, Volkswagens were heavily involved in Formula Vee (for VW) racing. The "Vee" class quickly grew into the largest single racing class in the United States (and the world). Starting in 1966, VW Motorsports established a tie to Formula racing/rallying, as a semi-official arm of the company.

Styled like Indy cars, single-seat Formula Vee racers used a 1200-cc engine (tuned and balanced, but only lightly modified apart from a megaphone exhaust), plus VW brakes, transmissions, and axles. Rear coil springs replaced the torsion bars. Weighing around 825 pounds,

Not just one, but both of these racing machines—pictured in 1983—are Beetles underneath. The open-wheel Formcar was the first successful Formula Vee racer, competing in the early 1960s.

Hannelore Werner of Germany began racing VW-powered Formula Vees in 1967, soon becoming Europe's top woman driver. (Phil Hall)

they could be purchased for about $2,500—complete—in the Sixties. Quite a difference from the amounts involved with other forms of racing, and they cost even less in kit form. At least 16 firms in the United States turned out Formula Vee racers or kits.

At the 1969 Chicago Auto Show, visitors could win a VW "Formula Vee." The accessory kit included "mag" wheels, racing stripes, and other goodies. Volkswagen also had a "science show" in Chicago, promoting space-age technology for vehicle design, production and testing.

Replicars and Neo-Sports Cars

Anyone who was unhappy with the basic appearance of a Beetle had no end of opportunities to give it an all-new personality, or transform it into something from another era. A Bugatti, perhaps? Maybe an ersatz MG-TD or Frazer-Nash? If a car from the past didn't appeal, VWs served as the basis for more futuristic sports cars—Elite Lasers to Kellmarks.

What these dozens of mini-size replicars that sprung up in the Sixties had in common was a Volkswagen chassis and drive gear, and a few VW components. Otherwise, it was a matter of "anything goes." Whether handmade or professionally crafted, the conversions ranged from crude to civilized. Many were poorly assembled, or used marginal-quality body components.

One of the first vehicles to make use of the Volkswagen platform was the Denzel, a sports car designed by Wolfgang Denzel of Vienna, Austria. About 160 were built, between 1949 and 1961. Early examples used highly modified VW engines, but later ones turned to 1600-cc Porsche engines. Handmade steel/aluminum bodies and

Taking advantage of its racing publicity, Volkswagen offered a Formula Vee accessory kit with "mag" wheels and racing stripes, in its exhibit at the Chicago Auto Show. (Phil Hall)

Replicars, whether produced in the early years or later, continue to appear at Volkswagen events. In August 1995, this FiberFab rendition of the MG TD participated in a Central Ohio show. To the rear are two Bradley GTs. (Photo: James M. Flammang)

frames used Italian *superleggera* techniques. Denzels fared well in Sports Car Club of America (SCCA) racing. Modification kits also were sold, using Denzel crankshafts, pistons and camshafts.

Enzmann was another Volkswagen-based sports car, with a door-less fiberglass body. Created by a Swiss physician, a hundred or so Enzmanns were produced over a decade-long period, starting in 1957. Most were equipped with Okrasa tuning kits or MAG superchargers. Another hundred MCA Jetstars left a shop in Bremen, Germany, in the early 1960s, with bodies from Bill Devin.

On the American side of the Atlantic, simulated Bugattis (sometimes spelled with a double "g") were among the most popular conversions, their bodies issued by several manufacturers. Most were painted blue, and many were shakily built.

Volkswagenwerk indulged in its own transformations, often focusing on safety. This Experimental Safety Vehicle first appeared at a Transpo exhibit in May 1972. (Phil Hall)

The Cimbria SS was a gullwing-door sports coupe with a pronounced snout, produced by Amore Cars Ltd. Weighing 1,650 pounds, the Cimbria could accelerate to 60 mph in 10 seconds and reach 110 mph.

Even quicker 0-60 mph times were claimed by the Kelmark GT Mk II. Styled like the Dino Ferrari, the shapely coupe from Kelmark Engineering came in kit form, and could allegedly be assembled in 30 hours.

Another fiberglass body topped the Bradley GTElectric, which coupled an electric motor to the Beetle's transmission. Electric Vehicle Corp., of Minneapolis, claimed a 75 mile range and 75 mph top speed.

Thoroughbred Cars of Redmond, Washington, turned out Tiger roadsters, resembling 1930s British sports cars. Like many conversions, the Tiger often used Beetle parts, but also could be ordered to fit other chassis.

Lindberg Engineering offered replicas of Mercedes roadsters and Auburn speedsters. Antique & Classic Automotive of Buffalo, New York, listed VW-platformed replicas of a 1930 Blower Bentley, 1927 Bugatti Type 37B, Jaguar SS-100 and 1934 Frazer-Nash. Fiberfab—one of the best-known companies—also issued a long list of fiberglass-bodied replicars.

BGW Ltd. produced a VW speedster that looked vaguely like a Porsche. Also available: a 1940 Willys opera coupe. Unlike most conversion kits, these two consisted of add-on parts, and did not require removal of the original body. They have to be seen to be believed.

This list barely skims the surface of the Volkswagen-based replicars that appeared in the Sixties. The replicar craze tapered off in the next decade or two. Many of the cars doubtless wound up in the crusher's jaws, but a few excellent examples still turn up at Volkswagen events.

Practical Tasks

Applications for the Volkswagen engine went far beyond automobiles. Farmers used it to power farm machinery—not unlike similar setups half a century earlier, with the Ford Model T's four-cylinder engine. Early in the 1950s, Dutch farmers found a way to run milking machines with the Beetle engine.

A German company used the VW four to power speedboats. Around 1960, a New York company, Inboard Marine Co., developed the Volks-Liner boat with a VW engine. It was to be sold at VW dealers, but failed.

More successful were VW-powered planes, taking advantage of the engine's light weight. Volkswagen of America did not officially encourage these installations, but *Small World* magazine reported on them periodically.

Mira Slovak, an airline pilot, put one into a European-built sailplane and flew it from Scotland to California—in a long sequence of short hops. Engines also were used in tiny one-man helicopters and "hovercraft."

Each ingenious installation added one more gold star to the VW's reputation for versatility and dependability, and the company did not hesitate to publicize the results.

Chapter 15

Trying Another Tack: Squarebacks and Fastbacks

Even before the Sixties began, voices within Volkswagen's market research department called for a model to supplement, if not replace, the Beetle. Voices from elsewhere, inside and outside the company, echoed that clarion call. Consumer demands were quickly changing, after all. An automobile that had filled the bill a decade earlier didn't necessarily earn comparable plaudits as the competition tightened.

"What an auto company loses in the market today," Heinz Nordhoff said in 1963, "it probably can't recover in the next 50 years." By then, Volkswagen ranked third in world production, behind General Motors and Ford.

Despite the recent debut of an economy-oriented Beetle, marketed only outside the United States, global Volkswagen sales had been slipping a bit. American sales were showing a stronger result, but hardly breathtaking: down 5.2 percent in the first four months of 1967—a period when domestically-built makes fell 17 percent.

By 1966, Americans had a new breed of VW. But even at the start of the Sixties, Europeans gained an alternate choice.

VW 1500—On Sale in Europe

Any analysts who'd predicted that Volkswagen would *not* introduce another model must have been stunned by news from the Frankfurt (Germany) motor show in September 1961. In addition to the expected revisions of the Beetle, the VW exhibit included a Type 3 (1500) squareback sedan. Development had been undertaken with some secrecy, the car's existence not even common knowledge at Volkswagen's main office.

Some called the 1500 a "Beetle in disguise," despite its far-different shape. Not only was the 1500 sedan six inches longer and three inches wider than a Beetle (though on the same wheelbase), but it exhibited a squarish profile, far removed from its Wolfsburg mate.

More modern and orthodox in appearance, the 1500 was akin to other European automobiles. With one big exception: its engine sat neatly under the rug of the rear trunk. Luggage fit into the rear as well as the front, with outside access.

Despite the rear-mounted engine, the 1500 had a noticeable, squared-up front hood. The engine was larger than a Beetle's, though not by much, displacing 1493 cubic centimeters.

The VW 1500 gave increasingly-prosperous Germans an opportunity to "trade up" to a fancier model, rather than "make do" with a Beetle. This way, they'd still be in the Volkswagen fold, and continue to enjoy familiar VW quality. A 1500 sedan cost the equivalent of $1,500 ($300 more than a Beetle 1200).

Because the original 1500 didn't fare so well, Volkswagen launched a fancier 1500S two years later. In addition to more chrome trim, the 1500S had a dual-carbureted engine rated at 66 horsepower (12 more than the initial 1500). Then came the 1600TL, with a 1.6-liter engine. Both fastback sedans and squareback wagons were produced, the latter named Variant.

Not everyone applauded the Volkswagen 1500, in any of its guises. Some found it seriously disappointing, unreliable and downright undesirable.

DM (Deutsche Mark), a product-testing magazine com-

Volkswagen had a completely different, conventionally-styled car ready late in 1961: the 1500 sedan. Never officially offered in the U.S. market, the 1500 drew some criticism in Europe.

A 1500 station wagon joined the initial two-door sedan in 1962, also for the European market only. Like the Beetle, the 1500 was powered by an air-cooled rear engine. (Volkswagen)

This handsome 1500 convertible was designed for 1962, but never marketed. (Volkswagen)

parable to the American *Consumer Reports*, was sued by Volkswagen for $2.5 million. Why? Because *DM* had given what *Newsweek* called an "unflattering verdict" on the 1500S sedan, after testing it for 30,000 miles. The magazine reported that its test car had been in the shop eight times, concluding that the car was unreliable and unworthy of recommendation.

VW alleged that *DM* testers had intentionally ruined the engine. A Volkswagen executive was quoted as saying the company was suing "for the sake of the eight million VW drivers throughout the world," because this nasty article "was an assault on their honor and trust in us."

Popular road tester Tom McCahill got his hands on a 1500 Variant station wagon in 1964, reporting in the January 1965 issue of *Mechanix Illustrated*. At the time, the car was available in Canada and Mexico, but not in the United States. Except via a virtual black market, that is. McCahill's secretary had obtained the 1500 through the efforts of a serviceman returning from Europe.

McCahill tested the car with 13,000 miles on the odometer. By then, it had suffered a number of small malfunctions, as well as problems with the brakes, "to such an extent you'd think it was a Detroit lemon." On the plus side, McCahill noted that the 1500 delivered "a magnificent ride for its size [and went] through potholes and dips like a car weighing a thousand pounds more."

Acceleration tests revealed a 0-60 mph time of 19.8 seconds—a snail's pace by domestic car standards, but brisker than usual for a VW. The 91-cid flat-four engine developed 54 horsepower and 82.5 pound-feet of torque, running on 7.8:1 compression.

Storage capacity was branded "remarkable," because the engine hid beneath the floor. McCahill predicted that the 1500 had "great potential," sure that "if they were readily available on these shores they'd go over like free booze on the Bowery." At the same time, he admitted that early models, at least, were not as well assembled as prior Volkswagens, and did not appear to be as reliable.

Through the 1960s, Type 3 Karmann Ghias also were produced, which differed sharply—literally—in appearance from the familiar coupes and convertibles. However, these were not sold in America.

Type 3 Squareback and Fastback Debut (1966-1973)

"It doesn't look like a Volkswagen," said the sales brochure of the new Squareback Sedan, "but it's sure built like one." The copywriters were correct on both counts. Volkswagen itself even admitted that in terms of technical features that had been "proven" in prior models, "the Squareback is a throwback."

A 1500 sedan leads the way off the ramp at the Wolfsburg plant, but Beetles and their offshoots accounted for more than 78 percent of production worldwide in 1964. The Wolfsburg facility in Germany turned out some 5,000 vehicles per day. (Volkswagen)

At last, in 1966, the U.S. market got a second model—and the Fastback touring sedan was a beauty. A 65-horsepower engine beneath the rear floor provided the power, and front disc brakes helped bring the car to a halt. (Volkswagen)

The new sedan came two ways: Fastback or Squareback (shown). Despite their good looks, the Fastback and Squareback never quite captured the public fancy—certainly nowhere close to the Beetle's charm and popularity. (Phil Hall)

Introduced in October 1965, as a '66 model, the Squareback looked much like the Type 3 (1500) wagon that had been sold in Europe through the early Sixties. By then, the 1500 had become Europe's top selling station wagon. The Type 3 Fastback Sedan, with a sloping rear end and long rear quarter windows, was a new body style, wearing what Volkswagen touted as a rakish roof line.

Although it gave the appearance of a small station wagon, Volkswagen billed the Squareback as a sedan, noting that "instead of curving or sloping the back, we extended the roof line, squared off the rear end and enclosed all the space that sits outside a conventional sedan above the trunk."

Both bodies held an air-cooled rear engine—slightly larger and more powerful than the Beetle's—plus a fully-synchronized four-speed transmission. Four-wheel independent torsion bar suspension was used. Unlike the Beetle, which stuck with drum brakes, Type 3 cars halted with front discs and rear drums. Each model seated five and could reach 84 mph.

Breathing through dual carburetors, the four-cylinder magnesium-aluminum engine developed 65 horsepower at 4600 rpm. Displacing 1584-cc (96.7 cubic inches), it ran a 7.7:1 compression ratio. The engine sat below the rear luggage compartment of the Fastback, and under the rear floor of the Squareback. The oil cap (with attached dipstick) sat under the back door, outside the engine compartment. Despite twin carbs, the engine ran on regular gasoline.

Volkswagen had quite a complete lineup in 1966, from station wagon and Karmann Ghia (top) to the new five-passenger Squareback and Fastback (center)—plus the ever-available Beetle. All had air-cooled rear engines. (Volkswagen)

In the 1967 Squareback, the rear seat folded to form a deck that held 42.5 cubic feet of cargo. Both the Squareback and Fastback could have an optional sliding steel sun roof. Each got a new third-gear ratio, plus a modified rear suspension and dual braking system. Twin carburetors sent the fuel mixture to the 65-horsepower rear engine. (Phil Hall)

For 1967, a new progressive spring system went into the rear suspension. Torsion bars were softened, and an auxiliary spring was installed. (Phil Hall)

● Tourist Deliveries—The Fun Way to Buy ● Your Beetle or Bus

As early as 1955, Volkswagen buyers in the United States didn't have to take delivery of their new cars in their hometowns. Instead, they could combine the new car purchase with a trip to Europe. A new Beetle could be picked up at Wolfsburg, driven through a few countries, then shipped back to America. For many, the price of such a program—made tempting as Volkswagen began to encourage such deliveries—was hard to pass up.

In the mid-1960s, Americans bought seven out of ten of the vehicles sold under the Tourist Delivery Program: nearly 15,000 Volkswagens for delivery in Europe, in 1966 alone. Not just Beetles, but also Fastbacks and Squarebacks, as well as buses and vans. Volkswagen had 950 authorized dealers in 1967, and people could easily arrange for European delivery.

By 1969, more than 100,000 VWs had been bought by Americans under the program. Cars could be delivered to any of 40 cities, in 15 countries.

Volkswagen offered Tourist Deliveries all through the Beetle era, and into the Squareback/Fastback period. Here, Mr. and Mrs. Gerard M. Schott of Arcadia, California, are ready to drive their new 1967 Fastback away from the Wolfsburg plant. It was the 100,000th car delivered under VW's International Tourist Delivery Program. Greeting the Schotts is Stuart Perkins, president of Volkswagen of America. (Volkswagen)

Flatter in configuration ("pancake" or "suitcase" style) than the Beetle's engine, the Type 3 engine was so well hidden that the sales brochure challenged readers to find it. Just 16 inches high, this was the most compact engine built by Volkswagen. It was almost VW's most powerful to date.

Wheelbase of the Type 3 (also known as the 1600 series) was 94.5 inches—just like the Beetle. Despite ample interior space, however, these two measured just six inches longer overall than the Bug. "So a parking space that's snug as a bug should fit the Squareback, too." Transmission gear ratios were identical to those in the Beetle sedan.

A compartment beneath the hood held 6-1/2 cubic feet of luggage. A trunk over the Fastback's engine held another 10.2 cubic feet, while interior space in the Squareback totaled 42.5 cubic feet (with the rear seat backrest folded). With the seat up, rear space dipped to 24.7 cubic feet. Because of the flat loading floor, sides and roof, Volkswagen claimed the Squareback's rear space was "almost like the inside of a packing case."

Cloth upholstery was standard; leatherette available (air-permeable for hot weather comfort). Upholstery, paneling, padding and carpeting were all in one matching color.

The spare tire sat in front of the forward luggage compartment, so there was no need to unload anything to change a flat. Also up front: see-through plastic containers for brake fluid and windshield washer fluid. An optional steel sliding sun roof gave 390 square inches of sunshine.

Fastbacks featured hingeless rear quarter windows made of flexible safety glass that bent as the window opened outward.

Squarebacks got an auxiliary rear spring, which came into play during hard cornering, on rough ground, or under severe load conditions.

Floor-level heater outlets for front seats were operated by levers on the dashboard. Rear occupants had a heater outlet lever between the seats. Front bucket seats adjusted to seven positions, fore and aft; backrests adjusted to seven different angles, for a total of 49 settings in all.

"In no way will these new and slightly larger cars replace our familiar Beetle," insisted Stuart Perkins, president of Volkswagen of America. The company's original car "has won a lasting place in America and...sales are hitting new highs this year." Perkins announced that Americans could expect to see just one of these new machines for every ten Beetles.

Volkswagen vowed average gas mileage of 28 mpg, further predicting that tires should be good for 40,000 miles or so. Prices started at $2,140 for the Fastback and $2,295 for the Squareback, which weighed a few pounds more. "When we make a fastback," the copywriters concluded, "we make a fastback. Not a fastbuck."

Initially optional, backup lights became standard for the 1967 models. Fastbacks added an auxiliary spring over the rear axle, like that on the Beetle (and the prior year's Squareback). Rear torsion bars were softened, in an attempt to ease the ride. Front seat lap belts in Fastbacks, Squarebacks and Karmann Ghias were retractable, like those in the Beetle. New safety door locks had push-button controls on lower edges of the door window frames, preventing unintentional opening from inside. Prices rose a little, to $2,148 for the Fastback and $2,295 for a Squareback—plus $125 for a sun roof.

VWs Get Automatic Transmission and Fuel Injection

During 1968, a fully automatic three-speed transmission became available for Fastback and Squareback models. Unlike the Automatic Stick Shift that entered Beetle option lists, this was a fully automatic unit. A six-position selector moved between P, R, N, D1, D2 and D3 ranges. Drive 1 was intended for steep downgrades and slippery pavement. A "kick-down" switch was incorporated, for acceleration when passing/merging.

Electronic fuel injection also was introduced during 1968—the industry's only system of that kind. Long before most manufacturers gave more than a passing thought to fuel injection in their regular vehicles, Volkswagen had such a system in all of its Fastbacks and Squarebacks.

Unlike the fuel-injection setups that had been installed in a handful of earlier vehicles, including high-performance Chevrolets and Pontiacs, the VW unit was electronic, not

Volkswagen had something new to attract Fastback/ Squareback buyers in 1969: a fully automatic three-speed transmission. Dashboards were more complete than the Beetle's. (Phil Hall)

Front occupants of the Fastback sedan got headrests in 1968, and the engine gained electronic fuel injection—long before such systems became common in domestic makes. (Phil Hall)

Nearly all the 1968 improvements were inside. Why did the Squareback and Fastback not sell better? In part, because they didn't look distinctive enough, compared to other imports that were gaining a foothold in the U.S. market by the late 1960s. (Phil Hall)

Little-changed outside, the 1969 Fastback sedan had a new rear suspension. Not everyone realized that Volkswagen's step-up models had rear engines, similar to the Beetle's, despite the visible air vents on quarter panels. (Phil Hall)

Luggage could be stored at both ends of the 1970 Fastback sedan. Lengthening the car by 4.5 inches gave the front compartment 25 percent more cargo space. The rear trunk sat above the engine. (Phil Hall)

By 1971, the Fastback was commonly known as Type 3 (its official designation). A new "memory" feature switched off the headlights automatically as the engine was turned off. Fastbacks and Squarebacks had a standard four-speed manual gearbox. A new Type 4 (411) series debuted this year. (Volkswagen)

As the decklid script indicates, this 1972 Squareback had the optional automatic transmission. (Phil Hall)

Type 3 Fastbacks (shown) and Squarebacks continued to compete against the Type 4 models in 1973, but were in their final season. They were aimed at buyers who wanted something bigger than a Super Beetle, but liked the smaller car's long-term economy. (Phil Hall)

mechanical. "Computers, widely used in auto plants," their May 1968 announcement stated, were "now being installed in cars themselves."

Described as little larger than a box of cleaning tissues, the control computer sat in the left rear quarter panel. This "little black box" (actually light gray in color) contained more than 200 transistors, resistors, diodes and capacitors. Promised benefits included a clean exhaust, faster accelerator response and improved fuel economy.

Except for the addition of an electric rear defroster, little was new for 1969 models. A Fastback sold for $2,295 that year, while the Squareback started at $2,470. A sun roof added $120. Prices rose just slightly for 1970, and a little more in 1971—two years of minimal change for the shapely duo.

Although Type 3 cars established a following of their own, they never approached the popularity that VW executives might have anticipated. Customers seemed to like them at first, but that early interest soon faded. As the Seventies decade got underway, sales hit a downhill slide.

Further refinements arrived for 1972, including longer-lasting front brake pads, a redesigned steering wheel, steering-column washer/wiper control, and new rear defogger switch. Speedometers now read to 110 mph, and a transistorized brake warning light was installed. Nothing crucial in that list, though higher-intensity taillights probably weren't a bad idea, and an improved rear backrest lock sounded practical. Compression dropped to 7.3:1, as the engines prepared to run on no-lead fuel. By now, the

Squareback had dropped the Type 3 designation, but it still applied to the Fastback.

Prices were up to $2,650 for the Fastback ($2,795 in deluxe form) and $2,995 for the Squareback in 1973, the duo's final season. Such minor changes as a modified handbrake lever and simplified heater controls weren't about to make much of a dent in sales at this late date. By now, too, VW had introduced two other non-Beetle series.

Type 4 Arrives (1971-1974)

If sales of the Type 3 turned out to be lackluster, the Type 4 proved to be a fiasco. Yet another evolution of the air-cooled rear-engine layout, the 411—and subsequent 412—failed to capture much notice at all, selling only 117,110 copies in the United States over a four-year period.

Marketed elsewhere in the world since 1969, the Type 4 became available in the United States for 1971. Billed as "our idea of a big sedan," the 411 came as a two-door hatchback or a four-door sedan. Both sold for the same $2,999 price—considerably higher than the Type 3.

"Designed and built from scratch," according to the sales brochure, the 411 had been "tested and proven in Europe for three years. On some of the worst roads in the world." Less than two feet longer than a Beetle, this was Volkswagen's first-ever four-door sedan.

The 1679-cc (102.5-cid) engine developed 85 horsepower at 5000 rpm, and 99.5 pound-feet of torque at 3500 rpm. Instead of a carburetor, it used electronic fuel injection. Unlike the Type 3 Fastback/Squareback, this engine demanded premium fuel (98 octane).

"They ride like much bigger cars," Volkswagen insisted, "but still maneuver like much smaller cars." The suspension consisted of coil springs and struts up front, and trailing wishbones with coil springs out back—no hint of torsion bars. VW claimed a top speed of 94 mph. Quad headlights helped give the cars a far different look than the Type 3.

Type 4 cars came with a standard three-speed automatic transmission. Fastbacks and Squarebacks had been available with automatic for several years, but the 411 had no stick at all.

Braking consisted of front discs and rear drums. A thermostatically-controlled auxiliary heating system let the driver set any temperature, which was maintained even when the engine wasn't running. Fully reclining posture-fitted bucket seats adjusted to 400 positions, and went up and down in five positions. The carpeted front trunk held 14 cubic feet, with an additional 6-cubic-foot luggage "well" behind the sedan's rear seat.

A $3,299 station wagon joined the initial two body styles for 1972. Engines now ran on no-lead fuel, automatic transmissions started in "Park" position and speedometers indicated 120 mph. Larger warm air outlets were installed, and the steering wheel got a fresh look; but nothing helped much on the sales charts.

If the Fastback and Squareback enjoyed so-so sales, the 411 sedan—introduced for 1971 as VW's first four-door model—ranked as a sales disaster. A standard automatic transmission and 85-horsepower engine didn't help. (Phil Hall)

VW 412 Displaces the 411

When a model fails to sell well, you can dump it. Or, you can touch it up and give it a new name. Volkswagen took the latter course. Thus, the marginally-moving 411 of 1971-72 became the 412 for 1973, billed as "a luxury you can afford."

Even those who *could* afford it failed to take heed. Marketers claimed that the car was fully restyled from the windshield forward. Rear taillights were redesigned, dashboards

Joining the new sedan and hatchback was a 411 station wagon. All Volkswagens, including the 411 series, still had rear-mounted, air-cooled engines. (Phil Hall)

Outside the United States, the 411 came in DeLuxe (left) or Standard form, the latter with single headlights. (Phil Hall)

displayed a new woodgrain inlay. Three body styles went on sale: four-door sedan, station wagon and two-door sedan. Customers did not exactly clamor for any of the trio.

A 412 measured 180 inches long (17-1/2 inches longer than a Super Beetle). Trunk capacity was 13.4 cubic feet (plus the space in a well behind the sedan's rear seat).

Under the new SAE net rating system, the fuel-injected 1679-cc engine delivered 76 horsepower at 4900 rpm, and 109 pound-feet of torque at 4500 rpm. (California cars had less-potent engines.) Modified camshaft timing promised a smoother idle, and a new nickel-plated muffler was installed. So were new 2-1/2-mph front bumpers.

The 411 evolved into a 412 series for 1973, offered in three body styles. Sales failed to improve, and the Type 4 became extinct after 1974. Volkswagen had other, more modern ideas in the works. (Phil Hall)

A three-speed automatic transmission again was standard, except in the two-door model, which came with a fully-synchronized four-speed manual gearbox. All models used recirculating-type steering.

Volkswagen claimed 0-60 mph acceleration of 17 seconds for the four-door and wagon, but a moderately swifter 14.5 seconds for the lighter weight two-door model. Claimed fuel consumption was a 20 mpg for the heavier models vs. 22 for the two-door.

Craftsmanship was expected to sell the car, starting "with an obsession with even the smallest detail, from the finish of a trunk lining to testing the engine before it goes into the car, and after." Volkswagen packed in plenty of standard fittings, but not much of it ranked as luxury, from the "posh cloth interior" to the "big, couch-like seats" and electric clock.

VW also touted two features offered in no domestic luxury car, at any price: electronic fuel injection, and a timed pre-heating system that heated the car in winter, without turning on the engine or sitting in the car. While you were pulling down that last cup of coffee in the morning, your 412 could be "making itself as warm as toast."

Increased prices didn't help at Volkswagen's 1,200-plus showrooms. The two-door sedan listed for $3,299, while the wagon started at $3,699.

For 1974, the final outing for Type 4, a larger (1795-cc) engine went into the four-door sedan and station wagon. Prices took a leap upward, topping at $4,200 for the wagon.

Customers still weren't clamoring for 412s, but Volkswagen definitely needed an alternative to the Beetle. If a bigger automobile wouldn't sell, how about a smaller one? Maybe even one with—Yikes!—front-wheel drive and a liquid-cooled engine!

Chapter 16

Second-Generation Transporters: Microbuses to EuroVans

When Volkswagen finally revised its Microbus line for 1968, the dimensions and basic structure didn't change much, but the vehicles adopted a whole new personality. A large expanse of glass yielded much greater visibility. A stronger engine gave the station wagons some much-needed zest. Still, while the updated models attracted a whole new generation of customers—and eventually, enthusiasts—many fans of the originals weren't quite so elated. Quite a few still yearned for the first-generation design, disdaining its modernized successor.

A New Breed of Wagons (1968-1979)

All-new for 1968, VW station wagons (the Microbus designation faded away) rode the same wheelbase as their predecessors. Still-boxy bodies measured 5.5 inches longer (now 174 inches overall), nearly an inch wider and an inch or so taller. Marketers believed the new wagons looked longer than the figures suggested. They were also a little heavier, shod with 5.00x14 tires. Volkswagen insisted the wagons were "virtually all-new inside and out,"

A dramatically new-look series of Transporters arrived for 1968. Like its mates, the station wagon (no longer dubbed Microbus, but still often referred to as a bus) featured "picture windows" and a sliding side door. Front legroom increased. (Phil Hall)

Volkswagen's new-style station wagons featured rounded corners and a wraparound windshield, but the rear-mounted, air-cooled engine hadn't changed much. Interiors held a safety-padded dashboard and a vent system that channeled fresh air to the rear via ducts running through the armrests. (Phil Hall)

Campmobiles were part of the new station wagon series. Greater glass area helped make the scenery easier to view. The "pop-top" option provided rooftop sleeping quarters for a child, while two more children—and parents—bedded down inside. (Phil Hall)

promising a "New Look, New Ride, New Convenience."

A one-piece wraparound windshield with rounded corners replaced the old split-pane front glass. Side windows were longer, larger and vented. These were "picture windows," a far cry from the little panes that had restricted the view from all prior Microbuses.

To ease loading of cargo or people, a sliding door supplanted the original double swinging door layout. Measuring 41.7 inches wide, that side door moved outward from the body as it slid rearward along three integral tracks.

Optional sun roofs were now made of metal—a lot less lengthy than the fabric originals. Safety features included a deep-dish steering wheel, padded dashboard and visors, impact-absorbing outside mirror and rubber-covered knobs. Drivers got a new seat, fitted with vinyl upholstery. A new fresh air vent system ducted into both front and rear compartments of passenger models, drawing air through an ornamental intake under the wide-angle windshield. All seats contained seat belts.

Volkswagen's new double-jointed rear suspension helped ease the ride and tighten handling. The rear-axle setup used two joints on each halfshaft, one on each side of the transmission case and one at each wheel. Therefore, diagonal trailing links could keep both rear wheels nearly parallel at all times, providing what copywriters claimed was "exceptional roadability" that was virtually "sedan-like." A wider rear track also helped stability, and front axles were equipped with ball joints.

Load volume increased to 177 cubic feet. Station wagons got a 28-cubic-foot luggage compartment, via a top-hinged rear door. The spare wheel sat in a well on the left-hand side.

Volkswagen's "1600" station wagon engine displaced 1584 cubic centimeters and put out 57 horsepower. A four-horse improvement, to be sure, but accelerating to 60 mph still took a leisurely 37 seconds. A thermostatically-controlled pre-heater helped control intake air temperature. Engine compression increased from 7.5:1 to 7.7:1.

Engine air intakes went high up on the bodysides, near the rear ends, to reduce the possibility of road dust flowing inside. New "dashpots" controlled exhaust emissions, holding the throttle slightly open during deceleration.

Convenience helped make the wagons user-friendly. Integral slip-proof foot steps, for instance, were formed into the end of the wraparound front bumper. The fuel tank increased from 10.6 to 16 gallons, for a range greater than 300 miles at an average consumption of 23 mpg. Peak and cruising speed was exactly the same as before: a modest 65 mph.

Passenger models for 1968 included a $2,269 Kombi, a $2,499 station wagon—and for $2,765, a Campmobile.

One of many Campmobile accessories, the free-standing tent added a separate "room," which could be left behind at a campsite for day trips in the countryside. Luggage fit into the optional "pop-top." (Phil Hall)

Station wagons for 1969 came in seven- and nine-passenger models, with or without a sliding steel sun roof. (Phil Hall)

While some people actually lived in Volkswagen Campmobiles—as they had with the first generation—most were used for vacations and camping trips. By 1970, the Campmobile cost more than $3,000. (Phil Hall)

The redesigned Type 2 lineup also included a full selection of commercial vehicles.

Except for the usual price hikes and addition of insulation to the engine compartment to cut noise (and dust), the 1969 Transporters were little changed. An electric defogger was new. So was an anti-theft steering lock. New trigger releases replaced push buttons for the front door locks. Station wagons came in seven- or nine-passenger configuration, with a $22 price differential. Kombis began at $2,414, and

Ingenuity seemed to know no boundaries when it came to thinking of ways to use a Volkswagen van to best commercial advantage. The straight-up bodysides were great for advertising messages. (Volkswagen)

the Campmobile again topped the list at $2,850.

Volkswagen maintained that its second-generation bus was the best seller of its type in the United States. Of course, that wasn't exactly a profound revelation, because there weren't many competitive vans of any sort in the American market.

Evolutionary Change, Into the 1970s

Wagons got reinforced front end frames for 1970, plus a safety steering column that tilted away in a front end collision. Gearshift levers grew longer, and day/night mirrors were installed. Nylon velour now was used to carpet the wagon's rear luggage compartment. The Campmobile cost a hefty $3,077, though an entry-level Kombi listed for just $2,495.

Power brakes entered wagons and trucks the next year—with front discs, no less. A brake-force regulator helped prevent premature rear wheel lockup. Thicker rear brake lining and perforated wheel rims gave better antifade cooling. Engines added three horsepower, employing a new dual-port manifold. Prices took a big jump, ranging from $2,720 to $3,440.

They leaped higher yet in 1972, with the Campmobile commanding a whopping $3,838. Wagons earned a 25 percent healthy power boost, adopting the dual-carbureted, 1679-cc (102.5-cid) engine from the 411 series, rated at 74 (SAE gross) horsepower. That move cut 0-60 mph times down to a civilized 22 seconds. Transporters also got a blower to boost heat flow into the passenger compartment, plus larger rear brake cylinders and air outlets on inside front door panels.

Four passengers (plus the driver) fit into a 1971 Double-Cab pickup truck. The open rear deck offered 31.2 square feet of load space, and under-seat storage added 10.6 more cubic feet. Single-Cab pickups also were available. Both were rated to haul more than a ton. Options included stakes and tarpaulins. (Phil Hall)

Panel trucks had long been part of Volkswagen's commercial lineup. The 1972 Delivery Van got a stronger engine with dual carburetors. Payload was 2,325 pounds. (Volkswagen)

The new 1700-cc engine for 1972 delivered 25 percent more power than before, for quicker acceleration. Note the single exhaust pipe. (Phil Hall)

Campmobiles showed little change for 1972, but carried the more potent engine. Neatly-fitted counters, plus a refrigerator and sink, really turned the wagon into a mini "home on wheels," especially with the optional screened lift-up top. (Phil Hall)

Not all VW campers were officially "factory" built. Outside companies also supplied camper conversions for Volkswagen wagons. This one was marketed by Sportsmobile, of Andrews, Indiana. (Phil Hall)

In addition to fresh front-end styling, with stronger bumpers, 1973 station wagons could have an optional automatic transmission for the first time. Wagons again held seven or nine passengers—or 176 cubic feet of cargo. The steering gear was new, headrests were optional on all seats, and front brake pads grew thicker for longer life. (Volkswagen)

Though not quite as roomy as a motel room, a 1975 Campmobile offered plenty of comfortable sleeping space—a welcome sight after a day on the road. Bunks served as seats during the day. (Volkswagen)

Engine compression dropped to 7.3:1, in keeping with changes throughout the U.S. industry. Improved transmission mounts and an insulated cargo floor cut noise, CV-joints were strengthened and the gas tank filler moved 16 inches rearward. An electric blower improved interior heating, and reduced clutch diameter made shifting easier. Radial tires now were standard, and a transistorized brake warning light was installed.

Something practically shocking arrived for 1973: a three-speed automatic transmission, for $235 extra. No longer were wagon drivers obligated to shift for themselves. The new front end held stronger bumpers, and front amber safety lights moved to a higher position. Under the SAE net rating system, the wagon engine developed 63 horsepower. Inflation was running rampant, sending the Kombi to $3,500 and the Campmobile all the way to $4,449. A seven-passenger wagon stickered at $3,799, its nine-passenger mate at $3,850.

The dual-carbureted engine got a bigger bore for 1974, displacing 1795 cubic centimeters (109.5 cubic inches). That was good for 68 horsepower (up 2) at 4200 rpm, and a torque rating of 91 pound-feet at 3000 rpm (up 10). A bigger clutch was installed, and the sliding side door became easier to operate. Campmobiles adopted an "upstairs room" with a double bed, and could be ordered with

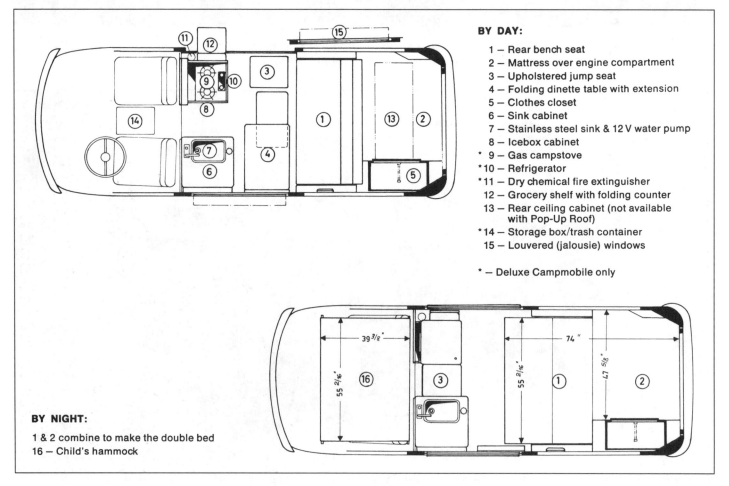

BY DAY:

1 – Rear bench seat
2 – Mattress over engine compartment
3 – Upholstered jump seat
4 – Folding dinette table with extension
5 – Clothes closet
6 – Sink cabinet
7 – Stainless steel sink & 12 V water pump
8 – Icebox cabinet
* 9 – Gas campstove
*10 – Refrigerator
*11 – Dry chemical fire extinguisher
12 – Grocery shelf with folding counter
13 – Rear ceiling cabinet (not available with Pop-Up Roof)
*14 – Storage box/trash container
15 – Louvered (jalousie) windows

* – Deluxe Campmobile only

BY NIGHT:

1 & 2 combine to make the double bed
16 – Child's hammock

Efficiency of layout was the watchword for VW Campmobiles. By day, the popular traveler carried five occupants in comfort. By night, it easily slept that same family group. (Volkswagen)

VW wagons served as spacious, easy-to-enter commuter cars, as well as practical family haulers. The 1976 model got a fuel-injected 2.0-liter engine, rated at 67 horsepower—but prices now started above $5,000. (Volkswagen)

an optional LP gas system. They also took another huge price leap, to $5,274—not exactly pocket change.

On July 9, 1975, Volkswagen built its four-millionth bus—affectionately referred to as "the box the Beetle came in." Marketers claimed—not without correctness—that VW had "launched the van craze in the U.S. and pioneered the mini-mobile home." More than 500,000 buses and 100,000 Campmobiles had come to the United States.

"It's a country home, a city bus and a family station wagon," said Volkswagen of mid-1970s Campmobiles. They offered "all the comforts of home, including the kitchen sink and a place to plug in the television." Campmobiles slept five with the optional pop-up top; even more with an extra-cost tent. Inside were "cabinets and closets galore, carpeting and curtains, louvered and screened windows, fold-out beds, swing-away dining table, food storage bin, icebox, sink and work counter." Deluxe models added a gas stove and electric refrigerator.

Transporters kept gaining potency. For 1976, they borrowed a 2.0-liter (1970-cc) engine from the Porsche 914, of all things. With electronic fuel injection, it made 67 horsepower and 101 pound-feet of torque (up from 90). That sent 0-60 mph acceleration time a hair below 20 seconds. A beefier clutch and exposed fuel filler cap were the only other changes, but the Campmobile now topped $6,100 and passenger wagons went for no less than $5,100. Buses earned an EPA mileage rating of 20/28

For its final season in this form, the 1979 Campmobile still attracted outdoors-oriented customers. (Volkswagen)

mpg. Options included the sliding steel sun roof, automatic transmission and air conditioning.

EPA mileage ratings dropped by 1978 to 18 mpg (city) and 25 mpg (highway) with manual shift—and a less-frugal 16/22 with automatic. Engines added hydraulic valve lifters, wagon bodies got two large sliding windows, and drivers faced a restyled steering wheel. The Transporter's second generation was drawing to a close—but Volkswagen wasn't ready just yet to dispense with its basic air-cooled, rear-engine layout.

Vanagons Arrive for 1980

If the second-generation Transporter lacked some of the charms of the original, the next era grew even more prosaic, albeit cleaner styled. As always, the Vanagons

The name and profile changed, but the 1980 Vanagon was similar to prior models under the skin. The new lineup consisted of four models, including the Camper. This deluxe edition had two full-size double beds (one in the pop-up top), plus a sink, stove, utility hookups, and screens for the sliding windows and hatch. Vanagons were roomier than the former buses, with rack-and-pinion steering and a revised driving position. (Phil Hall)

Vanagons looked more angular than their predecessors, but actually were more aerodynamic. A basic 1982 model started at $10,860. (Phil Hall)

have their modest legion of proponents; but on the whole, most Type 2 enthusiasts would just as soon stick with one of the earlier editions.

Volkswagen kept the rear-mounted flat engine, because it allowed more cargo space than other designs. Rear-engine traction also made the van more adept at climbing hills, and access to the rear compartment (from the front) was easy.

Though a bit longer and 3.3 inches wider, Vanagons otherwise were similar to their predecessors in dimensions. Wheelbase was 2.3 inches longer; front track a whopping 6.9 inches wider. Deeper, steeper windshields were one evident change. Side windows were larger, the back glass bigger yet, for a 22 percent increase overall. Vanagons got a front grille, though its utility was unclear. They also used rack-and-pinion steering, with a turning circle 4.9 feet smaller than the former vans.

Six models were produced, but only two came to the United States: the Vanagon (seven- or nine-passenger) and the Kombi (used as a base for Westfalia campers). At first, the sole engine was a 67-horsepower, fuel-injected 2.0-liter, with manual or automatic transmission. A new front suspension consisted of unequal length A-arms with variable rate coil springs. Vanagons stuck with the double-jointed rear end, but added variable rate coils. Volkswagen vowed that this was the safest van to date, and also the best handling. Vanagons weighed 3,290 pounds and cost nearly $10,000—a far cry from Transporters just a few years earlier.

Road & Track called it "the world's leading van." For a while, that designation made sense. Then, in 1984, Chrysler launched its earthshaking front-drive minivans—the Dodge Caravan and Plymouth Voyager—which began to push VWs far down in the pack.

Volkswagen also introduced a small front-drive pickup truck early in the Vanagon generation, to take the place of the Transporter-based pickups that had been offered all along.

New for 1980 was a Vanagon Camper, billed as a "fresh-from-the-drawing-board" replacement for the departed Campmobile. Retaining such features as the industry's first sliding side door, the new Camper also stuck with the proven, fuel-injected 2-liter engine. Four people fit comfortably inside the carpeted, curtained interior. The driver's seat swiveled 90 degrees, and the passenger seat turned all the way around, facing a stow-away swivel table. A second such table could go between the two front seats.

Deluxe Campers included a refrigerator that operated from liquid propane gas or electricity. A two-burner stove and sink were included, with a city water hookup. The back seat folded into a full-size double bed, while a pop-up top held another bed, with a zippered and screened window. With the top erected, a person could stand up inside.

A luggage rack fit over the driving compartment, food went into a pantry next to the stove, utensils fit under the sink, and clothes went into a mirrored wardrobe. In short, Campers promised space for just about everything needed for a day, a week or a month away from home.

The Camper's floor sat 2.4 inches lower than the prior Campmobile, and interior height was 2 inches greater. The rear hatch was 25 percent larger. Sliding side windows and the rear hatch opening were equipped with screens. For what amounted to a mini motorhome, the Vanagon Camper was frugal: rated 17 mpg in the city and 25 mpg on the highway by the EPA, with the four-speed manual transmission.

By 1982, the basic wagon stickered for $10,860, while the Camper brought $14,900. A total of 24,203 Vanagons were produced that year.

Vanagons Gain Liquid Cooling

Introduced as a 1983-1/2 model, the modified Vanagon "Waterboxer" (*Wasserboxer*) switched to a water-cooled engine—though still mounted at the rear. More powerful and economical than the air-cooled engine in prior Vanagons (and their predecessors), the new powerplant was again a horizontally-opposed "pancake" design. Employing multi-point fuel injection, it developed 82 horsepower at 4800 rpm, with 105 pound-feet of torque at 2600 rpm, using 8.6:1 compression. The water-cooled engine was standard in all three models: Vanagon L, GL and Camper.

The Vanagon was "the only vehicle in the U.S. to successfully bridge the gap between van and wagon," said Jim Fuller, vice-president of Volkswagen Division. Refer-

ring to the coming-soon Chrysler minivans, Fuller noted that competitors "still have to match the Vanagon's advanced 'Euro-Tech' design and its German fit and finish."

Maybe so, but sales figures over the next few years demonstrated that Volkswagen came nowhere close to the totals posted by the Dodge Caravan and Plymouth Voyager, first of the "garageable" domestic minivans.

The VW's water-cooled engine had 22 percent more horsepower than its air-cooled predecessor, and was 23 percent more economical on the highway, judged by EPA estimates. "Digi-Jet" fuel injection, redesigned combustion chambers and bigger valves contributed to the output increase.

The newest Vanagons had twin stacked grilles up front, the lower one serving as intake for the front-mounted radiator. Vanagons again had four-wheel independent suspension, rack-and-pinion steering and power front disc brakes. Forks and rods for the four-speed transmission were modified for easier shifting, and the final drive ratio was revised to match the engine's low- and mid-range torque characteristics. A new climate-control system included a standard rear-seat heater.

Installation of the water-cooled engine allowed Volkswagen to add a second heater under the back seat. Either a four-speed manual gearbox or three-speed automatic was available. Options included air conditioning and a sun roof. A diesel engine, introduced the previous year, also came in water-cooled form.

Volkswagen dubbed its 1983-1/2 Vanagon the "Waterboxer," because of its new water-cooled engine—still horizontally-opposed and rear-mounted. (Phil Hall)

Volkswagen's 1986-1/2 Vanagon GL Syncros were introduced to the press at Telluride, Colorado—high in the Rocky Mountains—along with the new Quantum Syncro wagon. These were the only permanent four-wheel-drive vans and wagons on sale in the United States.

A Wolfsburg Limited Edition option package became available during 1984, and much of that equipment became standard the next season. The Vanagon GL could get a "Weekender" option with a rear bench seat that turned into a double bed.

For 1986, Volkswagen introduced an automatic four-wheel-drive version of the Vanagon, called the Syncro. On smooth, dry pavement, 95 percent of power went to the rear wheels; but slippery surfaces sent the needed portion up front, until traction was restored.

Engines grew to 2.1-liter displacement and 95 horsepower in 1986. The Vanagon GL added a second sliding side door for 1987—first van in the U.S. market with that feature. A fancy Carat model joined in 1989, with color-coordinated bumpers and plush fittings.

Final Vanagons were considered to be the roomiest vans on the U.S. market, with 50 cubic feet of luggage space—even with all seats in position. Syncros became known for impressive traction. On the down side, some critics faulted the Vanagon's tall shape, which made it vulnerable to wind gusts. Not everyone favored the bus-like driving position with a non-tilt steering wheel, either—a stance that had seemed like fun in the Sixties, but perhaps more tedious in the Eighties. Most of the barbs, though, attacked the Vanagon's gross lack of power.

In mid-1989, Volkswagen introduced a Wolfsburg Limited Edition Vanagon GL.

Volkswagen launched the Eurovan (lower right) in 1992, as a 1993 model—the fourth generation of Volkswagen vans. Sales took off slowly as supplies were delayed. There was no '94 model at all. Not only was the engine liquid-cooled, it was mounted up front—heresy to traditional van fans.

Finally, Front-Drive: the EuroVan and Camper Today

For its fourth Transporter generation, Volkswagen finally abandoned the rear-engine configuration. An all-new EuroVan switched to front-wheel-drive and a five-cylinder powerplant.

Introduced at the Boston Auto Show late in 1991, Euro-Vans finally reached showrooms late in 1992, known as T4 (for fourth generation). These vans were intended as rivals to the Chevrolet Astro, Ford Aerostar and Toyota Previa, rather than to the ever-more-popular minivans from Chrysler Corporation.

The 2459-cc overhead-cam five-cylinder engine developed 109 horsepower, with Digifant fuel injection. Either a five-speed manual transmission or four-speed automatic could be installed. EuroVans displayed a far less boxy shape than prior VW vans. Torsion bars returned, but with a double-wishbone front suspension (not struts). Coil springs went at the rear, positioned by semi-trailing arms.

EuroVans used a new unitized space-cage frame. Power rack-and-pinion steering was standard, and anti-lock braking optional.

EuroVans rode on a 115-inch wheelbase, measuring 186.6 inches overall (vs. 180 for the Vanagon). They also weighed an extra 340 pounds. Three models debuted (CL, GL and MV), plus an optional "Weekender" package that included a pop-up roof with integral double bed, as well as window curtains and screens—in short, the most basic of campers. Prices started at $16,640.

No 1994 EuroVans entered the U.S. market, awaiting the arrival of a revised version with dual airbags. That one was delayed, so the 1995 season offered only a Camper, prepared with the assistance of Winnebago Industries. And only a handful of those hit the market. For 1996, Volkswagen still offered EuroVans only as the foundation for a Winnebago Camper, totally priced at $29,800. More civilized and refined than the old Transporters, EuroVans might be able to attract a new generation of customers— if basic versions finally become available.

Chapter 17

A Different Breed of VW

Noisy. Rambunctious. Boisterous. Bizarre. Joyful. Those are just a few of the words that might describe "The Thing," Volkswagen's 1970s descendant of the wartime Kübelwagen.

If they knew about it at all, most people would have assumed that the Kübelwagen had disappeared after its World War II service. The ungainly-but-useful military vehicle had no purpose in a civilian world, did it?

Not that it couldn't be fun. Writing in *Foreign Car Guide* for August 1962, Bill Haupt reported on a recent ride in a wartime military Volkswagen. "Its ability to climb steep snowbanks and out of 18 inches of mud or water was uncanny, particularly since it handled so well on good roads."

For guidance in deciding to promote such a machine, marketers might have simply looked at the military jeeps used by Allied forces, which were quickly transformed into a civilian version. For the next half-century, the rugged and reliable Jeep found an eager audience among the growing breed of off-road advocates.

Could Volkswagen executives have been pondering that success when they decided to issue a Type 181 in 1969? Perhaps not, since they skipped the U.S. market initially, releasing the curious vehicle elsewhere in the world in the early 1970s. In fact, Volkswagen indicated early on that it did not want—or expect—to bring the Type 181 to the United States. Production soon moved to Volkswagen's Mexican plant, still with the intention of selling the vehicle for its practical merits, elsewhere in the world.

Not until spring 1973 did the slab-sided machine finally find its way into American dealerships—and not because American VW dealers had been clamoring for it. Most of them trailed the pack in enthusiasm, preferring to concentrate on other Volkswagen products.

Meanwhile, in July 1971, *Motor Trend* had declared: "We liked the 181 as soon as we saw it but Volkswagen of America doesn't think we need it." The magazine suggested that similarly-inclined readers write letters to the company, insisting that the vehicle be made available north of the Mexican border.

Several "Things" competed in the 1972 Baja 1000 race, and one placed third in its class. Actor James Garner drove one to a second-in-class finish at the "Dam 500" off-road race.

Strictly Beetle-based, the Type 181 was billed as "another fun car from Volkswagen." Volkswagen of America itself coined the memorable name, "The Thing," which quickly fell into common usage among U.S. owners and observers. Among other distinctions, it was the first car to be imported from Mexico.

Described as "stark, rugged" in a 1974 press release, "The Thing" featured a fold-down windshield and detachable convertible top. The spare tire sat under the tall front hood, and off-roaders enjoyed a ground clearance slightly greater than eight inches—even when fully loaded. Unlike the Kübelwagen's rounded fenders, the Type 181 fenders were squared off.

Its 1584-cc, rear-mounted air-cooled engine, virtually lifted out of the Beetle sedan, developed 46 horsepower at 4200 rpm, using the SAE net rating system that became standard in 1972. The engine ran on 6.6:1 compression, to a four-speed manual transmission.

Wheelbase was 94.5 inches, the same as the Beetle. "The Thing" measured 148.8 inches long and 64.6 inches wide. Curb weight was just under a ton, and the fuel tank held 11.1 gallons.

Torsion bars borrowed from the Type 2 suspended each "Thing" at both ends. Tires were 165/14 size, on 5-1/2 inch rims. Drum brakes were installed.

Like the Kübelwagen of World War II, the Type 181 that debuted in the U.S. market for 1973 aimed at all-terrain action. Nicknamed "The Thing," the stark vehicle had a bare-bones look.

A gas heater was standard. Versatile? Well, not only could the windshield be folded down, but doors and side windows were removable. A folding convertible top was included, but a fiberglass hardtop also could be installed. Front occupants sat in bucket seats, while additional riders mounted the fold-down back seat.

Three vivid colors were offered in 1973: Pumpkin Orange, Sunshine Yellow and Blizzard White, each with a black convertible top and black leatherette interior.

If a plain old "Thing" just wouldn't do, Volkswagen offered a variant: the "Acapulco Thing," featuring a striped surrey top, striped seats and blue/white body paint. Quite a variety of extra equipment could be ordered by 1974, including a foam-padded steel roll cage, an outside-mounted spare tire (to increase trunk space), chrome wheels, trailer hitches (installed at the front and/or rear) and hitch-mounted power winches. Also available: a luggage rack, bumper overriders, sport horn set, foglights, front push bar, sports gearshift lever, tunnel console, steering wheel cover and—of all things—an air conditioner.

Volkswagen claimed a top speed of 71 mph, but safety advocates soon began to insist that "The Thing" wasn't so safe at velocities well below that. The vehicle was available in the United States for only two years, but sold in Mexico into 1978.

Fun wasn't the only function of this short-lived Volkswagen. "Our Thing does Your Thing," Volkswagen asserted in a brochure aimed partly at commercial applications. Potential users listed on the front page ranged from carpenters and delivery men to ranchers, news dealers, resort operators—and beachcombers. A likely prospect might be a "carpenter who likes to fish and hunt," one who

A rear-mounted 1584-cc engine, accessible via a hinged lid, powered "The Thing." Initial engines were rated at 46 horsepower, which was later increased to 55 bhp.

Typically used for fun in America, Type 181 vehicles also had commercial applications. Some were even used as police vehicles in Mexican towns. The 1973 models came in a choice of three colors. Windshields folded down, and doors and side windows could be removed.

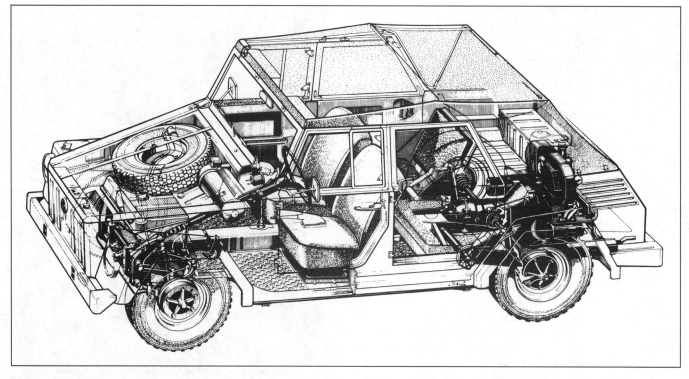

Cutaway of 1973 "The Thing" reveals front-mounted spare tire and typical Volkswagen air-cooled rear engine. A folding fabric top was standard. (Volkswagen)

A no-frills interior and dashboard greeted the "The Thing" driver. Note the lack of carpeting or insulation.

In addition to the standard "The Thing" (lower right), the 1974 VW lineup included an "Acapulco Thing" (lower left), with a striped surrey top, striped seats, and blue/white paint. (Volkswagen)

A fiberglass hardtop and luggage rack were available for the 1974 Type 181.

In 1974, its final season, "The Thing" could be ordered with a foam-padded steel roll cage and an external spare tire (to increase trunk space). Other extras included chrome wheels, front and rear trailer hitches, and hitch-mounted power winches. (Volkswagen)

could appreciate the virtues of a "vehicle that's rugged enough to take you where you want to go—even if that means leaving the road behind."

Though not a four-wheel-drive machine, it benefited from the Beetle's own brand of rear-drive traction, along with four-wheel independent suspension and high ground clearance. Only early models had a reduction gearbox, however, and true off-road capabilities couldn't approach those of a 4x4.

For off-road driving, the windshield folded forward and rested in retaining clips on the front hood. Clear plastic windows with vent flaps could be installed and removed easily. For real down-to-basics driving, all you needed to do was release a retaining spring, and lift the doors up and off their hinges.

Semi-gloss paint made scuffs and scratches less visible. The sloping hood was supposed to yield greater visibility, "a must when traveling the hills and dunes." A skid plate at the rear helped protect the engine from earthbound obstacles. All that and 21 mpg gas mileage (claimed, that is).

Hardly the most practical vehicle for everyday driving, "The Thing" found a small but hardy breed of customers who could appreciate its amusing and joyful qualities. Some liked its down-to-basics appearance. Others fell for the still-laudable merits of the familiar air-cooled, rear-engine powertrain. Top up or top down, "The Thing" slyly promised a memorable—even wild—experience behind the wheel, whether heading toward a Sun Coast beach or out into the midwestern woods.

Type 181 vehicles definitely had a utilitarian side, however. Some of them, in fact, saw service as police cars in Mexican towns in the 1970s. Typically painted bright orange, they might not have been able to keep pace with speeders and scofflaws, but they helped give the local *policía* a presence that was difficult to ignore.

Safety Advocates Take VW To Task

The Center for Auto Safety, a well-known watchdog group, presented its Second Annual Automotive Engineering Malpractice Award to Volkswagen of America. Center director Lowell Dodge and staff engineer Barney O'Meara singled out "The Thing." A VW employee accepted the "award."

Said Dodge: "The Center's criticism of 'The Thing' is not based on tests, but on common sense." He cited such distinctive hazards as fold-down windshield, removable doors and lack of shoulder harnesses, head restraints, roll bar and dashboard padding. "It is little more than the chassis of a regular Volkswagen Beetle," he insisted, "with a higher ground clearance...and heavier exterior sheet metal."

Earlier, Ralph Nader had urged the government to ban further importation and sale of "The Thing," because it did not comply with federal safety standards for passenger cars.

OWNER COMMENTS: Mike and Ann Fornataro

Mike Fornataro might not have owned too many Volkswagens in his life, but he started young. At the age of 8, he bought the remains of his grandfather's 1960 sun roof Beetle—basically, in a box—for $20. Being a bit too young to drive just yet, Mike "used it as a playhouse for years." It was "our version of a tree house."

That shouldn't be surprising, because Mike—who lives in Jacksontown, Ohio—came from a family with a fondness for special imported automobiles. His late father, a civil engineer, owned such seldom-seen vehicles as a Goggomobil, an Autobianchi and a Citroën DS-19. "I think he appreciated the engineering of them," Mike recalls today. The Autobianchi—a custom variant of the Fiat 500—is still in the family, and Mike wouldn't mind restoring it one day.

In 1978, Mike bought a 1969 Volkswagen. Before long, in a burst of "youthful enthusiasm," he "cut it up into a Baja Bug." While they were dating, his wife, Ann, owned a Super Beetle. Unfortunately, it was "rolled" one day, and the "body came off the frame." The car still ran, but "the whole body was cocked sideways."

Today, Ann drives a 1971 Karmann Ghia coupe. Mike—who writes an automotive column for *The Advocate* in Columbus—has a modified 1963 Beetle, which recently returned to the road with a new 1775-cc engine. He's also vice-president of the Central Ohio Vintage Volkswagen Club.

Chapter 18

On Dasher, On Rabbit: Away From Air-Cooled Engines

After nearly three decades on the market, the air-cooled rear engine didn't sound so tempting anymore. "Sooner or later," declared *Road & Track* in its February 1975 issue, "every good idea is likely to be surpassed by a new one, and so it is with the faithful old VW Beetle."

Already by that time, in fact, Volkswagen had a far different model on the American market: the front-wheel-drive (HORRORS!) Dasher, with a water-cooled engine no less. Soon afterward, for 1975, came the practical Rabbit and the sporty Scirocco.

Actually, Volkswagen had begun veering away from rear-mounted, air-cooled engines as early as 1971. In that year,

VW offered a variant of an Audi/NSU model with an inline four-cylinder engine. That occurred because VW had taken over NSU in 1969, just as it had obtained Audi earlier.

Dasher Flaunts Front-Drive

Who'd have believed it? After all those years of telling the world that a rear-mounted, air-cooled engine was the model of perfection, Volkswagen turned full circle. Not only did the Dasher look different from any prior VW, but it carried another breed of powertrain: a water-cooled, inline four-cylinder engine, atop a front-wheel-drive transaxle.

Introduced to the United States in 1974, the Dasher was VW's first water-cooled, front-engined model, with front-wheel-drive. This 1976 two-door hatchback sedan with folding rear seats got a larger engine with fuel injection. Interiors were restyled, with reclining front seats now standard. A console and heated rear-window defogger also became standard. (Phil Hall)

Styled by Giorgetto Giugiaro's Ital Design Studio at Turin, Italy, Dashers also came in station wagon form. Switching to front-drive and liquid cooling was quite a turnabout for Volkswagen, but the Dasher actually was based on an Audi model. (Phil Hall)

Essentially a variant of the Audi Fox, Dashers arrived in America for 1974, in two- and four-door hatchback sedan form or as a station wagon. The 1471-cc four-cylinder engine developed 75 horsepower. Seating up to five passengers, the four-door hatchback sold for $4,110, while the wagon brought $4,295.

Prices rose in 1975, ranging from $4,510 for the two-door hatchback to $4,875 for the wagon, with the four-door hatchback in between. Though Dashers changed little that year, in 1976 a larger (1588-cc) engine replaced the original unit. Not only did the '76 deliver gas mileage of 37 mpg highway and 24 mpg city, according to EPA es-

timates, but it could accelerate to 60 mph in 11.5 seconds (according to Volkswagen).

Reclining front seats and a center console now were standard. Metallic paint was optional, and bright trim highlighted the Dasher's wheel arches. The '76 grille had a different look, and open-up front vent windows became standard.

Mid-1977 brought a "Champagne Edition" of several Volkswagen models. Dasher's rendition was painted pale green metallic, with tinted glass and light green crushed velour fabric upholstery.

Quad round headlamps replaced the former single units on Dashers for 1978. Combined with a lowered grille and restyled hoodline, that gave the Dasher a fresh appearance, not unlike that of the new Audi 5000. Large amber wraparound safety lights were installed at front fender tips. A functional front spoiler was installed. Wraparound taillights went at the rear, above polyurethane-coated bumpers.

Trim was upgraded, and ride quality softened. Seats were upholstered in velour. Prices took their usual hike, from $5,975 for the two-door to $6,375 for a station wagon. Trunk openings were enlarged to extend down to the bumper. Dashers also got brake improvements. At this time, a Dasher could reach 60 mph in a claimed 12.2 seconds.

A diesel engine became available in 1979 Dashers. Little change was evident for 1980, and only diesel-engined Dashers were offered for the 1981 model year. That was the last outing for the Dasher, whose prices peaked at $7,970 for a two-door hatchback to a whopping $8,470 for the station wagon.

The Dasher wagon got new wheel covers and a restyled interior for 1977. Dashers had power front disc brakes, rack-and-pinion steering and radial tires. Options included air conditioning and a sliding steel sun roof.

Dasher showed a new front end for 1978, with a lower hood line and polyurethane-covered bumpers. Three body styles were available: four-door sedan (shown), two-door hatchback and four-door station wagon. Dashers could accelerate to 60 mph in 12.2 seconds, yet deliver 37 mpg on the highway. (Phil Hall)

By 1980, Dasher wagons could have a diesel engine. Unlike American diesels in the early 1980s, VW's version had a reasonably good reputation for reliability. (Phil Hall)

Second of VW's front-engine models—and far more important to the company's future—was the Rabbit, intended as a replacement for the departing Beetle. In 1976, its second season, the Rabbit gained a 1.6-liter overhead-cam engine, good enough for 0-60 mph times of 11.5 seconds. (1975 models had a 1.5-liter engine.) Rabbit hatchbacks came with two or four doors. (Phil Hall)

Rabbit Searches for Shoppers

Europeans got the Rabbit first, but under a different name: the Golf (a badge that would come to America much later). Design work had begun five years earlier. Finally, in June 1974, the press got its first look at that Golf, which was intended to replace the Beetle at Wolfsburg. (Beetle production would continue at other facilities.)

Volkswagen promoted the wide-opening doors and fold-away rear seat of its Rabbit, claiming it was virtually a mini station wagon. When converted for cargo-hauling, the Rabbit had 24.7 cubic feet of space. (Phil Hall)

Introduced for 1975—along with a sporty Scirocco coupe—Rabbits helped Volkswagen turn a corner in the U.S. market, even if they never achieved the popularity enjoyed by prior VW models. By 1978, Rabbits were being manufactured in the United States (see sidebar), though that venture wouldn't last through the 1980s. The Rabbit led to Golf and Jetta models of the 1980s, marketed along with a Rabbit-based Cabriolet (one of the few convertibles to survive in the U.S. marketplace). Diesel engines also would become part of the picture.

"Unlike the Beetle it replaces," wrote John Lamm in *Motor Trend* as the Rabbit debuted, "you laugh with it, not at it." At the same time, Lamm noted that "the Beetle is going to be one of the all-time tough acts to follow." Could the Rabbit, he asked, come up with its own version of the Beetle's "charm, its 'ugliness' to the point of 'beauty', its owners' right to be different," or its "anti-establishment" personality?

Even though front-drive, front-engine minicars had become popular in Europe, they were still new to the U.S. market. Rabbit was among the first to reach America in respectable quantities. Unlike Fiat and Honda in the mid-1970s, Volkswagen had an extra-strong dealer network to help move its new machines.

Giorgetto Giugiaro, the noted Italian stylist, lent his pen to the shaping of the Rabbit. Those shapes were tested in wind tunnels, not only to keep interior noise at respectable levels, but to reduce fuel consumption—no small matter at a time when the OPEC oil embargo and long lines at the gas pumps were highly recent history.

Workers complete installation of Rabbit engine accessories, at the Wolfsburg factory. The engine was then bolted to the transmission and other front-drive components, and installed in the car as a unit. (Volkswagen)

Inspectors run a final check of Rabbits on the Wolfsburg assembly line. (Volkswagen)

● VW Blazes Trail for Passive Restraints ●

A new passive seatbelt system underwent testing in Beetles in 1973. One end of the belt was anchored to the door, the other fastened to an inertia-reel retractor. A similar system, but with three-point belts, was employed in General Motors vehicles much later, in the 1980s. (Phil Hall)

Rabbits served as test beds for another phase of VW's passive restraint system. Over a 30-month period, some 65,000 Rabbits had been equipped with the setup, and not one suffered a fatality or life-threatening injury.

Long before airbags and other passive restraints entered the automotive lexicon, Volkswagen engineers were busy testing such safety features in the real world. Late in 1973, VW began a year-long highway test of 50 Beetles equipped with a new automatic seat belt system. Its goal: to find a way to eliminate the annoying ignition interlock systems that had been installed on all U.S. vehicles, and to find an "effective alternative" to the airbag that had been proposed.

No buckling-up was needed. One end of the belt was fastened to the rear edge of the door, the other to an inertia-reel retractor device behind and between the bucket seats. The occupant simply opened the door, sat on the bucket seat and shut the door. As the door opened, it pulled the belt from its retractor and provided access to the interior. When the door closed, the retractor automatically took up belt slack and adjusted it to normal wearing position, adjusting to the occupant's size. Any sudden deceleration immediately locked up the belt.

A foam padded knee bar took the place of a lap belt, to prevent sliding forward under the dashboard during an accident. The engine would not start until belts were properly connected, but emergency releases at the upper end of the belt provided quick-disconnect, if necessary.

Early in 1975, another passive restraint test began, starting with 200 Rabbits but escalating to a much larger fleet. After 18 months, 39 accidents had occurred—12 of them major—but only one severe injury. After 30 months, no fatalities or life-threatening injuries had been suffered in the 65,000 passive-equipped Rabbits. No other car had such a system, though thousands of experimental airbags had been installed in GM vehicles in the mid-1970s.

Two body styles went on sale: two-door and four-door, both with lift-up hatchbacks at the rear. Rabbits were unibodied, welded to a platform chassis. *Motor Trend* noted that all the Rabbits they drove were "as solid as any Beetle, even when two wheels were deliberately dropped off the pavement and into the rough."

Rabbits used the same engine as the Dasher: a 1471-cc (89.7 cubic-inch) overhead-cam four-cylinder, with a cast-iron block and aluminum cylinder head. Breathing through a Zenith two-barrel carburetor, with 8.2:1 compression, the engine developed 70 horsepower at 5800 rpm. Torque output came to 81 pound-feet at 3500 rpm. Unlike the longitudinal layout under Dasher hoods, the Rabbit's powerplant was mounted transversely. The compact engine fit into a roomy compartment, allowing plenty of working space.

A catalytic converter was used to control exhaust emissions. Rabbits came with either a four-speed manual gearbox, or three-speed automatic transmission.

The Rabbit's suspension consisted of MacPherson struts up front, with asymmetrical lower control arms. No stabilizer bar was installed. At the rear, Volkswagen installed a "Connected Trailing Arm Rear Axle." *Motor Trend* described it as a "combination axle, torsion bar and stabilizer bar," consisting of a T-shaped bar, with a tubular trailing arm welded to each end. "When one rear wheel hits a bump, the axle twists to absorb the wheel movement, but without really affecting the opposite wheel." It offered the benefits of a rigid axle (unchanging track width), and also those of an independent suspension (low unsprung weight).

Americans did not know what Volkswagen's next model would be called, until the Environmental Protection Agency spilled the beans, including the new name in its 1975 fuel-economy listings. Marketers hoped the Rabbit badge would help give the hatchbacks a cuddly image, comparable to that of the Beetle. The car's EPA rating with manual shift was 39 mpg highway and 25 mpg city. (Phil Hall)

Steering was rack-and-pinion type. Initial Rabbits had all-drum brakes, but by 1976 front discs were standard.

Rabbits earned an EPA mileage rating of 38 mpg on the highway, or 24 mpg around town. Only the Datsun B-210 got a higher rating. A Rabbit could accelerate to 60 mph in a reasonably brisk 11.8 seconds—not so bad in 1975, when economy had shoved performance aside as a driving force.

After producing a million Rabbits in 1975-76, Volkswagen switched to fuel injection, boosting horsepower by 10 percent. New equipment included front headrests and headlight flashers.

Hatchback versatility was a selling point in 1977, for the Rabbit and other imported models.

Apart from excess engine noise, *Motor Trend* found few flaws with the early Rabbit. Ride quality was deemed "more than reasonable for a car of such size and weight," and the Rabbit was declared fun to drive—not unlike the Beetle. Steering was considered sufficiently light for ordinary driving, yet precise.

"Try and maintain a Rabbit's pace with a Beetle," *Motor Trend* warned, "and you scare yourself silly."

Dashboards contained rocker switches and warning lights, earning plaudits for easy instrument reading and convenient controls. *Motor Trend* described the seats as comfortably firm "with good lower back support, but with-out being thin and hard as in many smaller cars." Back seats had enough space for adults.

Doyle Dane Bernbach, VW's advertising agency, took partial credit for the "Rabbit" name. "Volkswagen of America wanted a name," the announcement read, "that would combine practicality with the whimsical tone that Beetle or Bug conveys. The furry, but productive rabbit was selected as one which would stand out in a field of powerful and sometimes vicious automotive animals." Already, of course, the field was cluttered with Cougars, Mustangs, Rebels, Tigers and other assertive creatures.

Before the company had a chance to announce the car's name officially, the Environmental Protection Agency let the cat (or rabbit) out of the bag, including the new name with its list of fuel-economy estimates for 1975.

More than the Dasher that appeared a year earlier, the Rabbit was viewed from the start as the Beetle's true successor. Five models went on sale, priced from $3,330 to $4,030 (for a DeLuxe four-door).

Why the switch to front-drive, with a transverse-mounted front engine? What had been a model of efficiency, Volkswagen engineers suggested, was no longer up-to-date. Not since a host of other makes had produced small cars with the front-engine, front-drive layout—from the British-built Mini to Fiats, Simcas, Hondas and Datsuns.

Rabbits went on sale in January 1975. When that year ended, the new model showed the best "first year" ever for an import. More than 100,000 were sold in all (98,215 through December).

After one year with the 1471-cc engine, the Rabbit adopted a larger (1588-cc) four with a bigger bore. This new overhead-cam engine developed 71 horsepower and 82 pound-feet of torque (each figure up by one). Volkswagen claimed a 0-60 mph acceleration time of 11.5 seconds.

Numerous "extra-cost" items became standard, and Rabbits could turn in a tighter circle, helped by easier steering. An electric rear defogger was installed. Models with automatic transmissions had a device that told when to replace front disc brake pads (the pedal vibrated noticeably). Front seats were redesigned for greater seatback adjustment, and rear knee room was increased.

Fuel injection went into all 1977 models, and the standard-equipment list grew. Horsepower got a boost, from 71 to 78. Deluxe Rabbits added open-up vent windows and adjustable headrests.

Introduced at the Detroit auto show, a diesel engine became available during 1977, striving to satisfy customers who craved the utmost in economy during this era of fuel worries. The 1973-74 OPEC oil embargo and its resultant gas shortages remained vivid in motorists' memories. Another crisis was looming, to be felt later in the decade. The diesel earned an EPA rating of 52 mpg city/39 mpg highway, sure to please the most frugal owners.

To mark the sale of the millionth Rabbit in 1977, Volkswagen released a "Champagne Edition." Marketed in limited quantity, "champagne" Rabbits had special metallic paint (silvery green or light gold), side striping and wider (175/70SR13) tires. They were upholstered with crushed velour.

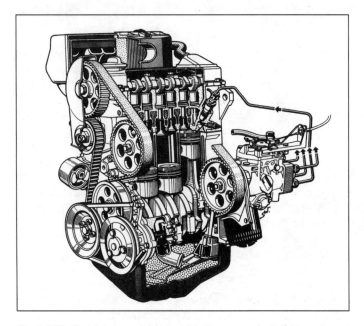

By 1977, Rabbits could have Volkswagen's 1.5-liter diesel engine. (Phil Hall)

Rabbits were even more economical in 1978: 25/38 mpg with a manual shift gas engine, or 40/53 mpg for the diesel. In addition to the basic models, a Rabbit "C" had custom features, while an "L" had a deluxe interior and styling touches.

A smaller (1457-cc) engine went into 1978 Rabbits, cooled by a bigger radiator. Starting this year, Rabbits also were produced in America. German-built Rabbits kept their round headlights, while those that hailed from Pennsylvania switched to rectangular lamps.

Volkswagen still had a Bonds-for-Babies program, extended to the Rabbits. More than 330 children had been born in VWs between 1964 and 1979 (74 in California alone). This was one of many ways in which Volkswagen attempted to extend the Beetle's legacy to encompass the Rabbit—an effort that was largely doomed to failure. For many a devotee, air cooling was—and still is—the only way to travel.

VW Gets Sporty: The Scirocco

Named after a hot wind that blows off the desert across the Mediterranean Sea, Scirocco was the first of the 1975 models to be unveiled. Serving nominally as a replacement for the extinct Karmann Ghia, the Scirocco instead sent Volkswagen scurrying in a new direction. In essence a sporty version of the basic Rabbit sedan, this was VW's first all-out sport coupe, handling like no prior model and attracting a totally new breed of customer.

As Paul Frére explained in *Road & Track*, in June 1974, the Dasher had been "no more than an Audi Fox with a different rear treatment...the essential move of a crash program...to get the company out of the red figures." Scirocco was to be the first of an all-new line.

Scirocco's lines were "quite outstandingly elegant," with a wedge-shaped nose that, in Frére's opinion, ranked as "a masterpiece of the styling art." He test drove the car in Europe, prior to U.S. sale, calling it "an almost perfect combination of a shopping car and a lively, sporting GT."

Front wheels, said *Road & Track*, were "driven by unequal-length hollow shafts with constant-velocity joints at each end. The two shafts are of different diameter so that despite their different length they will be twisted by equal angles when the driving torque is applied." The rear suspension was called "both very simple and very clever," featuring rear trailing arms joined by an L-shaped welded crossmember.

Sciroccos were produced not at Wolfsburg, but at the Karmann factory (where bodies also were built). Frére described performance of the top European version as "extremely lively," but "very safe to handle."

Styled by Giugiaro's Ital Design studio in Turin, Italy, Sciroccos were tested in wind tunnels. Golf/Rabbit chassis were shipped to the Karmann factory at Osnabrück (where Porsche 914s were assembled), to get a four-seat Scirocco body.

Except for 175/70SR13 tires on alloy wheels, the Scirocco's chassis was identical to the Rabbit's. Because of its lower center of gravity, the coupe delivered handling matched

Rabbits even saw service as taxis. The Yellow Cab Company in Lexington, Kentucky, had a fleet of 11 Rabbits. The company estimated it would save $135,000 per year by converting its 39-car fleet to smaller, more fuel-efficient vehicles. (Phil Hall)

Yes, that's a Rabbit—circa 1978—engaged in police duty. (Volkswagen)

by few cars in its class. "For once," *Motor Trend* proclaimed, "the Scirocco performs in character with its looks."

In the U.S. market, which received premium versions of the cars sold elsewhere in the world, all three models—Dasher, Rabbit, Scirocco—used the same overhead-cam engine. Otherwise, they differed considerably. In the Dasher, the four-cylinder engine occupied a longitudinal position. Rabbit and Scirocco engines were transverse-mounted. Dasher rear suspensions incorporated a beam axle, whereas the Rabbit and Scirocco employed independent suspension all around. The Rabbit and Scirocco also were considerably smaller than a Dasher.

Compared to a Karmann Ghia, the new Scirocco was quicker, smaller and lighter in weight. It was also more spacious inside, and consumed less fuel. The 2+2 hatchback body looked the part of a sport-performance machine and, unlike the Karmann Ghia, delivered action to match. *Road & Track* considered the Scirocco to be VW's entry in a new class: a "stylish GT car...that appears to be perfectly suited for our time."

To attract the sporty crowd, Volkswagen issued the Sciroc-co 2+2 coupe. For 1976, its engine grew from 1.5 to 1.6 liters, for greater performance at low rpm. New seats had adjustable height and backrests. Sciroccos could accelerate to 60 mph in 11 seconds, yet earned a 39 mpg EPA highway gas-mileage rating. (Phil Hall)

Scirocco had a "pronounced wedge shape, the appearance of a long hood...and a commendable amount of space inside for a car that's fully 10 inches shorter than the Karmann Ghia." Despite new U.S. regulations, the American version got the same bumpers as Europeans; their hydraulic impact cylinders increased length by only 3.5 inches. Deep cargo space was hidden by a hinged partition. Rear space was on the tight side, especially limited in headroom, thus adequate, according to *Road & Track*, "only for small children."

Initial models started at $4,450 (though the price rose quickly) and weighed 1,930 pounds at the curb. Wheelbase was 94.5 inches (identical to the Beetle), and a Scirocco measured 155.7 inches long and 51.5 inches high. The 1471-cc engine developed 70 horsepower at a high-revving 6000 rpm, and 81 pound-feet of torque at 3500 rpm. A Zenith two-barrel carburetor was used, and 91 octane no-lead fuel was required.

A four-speed manual transmission was standard. So were front disc brakes. MacPherson struts with lower A-arms and coil springs made up the front suspension, while the rear used trailing arms, coil springs and an anti-roll bar. Rack-and-pinion steering was installed.

Scirocco's slogan read: "German sportscar, Italian style." The dashboard was stock Rabbit, with a tachometer replacing the clock and a pair of extra gauges popped into the console. A sport steering wheel was installed. Tartan plaid inserts occupied the reclining bucket seats. Options included air conditioning and an automatic transmission—mounted transversely, an industry "first."

In the hands of *Road & Track* test drivers, the Scirocco accelerated to 60 mph in 12.7 seconds, ran through the quarter-mile in 19.4 and could reach 102 mph. Normal driving yielded gas mileage of 29.5 mpg.

Road & Track noted "no particular problems with controls," adding that "an enthusiastic driver can even indulge in good old-fashioned throttle-blipping while downshifting with ease because the brake and accelerator pedals are placed just right for it." Highest marks went to the car's

Fuel injection went into the 1977 Scirocco, boosting horsepower by 10 percent. The 2+2 coupe featured a redesigned front spoiler and restyled sports steering wheel.

Volkswagen offered a Limited-Edition Scirocco in 1979, with a five-speed transmission, racing-style bucket seats, front air dam and special black or white paint. Its steel-belted radial tires had raised white lettering. (Phil Hall)

performance, ride and handling. Scirocco was nothing less than "state of the art in 1975 and will surely set standards for others to meet over the next few years." Although the Dasher had exhibited "lively acceleration with remarkable fuel economy," it had been noisy. The Scirocco scored better all around.

The Scirocco's suspension also achieved "what might have been considered impossible a few years ago: a very good ride in a car weighing less than a ton. Over a variety of road surfaces we found the Scirocco impressively competent and well controlled." *Road & Track* test drivers noted that there was "no waste, not an ounce of fat on it; and yet it's exciting to look at, delightful to drive and technically fascinating."

Evidently, VW had another winner on its hands. Or did it? Management certainly hoped so, as Volkswagen was losing money far too fast for comfort.

After one year with 1471-cc, the Scirocco adopted a larger (1588-cc) four, delivering greater torque at low revs. Sciroccos got a smaller turning circle and a more positive reverse-gear lockout. Sciroccos had a single wiper at the center, whose intermittent mode swept about every seven seconds.

Volkswagen claimed a 103 mph top speed (100 mph with automatic). The Scirocco's 11-second 0-60 mph time wasn't so much swifter than a Rabbit's, but the coupe excelled in handling. Its rear axle consisted of a transverse T-bar with attached trailing arms. When one wheel hit a bump, the T-bar twisted, resisting further individual wheel movement.

In July 1976, a Super Scirocco debuted, with a 78-horsepower fuel-injected engine (7 more horses than stock). This one got such extras as front vent windows, rear wiper/washer, brown metallic paint with gold lettering.

Sciroccos got a sleeker front end for 1978, along with restyled trim, a woodgrain dashboard, remote mirror and improved sound insulation. A smaller (1457-cc) engine was installed, but the 1588-cc four returned by 1979.

The 1979 model added a bright molding surrounding the grille. By then, either a four- or five-speed manual gearbox was available. Scirocco's price edged past the $7,000 mark. Spring's Limited-Edition included a five-speed, large air dam and race-type seats.

Sciroccos remained on sale in the United States through most of the 1980s (see Chapter 19). By 1980, Europeans could get a turbo Scirocco, but that wasn't ready for America.

For 1978, the Scirocco coupe gained a sleeker front end, but dropped—temporarily—to a smaller engine.

Volkswagen—Built in the U.S.A.

Volkswagen's first attempted foray into U.S. manufacturing, in the 1950s, had failed. A Studebaker-Packard plant in New Jersey had been purchased, but production costs would have been too high. Heinz Nordhoff wound up selling that plant—reportedly for a million-dollar profit.

The value of producing cars in their strongest market lingered in the minds of Volkswagenwerk executives. Finally, in September 1976, VW inked an agreement to set up shop in Pennsylvania. The company invested more than $300 million in the Westmoreland facility, near Pittsburgh, with the capacity of turning out 200,000 Rabbits yearly. So, Volkswagen became the first "transplant" operation—an import make producing some of its automobiles right in America. Not until well into the Eighties would other automakers make such a foray, led by the Japanese brands.

First president of Volkswagen Manufacturing Corporation of America was James McLernon (formerly manufacturing manager at General Motors). About half of the Rabbit's content came from domestic suppliers. Later on, a VW metal stamping plant went online in South Charleston, West Virginia.

Volkswagen stuck with the Westmoreland facility until July 1988, continuing production of Golfs (and some Jettas) after the Rabbit was discontinued.

OWNER COMMENTS: René Rondeau

"Like many baby boomers," says René Rondeau of Corte Madera, California, "I grew up with Volkswagens. My dad was seduced by the classic DDB ads...and one day he drove home a shiny, almost new 1962. It was love at first sight, for him and for me."

Rondeau learned to drive in that '62, which tends to "put VWs into your blood." Having read *Small World* magazine, he wanted a bug of his own—preferably a pre-1952 split window.

Finally, one snowy night in 1966, he found one: a 1950, original except for paint, solid and dent-free, complete with original owner's manual. It even had the cylindrical bolsters, serving as back seat armrests. Just before delivery, the engine "blew." So, Rondeau dickered the price down to $85. He had the car painted Bordeaux Red, matching the dashboard. NOS grooved bumpers were obtained through the local dealer, who sent to Germany for NOS semaphores.

"When I first got the car no one paid a second glance to it," Rondeau recalls. "There were zillions of bugs on the road and this just looked like an old jalopy. But, with new bumpers and fresh paint the transformation was miraculous.... Lack of window trim and the low, thin bumpers made it stand out in a sea of newer VWs."

Rondeau drove that '50 through the end of senior high school. His "friends thought I was nuts," but "I thought it was the coolest car on earth."

Not that mishaps didn't occur. On a date with his girlfriend, the metal bar that held the roller gas pedal split in half. Rondeau fixed it with wire, tying one end to the pedal and holding the other in his hand—pressing the wire with his foot to nudge the VW home. "So much for romance," he reminisces today.

A letter to Wolfsburg brought the news that Rondeau's car was one of the "minuscule few" sold to Hoffman Motors in New York, "an official export."

While Rondeau was in Europe for his junior year of college, the '50 went up on blocks, in a barn. When he moved west after graduation (in a 1966 bug), the '50 stayed behind. "Mice moved in," he recalls; "kids played on top of it." In the end, "it was a pretty sad looking vehicle." Eventually, it was sold to a Pennsylvania collector. Today, Rondeau has a '57 oval-window, painted the same color as that old '50, with euro bumpers.

Rondeau's recollections of that 1950 VW appeared in an issue of the VVWCA newsletter, under the title "Split Window Memories."

Chapter 19

Into the Eighties and Beyond

With the demise of the Beetle, Volkswagen turned into a different breed of auto company. Obviously, it needed another automobile that could firmly capture the public fancy. As things turned out, however, that homely-but-loved Type 1 was too tough of an act to follow.

As one model after another—Rabbit to Jetta to Golf and beyond—failed to produce sufficiently strong sales in the United States, Volkswagen's management began to distance itself from Beetle history. After a time, they almost appeared to deny that the Beetle had ever happened.

Instead, VW concentrated wholly on its current models—even if those sold in modest to minuscule quantities, compared to their illustrious predecessor. Promotional efforts had to focus solely on the present, executives believed, if VW were to remain a going—and growing—concern.

Globally, Volkswagen remained a dominant force. But in the United States, the German company suffered slippage from which it couldn't seem to recover.

Not that sales of the Rabbit and its Golf and Jetta offshoots weren't respectable. Those models kept Volkswagen alive in the U.S. market. Most VW owners of the 1980s and early '90s were pleased with their purchases. Still, those models couldn't begin to approach the affection with which the hard-to-ignore Beetles had been greeted.

Beetles continued to sell well in Latin America, prompting some former owners to long for a chance to buy one. In a curious aside, several years after the extinction of the Super Beetle, the Peoples Car Company in California tried to import Beetles from Mexico. They sold about 1,500 in 1983-84, modified to meet federal requirements. As EPA regulations tightened further, however, that venture proved to be unprofitable and expired.

Continued: Rabbit and Scirocco

Rabbits had a few more seasons to go before giving way to a Golf successor, which would carry Volkswagen into the late 1980s and '90s. VW's sporty Scirocco coupe was destined to last through the 1980s decade.

Not only did 1980 bring a brand-new Rabbit convertible (see Chapter 20), but Volkswagen launched a Rabbit-based pickup truck. VW had been pondering the tempting mini-truck market for quite a while and finally decided to take the plunge, developing a rival to the increasingly popular Japanese-built trucks. Unlike most small pickups, it was front-wheel drive. Essentially, the pickup was a Rabbit sedan with its roof snipped off, to the rear of the front seats. Its standard fuel-injected 1588-cc (97-cid) four-cylinder engine developed 78 horsepower. An optional 1471-cc (89-cid) diesel also became available, rated at 48 horsepower.

Meanwhile, the 1980 Rabbit hatchbacks reverted to a standard carbureted version of the 1471-cc gasoline engine, making 62 horsepower. A fuel-injected 76-horsepower, 1588-cc engine was optional. So was the 1471-cc diesel powerplant.

Starting in 1979, all Rabbits were produced in Pennsylvania, thus qualifying as domestic models. For the 1980 model year, Volkswagen produced 223,261 Rabbits vs. 132,822 in 1979, for a 3.16 percent share of the market.

Growing competition in the front-drive hatchback field compelled Volkswagen to face-lift its Rabbit for 1981, installing a fresh front end—akin to that on the Scirocco

Volkswagen also released a series of small pickup trucks in the early 1980s, based on the Rabbit. (Phil Hall)

These folks were appropriately dressed, to step into the "Black Tie" special-edition Rabbit that VW issued in 1982.

coupe. Front bumpers grew thicker, with wraparound parking/side marker lights. Both the gasoline and diesel engine grew in size, to 1.7 liters (105 cid) and 1.6 liters (97 cid), respectively.

Though road testers continued to praise the Rabbit's assembly quality, interior space and visibility, some—including *Consumer Guide*—complained that American-made Rabbits didn't handle as well as the prior German-built models. *Consumer Guide* also faulted the car's price, considered too high to be a good value against various domestically-produced subcompact rivals. In fact, Rabbit sales fell by almost 50 percent in the 1982 model year. By then, too, earlier VW Rabbit engines had begun to establish a less-than-enviable reputation for excessive oil consumption and leakage, as well as premature valvetrain wear.

Though far better than American-produced diesel engines of the period, VW's "oil-burner" was deemed noisy at idle and low speed. Even so, its fuel economy proved to be phenomenal. Some road testers even were able to beat the 41 mpg EPA estimate for city driving, though performance was not exactly a "plus."

Rabbit fans had a sporty version in the early 1980s. This 1983 GTI hatchback carried an enlarged (1.8-liter) version of the Rabbit's fuel-injected 1.7-liter four. A close-ratio five-speed manual gearbox was standard. So were a tuned exhaust system, special instruments, and flared wheel wells.

At the Westmoreland plant in Pennsylvania, Rabbits neared completion (top), then went through final inspection. About 2,500 employees turned out 470 cars each day. (Volkswagen)

Rabbits of the early 1980s could have either a four- or five-speed manual gearbox, or a three-speed automatic transmission. Two- and four-door hatchback bodies were available. Costlier LS editions added such extras as open-up front vent windows, dual remote mirrors, full wheel covers, intermittent wipers and a woodgrain instrument panel applique. Sticker prices in 1982 ranged from a modest $5,990 for a base two-door hatchback to $7,305 for the top S edition, which featured red accent striping, black body moldings, a sport steering wheel and full instrumentation including a tachometer.

Worldwide, Volkswagen produced 974,140 passenger cars in 1982. In addition to the domestically-built Rabbits, a total of 67,350 imported Volkswagens were sold in the United States that year, rising to 77,009 in 1983 and an impressive 103,479 in '84.

Rabbit buyers got another choice for 1983: a sporty new GTI two-door hatchback, containing an enlarged (1.8-liter) high-output version of VW's fuel-injected 1.7-liter four-cylinder engine, making 90 horsepower. Meanwhile, the 1.7-liter engine was now standard in LS/GL models, while the budget-priced Rabbit L stuck with a carburetor.

List-priced at $7,990 ($500 more than a Rabbit GL and $1,575 higher than the cheapest model), the GTI included a close-ratio five-speed manual gearbox, as well as front/rear stabilizer bars, a flexible urethane front air dam, black body trim and flared wheel wells. Wider (six-inch) alloy wheels held Pirelli P6 performance tires. A sport-style steering wheel and front seats, full instruments and a tuned exhaust system and suspension rounded out the GTI equipment list.

Along with the new turbodiesel option for Jettas and Quantums (see below), the GTI provided what James R. Fuller, Volkswagen of America's vice-president, believed "car buyers are looking for: quality construction, straight-line and cornering performance and VW's traditional economy.... Behind the wheel of the GTI, one can experience potent, G-generating performance not found in any other comparable priced car." Volkswagen claimed a 0-60 mph acceleration time of 9.7 seconds, and a top speed of 108 mph. Soon dubbed "pocket rockets" and "nickel missiles" by enthusiasts, GTIs helped spawn a whole new genre of small, high-performance hatchbacks.

Initial GTIs came with black, red, white or silver metallic

In mid-season of 1984, shortly before the model faded away, Volkswagen issued a Wolfsburg limited-edition Rabbit L. (Phil Hall)

paint, and cordovan or midnight blue (special-ordered) interiors. No automatic transmission was available. Through the 1980s, the GTI gave Rabbit buyers the option of a little extra zest—not quite a Scirocco, but with some of that coupe's hearty personality.

Volkswagen claimed to have made 1,300 changes to the 1983 Rabbits, the most significant affecting the car's seating and suspension. All models got a retuned suspension with stiffer spring rates and revised shock valving, for a tauter, more controlled ride. This year's GL was promoted as "the most luxurious and fully-equipped Rabbit ever offered," with such features as power steering, wider

Starting in 1982, Scirocco coupes wore an all-new, more rounded body—intended to reduce air drag. Increased length added space to the rear-passenger area and luggage compartment. (Phil Hall)

wheels and a rear wiper/washer. The low-priced base model was deleted, signaling a more upscale emphasis.

Rabbits could again have a 1.6-liter diesel four—or even a new turbocharged diesel. Rabbits continued to be made in the United States, whereas Jettas and other models hailed from Germany.

Scirocco in the 1980s

VW's sporty coupe entered the Eighties with a standard 1588-cc four-cylinder engine and four-speed manual gearshift. A five-speed and an automatic transmission were available at extra cost. Europeans could get a turbocharged Scirocco by this time, but Americans could only fantasize about that possibility.

Scirocco engines grew to 1.7 liters (105 cid) for 1981, but horsepower rose only slightly—to 76 bhp at 5500 rpm. Road testers still liked the Scirocco's sporty personality. This was a car that "loves to be driven hard," said *Consumer Guide*, "and responds well in tight cornering." Furthermore, its "gutsy, free-revving engine and lightweight design equal[ed] fine acceleration with excellent fuel economy." The ride was described as "fairly jiggly," but "not jarring except on severe bumps." One notable flaw was price. "Like all VWs," *Consumer Guide* reported, Scirocco had been "pushed out of its natural price class by inflation."

Mechanical details of its Rabbit-based chassis changed little, but the sporty Scirocco coupe wore an all-new Karmann-built body for 1982—roomier inside and more rounded outside, to reduce air drag. Wheelbase and width remained the same, but the car grew 6.5 inches in overall length, which added space to the rear seat area and luggage compartment. An expanded window area included a deeper back window, which curved downward to reach the hatchback door. Weight rose by close to 100 pounds, due to the addition of more sound insulation. A small under-the-bumper lip spoiler was installed at the front end, and the rear also held a spoiler.

List-priced at $10,150, all 1982 Sciroccos had power brakes, an electric rear defroster, tinted glass, a remote driver's mirror, AM/FM stereo radio with cassette player, reclining front bucket seats (with height adjustment) and a four-spoke sport steering wheel. A GL option package included power windows and mirrors, and a powered antenna. The standard 1.7-liter (105-cid) fuel-injected engine developed 74 horsepower and 90 pound-feet of torque. Scirocco's sole options were power windows and steering, cruise control and air conditioning.

Late in the 1983 model year, Sciroccos switched to a 1786-cc (109-cid) enlargement of the overhead-cam four-cylinder engine. That one made 90 horsepower at 5500 rpm, and an even 100 pound-feet of torque at 3000 rpm. A close-ratio five-speed gearbox also became standard, as the Scirocco price rose to $10,870. Options in 1984 ranged from air conditioning ($700) and power steering ($265) to a slide/tilt sun roof ($445) and leather interior trim ($695).

Only 500 limited-edition Sciroccos were produced in mid-1983, specifically for the Southern California market. Note the dramatic fender and rocker extensions, the deep front air dam, and alloy wheels. Sciroccos remained in VW's lineup into 1988. (Phil Hall)

In 1987, a stronger 16-valve engine, rated at 123 horsepower, was installed in the 16V edition of the Scirocco. Base models stuck with the 90-horse four. A 16V retailed for $12,980 vs. $10,680 for the base coupe. Sciroccos remained available into 1988, but then disappeared, as VW prepared to launch a new Corrado replacement for 1990.

After launching the Jetta sedan in 1980, Volkswagen decided to give it a diesel-engine option during 1981. With an EPA rating of 41 mpg city and 57 mpg highway, the Jetta diesel was the second most fuel-efficient car in America—trailing only the Rabbit diesel. (Phil Hall)

By 1983, the Jetta—built as a two- or four-door sedan—was garnering respectable sales totals in America. Regular diesel and turbodiesel engines were available, in addition to the standard gasoline powerplant. (Phil Hall)

Volkswagen offered this Wolfsburg Limited Edition Jetta GLI 16V as a 1989-1/2 model.

Into the early 1990s, the four-door notchback Jetta shared its platform with the hatchback Golf. This is a 1991 Carat model. A higher-performance GLI 16V also was available, with a bigger dual-cam engine.

Jetta (1980-1992)

During 1980, Volkswagen announced that American buyers could get a notchback sedan companion to the Rabbit—also front-drive and initially powered by a 1588-cc fuel-injected four-cylinder engine. VW's first notch-backs to be sold in the United States, Jettas came in two-door or four-door sedan form, on a wheelbase identical to the Rabbit's (94.5 inches) but measuring more than a foot longer overall. All body trim was matte black, with an under-the-bumper front spoiler.

Only one trim level went on sale, dubbed "deluxe." Prices began at $7,650 for the two-door, and $7,870 for the four-door, with an automatic transmission adding $375 to the tariff. The brief option list also included a sliding steel sun roof, air conditioning, tinted glass and alloy wheels.

Unlike Rabbits, Jettas were manufactured in Germany. Interior fittings were plusher than the Rabbit's. Like the Rabbit, Jettas gained a larger (1.7-liter) gasoline engine for 1981, rated at 74 horsepower, along with a diesel option.

Prices for 1982 rose to $8,375 and $8,595 (for the two- and four-door, respectively). Standard equipment included a five-speed manual gearbox, power brakes, electric rear defroster, dual remote mirrors, AM/FM stereo radio, intermittent wipers, tinted glass, floor console, padded steering wheel and woodgrained instrument panel.

Volkswagen promised "Scirocco-like performance and handling" from its 1983 Jetta, also touting the car's "formal European roofline" and impressive fuel-economy rating. A new 68-horsepower turbodiesel engine joined the option list, or buyers could choose a conventional diesel.

Sedan buyers didn't have to skimp on performance in 1984, as Volkswagen launched the GLI—a notchback equivalent to the Rabbit GTI, with that model's more potent 90-horsepower engine. At $8,690, the GLI cost only $480 more than a GL sedan.

Not only did Volkswagen issue a new Golf hatchback (see below) in 1985, but it reworked the notchbacked Jetta in a similar aerodynamically-improved manner—including aero halogen headlights. Like the Golf, each Jetta boasted a more spacious interior, along with a 25 percent larger trunk. Front and rear suspensions were modified, and a new rear axle was installed. Rated for carrying five passengers, this modified Jetta started at $7,975 for the base two-door, topped by a GLI four-door at $9,995. Four-doors also came in base and GL trim.

With the 1.6-liter diesel engine, a Jetta warranted an EPA gas-mileage rating as high as 57 mpg. By 1986, some Jettas were being produced in Pennsylvania, as were *all* Golfs.

By the late 1980s, a Jetta GLI/16V was available, in addition to the basic GLI, a GL four-door sedan and base two- or four-door models. The sporty GLI/16V held a 16-valve engine and five-speed manual gearbox, and sold for $13,725 in 1987 vs. $11,690 for the GLI. Anti-lock braking arrived as an option in 1989, but only for top models.

Nicely-fitted Carat editions became available late in the decade and into the 1990s, bridging the gap between GL Jettas and the GLI/16V. Two-door Jettas departed after 1991, and a new turbocharged ECOdiesel engine became available in 1992.

Replacing the Dasher, VW's Quantum debuted in 1982, with a 1715-cc engine. Three body styles were offered: fastback (hatchback) coupe, four-door sedan, and four-door station wagon.

Quantum (1982-1988)

Every VW model seemed to have a direct successor. In the case of the 1970s Dasher, its replacement for the Eighties was named Quantum.

Introduced for 1982, Quantums rode a 100.4-inch wheelbase—six inches longer than the Jetta's. VW's "flagship" came in three body styles: fastback (hatchback) coupe at $10,770, four-door sedan for $11,070 and four-door station wagon stickering for $11,470. A five-speed manual gearbox was standard, with a three-speed automatic transmission optional. Standard equipment included an electric rear window defroster, clock, reclining front bucket seats, tinted glass, dual remote-control mirrors and alloy wheels. A GL option added cruise control, power door locks, electric remote mirrors, a lighted visor vanity mirror and power windows.

Beneath each Quantum hood sat the same 1715-cc (105-cid) overhead-cam four-cylinder engine used in Jettas and Sciroccos, developing 74 horsepower at 5000 rpm and 89.6 pound-feet of torque at 3000 rpm. The engine was mounted longitudinally, above the front wheels. Power rack-and-pinion steering was standard. Quantums had four-wheel independent suspension, with MacPherson struts and a stabilizer bar up front.

A turbodiesel engine became available in 1983 Quantums (except for the coupe). Turbodiesel models could have an "E-Mode" transmission with a special economy position, which employed a form of freewheeling (disconnecting the engine whenever the gas pedal was released). An Audi five-cylinder engine could be installed in Quantums at mid-year, making 100 horsepower and 112 pound-feet of torque.

Only a four-door sedan and a station wagon were available in the Quantum series for 1984, with the 2144-cc (131-cid) five-cylinder Audi engine and a five-speed gearbox (or optional automatic). The turbodiesel four remained available, too. "Wolfsburg Edition" sedans and wagons arrived at mid-season, promoted as luxury grand touring machines with deeply contoured sport seats, black window trim and a leather-wrapped steering wheel and gearshift knob. Wolfsburg Quantums also had six-inch alloy wheels with low-profile tires.

The 1983 Quantum GL5 had a 2.2-liter, 100-horsepower five-cylinder gasoline engine—the largest and most powerful engine ever in a Volkswagen. Featuring fuel injection and electronic ignition, it was 35 percent more powerful than the prior engine. Quantums remained on sale through 1989, when they were replaced by a Passat.

Europeans had a Golf model since the early 1970s, and the name finally came to America for 1985, on the redesigned replacement for the Rabbit. Larger dimensions caused the EPA to reclassify these cars as compacts, rather than subcompacts. Wheelbase was almost three inches longer than the Rabbit's. Golfs came only in hatchback form, while Jettas were notchback sedans. (Phil Hall)

By 1985, that 2.1-liter Audi five-cylinder engine no longer was available, but a 2.2-liter (136-cid) version became standard in the Quantum sedan, rated at 110 horsepower. Wagons reverted to a 1.8-liter four. Both engines adopted new Bosch KE-Jetronic fuel injection for improved driveability and performance. The GL5 sedan had a wraparound front air dam, smaller-diameter steering wheel (leather-wrapped) and a storage tray built into the folding rear center armrest. For 1986, the wagon was dropped, leaving only the GL sedan with its Audi five-cylinder engine.

A four-wheel-drive (Syncro) wagon debuted during the 1986 model year, joining the two-wheel-drive models. The Syncro stickered for $16,645, as opposed to $13,450 for a two-wheel-drive wagon and $14,985 for the sedan. Syncro wagons weighed close to 3,000 pounds vs. 2,745 pounds for a two-wheel-drive wagon. Each model used the Audi five-cylinder engine. Quantums dropped out after the 1988 model year.

Golf (1985-1992)

Volkswagen had used the Golf nameplate elsewhere in the world for a decade. Now, for 1985, restyling of the Rabbit was accompanied by a switch in designation. Hatchbacks adopted the Golf name, while notchback sedans—comparably redesigned—retained the Jetta badge.

Expanded dimensions caused the EPA to reclassify both the Golf and Jetta as compacts, rather than subcompacts. Each ranked as a full five-passenger vehicle. Wheelbases were 2.6 inches longer than before, overall length grew by 4.7 inches and tread dimensions were wider. Overall width expanded by 2.1 inches, while the rear

Continuing in the tradition started a couple of years prior by the Rabbit, the 1985 Golf line included a sporty GTI hatchback. (Phil Hall)

In their first season on sale, Golf sedans swept the first six spots in the compact class at the Firestone Firehawk Endurance Championship at Sebring, Florida. Karl Hacker won first prize, with the quickest lap of 81.621 mph. (Phil Hall)

seat measured 3.5 inches wider. Interior volume thus improved by 12 percent, and trunk space was 30 percent greater. Not only was aerodynamic drag reduced by 17 percent, but this modification of the formerly-used 1.8-liter engine developed 15 percent more horsepower (now 85), for improved performance.

The Golf came in two- and four-door hatchback form, while Jettas remained notchback sedans. VW's 1.6-liter diesel engine also was available in Golfs and Jettas.

Built in the United States, a two-door Golf stickered for $6,990 ($200 less if it had a diesel engine). The four-door brought $210 more. The $8,990 GTI two-door was listed as a separate model, with a 100-horsepower engine, 116-mph top speed and a claimed 0-60 mph time of 9.5 seconds. Aero headlights and a rear window spoiler helped give the GTI a distinctive look. GTIs also had four-wheel disc brakes, front and rear stabilizer bars and stiffer springs/shocks. A close-ratio five-speed gearbox helped the driver make the best use of the car's potential. *Motor Trend* named the GTI its "Car of the Year" for 1985.

A total of 140,505 imported Volkswagens were sold in the United States during 1985, followed by 143,319 in 1986, 130,641 in 1987, 128,503 in 1988 and 129,705 in 1989. During 1987, as a comparison, Volkswagen produced 66,696 Golfs and Jettas in the U.S. plant, down from 84,397 in '85.

In 1987, the 16-valve engine from the Scirocco 16V became available in the Golf GTI (as well as the Jetta GLI), developing 123 horsepower. Sticker price: $12,240 vs. $10,325 for the GTI with its 102-bhp engine. Golfs adopted aero headlamps and moved a tad upscale—a result of the arrival of the Fox as VW's new entry-level model.

Late in the 1980s, the 16-valve engine from the Scirocco 16V became available in the GTI hatchback, developing 123 bhp. Shown is a 1988 GTI 16V.

In 1991, the Golf hatchbacks were nearing the end of their lifespan in this form. In addition to the GL edition (shown), a more vigorous GTI became available.

Engine horsepower ratings rose in 1988, to 100 bhp for the base 1.8-liter four and 105 bhp for the high-output version. For 1991 a larger, more potent (134-bhp) 2.0-liter engine went into the GTI 16V, following the lead of the previous year's Jetta GLI 16V. Only a five-speed was available with that hot powerplant.

Through much of the 1980s, Golf and Jetta models earned one unwanted distinction: a high ranking on the auto-theft list, because their high-mounted stereo units were too easy to remove. An anti-theft system helped cut the toll, later in the decade. By the early 1990s, after the closing of the Pennsylvania plant, Golfs were produced in Mexico, while Jettas arrived from Germany.

Fox (1987-1993)

When Volkswagen introduced another front-drive model early in 1987, it wasn't built in Germany or the United States. Instead, the subcompact Fox—offered as a two-door sedan, four-door sedan or two-door station wagon—came from Brazil. Beneath the hood sat VW's familiar 1.8-liter engine, developing 81 horsepower at 5500 rpm. Prices began at $5,690, but the GL wagon went for $6,590.

Based on the Brazilian Voyage sedan and Parati station wagon, the Fox was considerably modified for sale in the United States. Only a four-speed manual transmission was available in early models, but a five-speed arrived for 1989 (in upper models). Hampered in part by lack of an automatic transmission, and by lackluster design, the Fox

never became a strong seller and disappeared after the 1993 season.

Corrado (1990-1994)

After the departure of the Scirocco, Volkswagen had no full-sport model for the 1989 model year. Then came the hot little Corrado hatchback coupe, on a 97.3-inch wheelbase, containing nothing less than a supercharged en-

Volkswagen do Brasil produced the subcompact Fox, which arrived in the U.S. market for 1987. Throughout its brief lifetime, the Fox was one of the few cars that had no automatic transmission available. Sales never quite took off, so the Fox was dropped after 1993.

After the Scirocco departed, Volkswagen issued a sharp new Corrado sports car in 1990. Beneath its hood sat a "G-Charger" engine (so called because the supercharger was G-shaped), whipping up 158 horsepower. VW called the Corrado coupe its "first full-blooded sports car." Only a five-speed manual gearbox was available.

gine, and promoted as VW's "first full-blooded sports car."

The four-seat, front-drive G60 coupe carried a "G-Charger" engine (so called because the supercharger was G-shaped) that developed 158 horsepower at 5600 rpm. Only a five-speed manual gearbox was available at first; a four-speed automatic transmission arrived in 1991, with Normal and Sport shift modes. Four-wheel disc brakes were standard, with anti-locking optional. Corrados also had an automatic "active" rear spoiler that rose

Inside, the 1993 Corrado offered a driver-oriented cockpit, centering around the five-speed's gearshift lever. VW's sports car lasted into 1994.

at speeds above 45 mph to reduce lift, then retracted when road speed fell below 12 mph.

Initially priced at $17,900, Corrado escalated to $25,150 at the time of its demise, after the 1994 model year. Road testers and enthusiasts tended to like the Corrado, but sales never quite took off as anticipated, even when VW's narrow-angle VR6 (V-6) engine became available during 1992, shoving aside the blown four.

The new V-6 made a "huge difference" in performance, said *Consumer Guide* of the '93 model. Acceleration from this costly but "wonderful driver's car" was deemed "strong at low engine speeds and robust as the revs rise."

Billed as the fastest production Volkswagen ever, that Corrado SLC (Sports Luxury Coupe) could accelerate to 60 mph in just 6.8 seconds. A "Plus Axle" suspension system promised precise handling, while electronic traction control helped eliminate wheelspin. A four-speed "adaptive," electronically controlled automatic transmission in 1994 could replace the standard five-speed manual gearbox.

Passat (1990-)

VW's new German-built Passat sedan and station wagon arrived during the 1990 model year, powered by a 2.0-liter engine, to replace the Quantum. Rivaling such popular models as the Honda Accord and Toyota Camry, front-drive Passats ranked as VW's biggest cars ever. Previously well-known in Europe, Passats exhibited far different styling than other VWs, led by a no-grille nose.

With 10.8:1 compression, the Passat's engine developed 134 horsepower at 5800 rpm, and produced 133 pound-feet of torque. Both models rode on a 103.3-inch wheelbase and were loaded with standard features. A single GL trim level was offered, with only a handful of options.

For 1993, Passats could get VW's innovative new narrow-angle VR6 engine. Rated at 172 horsepower, that 2.8-liter V-6 engine is the same as that used in the GTI, with a five-speed manual gearbox or an automatic transmission. *Popular Science* magazine gave the VR6 engine its "Best of What's New" award, and *Popular Mechanics* delivered a "Design and Engineering" award. *Ward's Auto World*, an industry magazine, named the VR6 one of the top ten engines for 1995.

During 1993, Passats abandoned the initial automatic transmission with Economy and Sport shift modes. Its replacement was a new "adaptive dual mode" unit, which constantly altered shift points to conform to the driver's habits.

Face-lifted for 1995, Passats gained dual airbags and traction control. *Car and Driver* tested a Passat GLX with the new dual airbags, ranking it in first place among a group of family station wagons. They praised the Passat's "ardent chassis, remarkable space efficiency, [and] superb cockpit."

After a two-year period with only the V-6 engine available, Passats in 1996 also could be ordered with four-cylinder power. Also available: VW's ingenious new TDI (turbo direct injection) diesel.

A new Passat sedan and station wagon arrived during the 1990 model year, powered by a 134-horsepower, 2.0-liter engine, and replacing the Quantum.

Golf III and Jetta III (1993-)

Anyone awaiting the arrival of the redesigned Golf and Jetta had to wait a little longer than expected. Instead of appearing around the country as 1993 models, the Mexican-built duo emerged first only in the San Diego area. Not until months later, as '94 models, did Golf III hatchbacks and Jetta III notchbacks finally began to trickle into dealerships across the country.

In 1996, the Passat could have either a four-cylinder or V-6 gasoline engine. A new Turbo Direct Injection (TDI) diesel engine also became available. Shown is a GLX station wagon.

Announced for a 1993 debut, the redesigned Golf III (shown) and Jetta, now built in Mexico, were available initially only on the West Coast. Not until 1994 did the new models arrive at dealerships nationwide.

Labor unrest at the plant in Puebla, Mexico, was the major cause of the delay of this third generation of the original Rabbit design—sleeker, more rounded, and more powerful than the prior Golfs and Jettas.

The first Golfs started at $11,600, while Jettas stickered for no less than $12,900. Dual airbags became standard after the start of the 1994 model year. The 2.0-liter four-cylinder engine developed 115 horsepower and 122 pound-feet of torque. A new four-speed electronically con-trolled automatic transmission was optional. Like the prior generation, *Consumer Guide* reported, the Golf had "sporty moves for a family hatchback."

Launched in Europe in 1992, the Golf III tallied global sales of 1.4 million cars by the time the 1994 model year began. Volkswagen described it as "the most loved car in the world."

Volkswagen also continued the sport-performance tradition with a Jetta GLX for 1994 and a Golf GTI edition for 1995, powered by the VR6 engine that had first appeared in Passats. That V-6 powerplant had a narrow (15-degree) angle between its cylinder banks. Road testers praised the $18,875 GTI's nimble handling and fine steering response, as well as impressive acceleration.

By 1994, Volkswagen claimed that the Jetta was the top-selling European nameplate in America, ahead of BMW's 3-Series.

Height-adjustable front seat belts went into 1995 models, and Daytime Running Lights were installed. For 1996, a dashboard glovebox returned, having been displaced in 1994 by the addition of the passenger-side airbag.

Though criticizing the Corrado as an overpriced entrant, and branding the early 1990s GTI as "an orphan with asthma," *Car and Driver's* John Phillips praised the "sweet V-6" engine and "rock-solid structure" of the new 1995 edition. That GTI VR6 could reach 60 mph in just 6.7 seconds and run a quarter-mile in 15.3 seconds (hitting 91 mph), but cost only $19,190. Negative points included the car's "antiquated styling, zero cockpit storage space, [and rigid] sports car ride."

Like their predecessors, Jetta IIIs were four-door notchbacks, while Golfs had rear hatches. This is a 1993 Jetta GL.

Volkswagen's Future—Looking Bleak, But Hopeful

In 1994, VW's Golf passed the Ford Model T's record for continuous production, following the lead of the Beetle more than two decades earlier. Even so, Volkswagen AG was in financial trouble—despite its status as the fourth biggest automaker in the world, and the largest in Europe. Production cuts and a cost-cutting program had been initiated in 1993, when the company suffered a half-year loss of $860 million.

Sales in the United States were worse yet—a mere shadow of the totals logged by the Beetle, so many years previous. Analysts charged that VW's economic ills evolved from the Rabbit, which had earned a reputation for unreliability. Furthermore, VW of America had for years been trying to distance itself from its Beetle-related history. Executives were convinced that the company needed to move upscale to survive, and that memories of the Beetle tugged in the wrong direction.

Between 1970 and 1992, U.S. sales dropped by 87 percent. Only 75,000 cars were sold in the United States in 1992, and fewer yet the next year. In 1994, on the other hand, U.S. sales nearly doubled. Globally, 3.3 million Volkswagens were sold in 1993.

Construction of a new Design Center in Simi Valley, California, was completed in 1991. At that time, Volkswagen of America also moved its corporate headquarters to Auburn Hills, Michigan.

A 1993 ad campaign began to resurrect the Beetle as a drawing card for Passat sales. Produced by DDB Needham Worldwide, a successor to Doyle Dane Bernbach, the ads used the theme: "The Most Loved Cars in the World."

A year earlier, Volkswagen of America had advertised that it would guarantee to cover car payments of any purchaser who lost his or her job—an acknowledgment of the economic woes that had beset the United States. As another form of inducement to buy, VW later trotted out a startling new warranty: 10 years or 100,000 miles.

Advertising Age magazine dissected Volkswagen's "stunning U.S. decline" in 1993, in a story titled "From Beetle to Bedraggled." Consultant John Bulcroft, a former VW marketing executive turned president of Advisory Group, noted that "the Beetle was basic, bulletproof transportation, which is what Volkswagen should be selling today." VW's marketing director, William Gelgota, explained that the company needed "home runs." Soon. Ad director Greg Stein noted that Volkswagen should realize it was a major brand, worldwide. "If people think you're an insignificant brand," Stein advised, "then you become a risk."

Volkswagen celebrated its 40th anniversary in the American market in 1995. (Yes, VWs had been available since 1949, but the first official company headquarters was established in '55.) As part of the festivities, Volkswagen issued a 30 minute video, called *In Our Time: Volkswagen Reborn.*

A fresh ad campaign emerged during 1995, taking the place of the *"Fahrvergnügen"* theme earlier in the decade—which few customers seemed to understand. (That term supposedly meant "the rewarding and distinctly European driving experience unique to Volkswagen.")

"On the road of life," said the subsequent slogan, "there are passengers and there are drivers. Drivers wanted." Under this later theme, the company is attempting "a return to the essence of the Volkswagen brand." Marketers want to identify "the rational and emotional truth of Volkswagen." Between 1960 and 1975, after all, Volkswagen became one of the most recognizable brands of all time. Now, they want customers of the late 1990s to recognize that VW offers "technology that invigorates—never isolates." They're trying to show that owning a VW is part of "the difference between just living and being alive."

For the late 1990s, Volkswagen in America continues to face sluggish sales. But the future looks more promising, regardless of the impact of the new Beetle (Chapter 22) that's expected in 1998. Favorable evaluations from U.S. road testers have helped. Jack Gillis, for instance, rated all Volkswagen models as "Best Bets" for his 1996 edition of *The Car Book*. A year earlier, Gillis had estimated that Volkswagens cost 47 percent less to maintain than the average car.

Not too many shoppers fully understood what "Fahrvergnügen" meant when VW introduced the term in late 1980s ads. The advertised explanation didn't exactly make it clear, either.

Volkswagen's Futura concept car first appeared at the Frankfurt (Germany) auto show in September 1989; then at the North American International Auto Show in Detroit, a few months later. The four-passenger experimental automobile converted into an open recreational vehicle.

During 1996, Volkswagen introduced the new 1.9-liter Turbo Direct Injection (TDI) diesel engine in a series of models—first the Passat, and later the Golf and Jetta. The engines first appeared at the North American International Auto Show, in Detroit.

Outdoor-oriented customers had a special choice of Jettas during spring-summer 1996: the limited edition Jetta Trek, supplied with a 21-speed Trek/Jetta performance mountain bike. Though obviously not for everyone, the $14,500 Jetta Trek was the first time an automaker offered a standard mountain bike with an automobile.

Volkswagen Expands Its Diesel Image

Early in 1996, a TDI (Turbo Direct Injection) engine became available in the Passat. Billed as "lean" and "green," the turbocharged 1.9-liter four-cylinder engine, developing 90 horsepower and 149 pound-feet of torque, later became available in Golf and Jetta models. The turbocharger forces extra fresh air into the cylinders, for more efficient combustion and reduced exhaust emissions. Volkswagen also promises "surprisingly responsive performance" from its TDI trio, along with high fuel mileage.

Volkswagen had offered diesel engines since the 1970s, installing them in a modest percentage of U.S. models (but far more elsewhere in the world). Diesels had been criticized for excessive noise and emissions, but Volkswagen vowed that TDI technology nearly eliminated those ills.

Available in Europe since 1994 and introduced to North America at the New York Auto Show in spring 1995, TDI—according to VW—"performs on a par with a comparable gasoline engine, is cleaner than most gas engines and provides significantly better fuel economy." As installed in a European Golf, the TDI yielded a 111 mph top speed and had a nearly 700 mile range per tank of fuel. Volkswagen promised a "remarkably flat" torque curve, peaking at just 1900 rpm. That TDI Golf could accelerate to 30 mph as quickly as a European GTI. The TDI engine also emitted 20 percent less carbon monoxide than many gasoline engines.

Other diesel engines use a separate swirl chamber to ignite the fuel-air mixture. TDI injects fuel directly into the cylinder, yielding almost 20 percent greater fuel efficiency.

There's a "fairly significant market out there" for diesels, said VW spokesman Tony Fouladpour in 1995—especially since the TDI engine is "unlike any we've ever sold." Electronic control eliminates the noise and soot problems that had plagued earlier diesels, making the TDI "a leap forward." The engine can deliver a "tremendous amount of low-end torque [and is] a joy to drive, especially on the freeway."

To date, Volkswagen has sold seven million diesels worldwide. One in every seven Golfs sold in 1995 were diesel-powered, as were one-third of the Passats sold in Germany.

Because engineering has long been a Volkswagen strong point, it's just possible that the TDI might trigger a fresh surge in VW sales, even if diesels no longer seem as attractive as they did during the fuel crises of the 1970s and early '80s.

Chapter 20

Style and Fun: Rabbit Convertibles and Cabrios

Almost since the beginning, convertibles had been a vital part of the Volkswagen picture. First exhibited on July 1, 1949, they were built by Karmann throughout the Beetle era.

Though never the strongest sellers in Volkswagen's annual lineup, these were the cars that helped maintain a glamorous image. And glamour could be just as essential for a low-priced car as for a costly make, if not more so.

Affirming that reputation, the VW convertible was even named "snobbiest car of the year" in Paris, in 1973. Basic black ones were dubbed "ultra chic," driven by such luminaries as Marcello Mastroianni, Alain Delon and Yves Saint Laurent. Convertibles, then, had always topped the VW line and also carried the biggest load of equipment.

The Final Beetle Convertibles

When Volkswagen deleted the Beetle sedan from the U.S. market in 1977, the convertible—its body still built by Karmann—hung on a little longer. By then, some 270,000 had been built—slightly more than half of them going to America. Volkswagen declared that its open Beetle was the longest-produced four-seat convertible in automotive history. With the demise of American-built ragtops, apart from a handful of specially-built models, it was also one of the few that remained on sale in the late 1970s.

About a thousand special editions went to dealers in 1976, wearing light ivory paint and white upholstery, plus

The last Beetle convertibles sold in the United States didn't look remarkably different from those sold a decade or two earlier, but details had changed considerably. Note the front-seat headrests and bulged front hood. Only 10,681 went to U.S. customers in 1979, the final season. (Volkswagen)

Even though the American market had been without do-mestically-built convertibles since 1976, Volkswagen wasn't about to abandon the ragtop. For 1980, an open Rabbit with roll bar arrived. This is the Canadian version. (Phil Hall)

an off-white top. Each had a simulated woodgrain dashboard, four-spoke steering wheel with padded rim, adjustable headrests and sport-style rims. By that time, Volkswagen was producing 50 convertibles per day (up from 33). Interiors were now fully carpeted, while front seats got greater backrest adjustment. Standard models came in Scarlet Red, Sunflower Yellow, Fiesta Orange and Laguna Blue.

Car and Driver declared in 1977 that the top-down Beetle "can be one of the world's finest convertibles." Though "terribly slow...the flat-out driving style required to keep it

moving compensates for a lot of flaws." With so few weaknesses remaining, they added, it should be regarded "as an institution rather than an automobile."

Alas, all good things must end one day. So, 1979 saw the final appearance of the long-lived Beetle convertible—victim, in part, of tightening emissions and safety standards. By that time, it sold for an eye-opening $6,800, but its zealous fans were happy to pay the price. For other fun-in-the-sun drivers, VW had a far different breed of ragtop in mind for the 1980s.

Topless Rabbits Go On Sale

With the Beetle-based convertible gone, Volkswagen needed a replacement ragtop. So, stylists created one with the Rabbit Cabriolet. Introduced for 1980, this new convertible had a Targa-style roll bar for extra structural rigidity, but was otherwise an open car. Unfortunately for some who swooned over the convertible's intriguing shape, it stickered for a whopping $9,340—more than $3,000 higher than a Deluxe hatchback sedan.

No matter. For the next 14 years, the Cabriolet would capture the hearts of a small, but enthusiastic group of fans. It would also gain distinction as a vehicle with one of the highest resale values on the U.S. market—just as popular secondhand as it was when brand new. Women, in particular, took a liking to the open VWs of the 1980s, but buyers came from a variety of demographic groups.

Seating four adults, Rabbit convertibles featured an easy-to-open waterproof top. They carried 9.9 cubic feet of luggage (21.8 cubic feet with the rear seat folded

Rabbit convertibles soon matched, if not exceeded, their Beetle predecessors in popularity. The 1982 model had a standard 1.7-liter gasoline engine. (Phil Hall)

Wolfsburg Limited Edition Rabbit convertibles appeared at mid-season in 1984. (Phil Hall)

down). Standard equipment was similar to that of the Deluxe Rabbit hatchback, along with a five-speed manual gearbox, tachometer, oil temperature gauge, trip odometer, cassette stereo system, lockable gas cap, vent windows and 175/70 steel-belted radial whitewall tires.

A carbureted version of the Rabbit's 1457-cc engine replaced the fuel-injected edition in 1981, but a larger (1588-cc) fuel-injected four was optional. So was the diesel engine. Like other Rabbits, the convertible earned a 1981 face-lift, including a new front end similar to that used in the Scirocco. Inside was a new dashboard.

Priced at $10,595, the 1982 Rabbit convertible included a floor console, integral roll bar, passenger vanity mirror, lockable gas cap, dual-tone horn, digital clock, padded steering wheel and carpeted lower door panels.

Volkswagen billed its open 1983 Rabbit as the "least expensive four-passenger convertible on the market." Equipped with a fuel-injected 1.7-liter engine and five-speed gearbox, the ragtop had full instruments, an electrically-heated glass rear window, fully padded (lined) top, "Heidelberg" four-speaker cassette stereo and a fold-down rear seat. Bumper guards now were standard. Power steering remained an option, along with an automatic transmission and air conditioning.

For 1984, convertibles got the same 1.8-liter engine used in the hot GTI hatchback. A mid-season "Wolfsburg Edition" came in metallic black-on-black. Convertible buyers could also get the "triple white" version, with an Alpine white body, top, fender flares, wheels, mirror housings,

upholstery and bumpers. Those pure white ragtops are still a stunning sight, when one is spotted on the road.

Rabbit hatchbacks faded away after 1984, replaced by the new Golf. But the Rabbit's basic design was destined to continue for another decade with the convertible—now commonly called a Cabriolet. A bigger fuel tank went into 1985 models, again propelled by a 90-horsepower, 1.8-liter four-cylinder engine.

Each succeeding season brought an improvement or two, along with a succession of price hikes—from $11,595 in 1985 to $15,195 in 1989. A driver's airbag became standard in the Cabriolet for 1990 (but not in other VW models). A power top arrived in 1991, available on the top model—called Carat—but it lasted only two seasons. A special edition Etienne Aigner Cabriolet the next year was named for a European designer of leather goods. Then, a Cabriolet Classic replaced the Carat for 1993.

Though never a powerful seller, the Cabriolet continued to draw avid buyers each year. A disproportionate number of owners were female, prompting certain male motorists to brand the VW Cabriolet as a "chick car." Even if such narrow-minded fellows fully appreciated this cute German-built convertible's eager personality and solid build quality, they couldn't quite bring themselves to purchase one, leaving that pleasure to the "girls."

By the 1990s, the Rabbit-based convertible was looking rather dated—if still attractive in its own distinct way. Fortunately, Volkswagen had another idea waiting in the wings: a gracefully rounded Cabrio, evolved from the Golf III.

Special editions of both the Cabriolet and the Scirocco coupe were issued by such companies as BBS, GMP, and Neuspeed in the mid-1980s.

By 1989, the Rabbit was long gone (replaced by the Golf), but the convertible—dubbed Cabriolet—carried on, following a 1988 face lift. This is a Wolfsburg Limited Edition, issued at mid-year. VW convertibles had some of the highest resale values in the U.S. used car market.

In 1993, the Rabbit-based Cabriolet was nearing the end of its long-term run, but continued to capture the hearts of many an American VW fan.

Volkswagen finally abandoned the long-lived Rabbit configuration for its Cabriolet, issuing an all-new, neatly-rounded Cabrio for the 1995 model year. Its spirited 2.0-liter engine made 115 horsepower.

Cabrio (1995-)

After a decade and a half, the Rabbit-based convertible finally had to go. In its place came a just-as-cute, but much more rounded, Cabrio. Launched as a 1995 model, the Cabrio clings to the tradition of including a Targa-style integral roll bar. Not only does that unit add structural rigidity, but it contains mounting points for the front seat belts. The Cabrio's 2.0-liter four-cylinder engine develops 115 horsepower. No V-6 is available.

Like the Rabbit-based Cabriolet that preceded it, the new Cabrio contained a Targa-style roll bar. Initial models were built in Germany, but production moved to Mexico in 1996.

Bigger inside and out than their predecessors, Cabrios came with dual airbags, anti-lock braking and a manually-operated top. Not merely a topless hardtop, they're purpose-built as convertibles, thus providing greater chassis rigidity, better corrosion resistance and improved collision energy management. Cabrios have four-wheel independent suspension, power rack-and-pinion steering and an impact-resistant polyethylene fuel cell.

Because the Cabrio's six-layer top now folds flatter than in the Rabbit version, it interferes less with rearward visibility. Lowering the top, said *Road & Track* magazine, "takes less time than eating a burrito...one of the easiest-lowering tops we've experienced."

Well-equipped in standard form, Cabrios have power windows and mirrors, central locking, an anti-theft system, folding rear seat, cassette stereo and intermittent wipers. A glass back window contains a defogger. The short option list included a trunk-mounted CD changer, leather upholstery, air conditioning and seven-spoke alloy wheels. An "adaptive" four-speed automatic transmission, with shift action to match the driver's habits, can replace the standard five-speed manual gearbox.

Initial Cabrios hailed from Germany. Karmann Coachworks started with a Golf III, transforming it into a convertible. Beginning early in 1996, all Cabrio production took place at the Puebla plant in Mexico.

Naturally, Volkswagen hopes the Cabrio will be another near-classic. And until the "New Beetle" (see Chapter 22) arrives, the Cabrio undeniably comes closest to capturing the essence—the mystique—of the original VW models.

Chapter 21

Volkswagen Today—A Global Powerhouse

Because Volkswagen in the 1990s appears to be a mere shadow of its former self in the U.S. market, not everyone realizes that it's the number one auto manufacturer in Europe. Obviously, VW sales have done better elsewhere in the world of late, than in America. Not only have Beetles remained in production in Brazil and Mexico, but Volkswagen has launched dozens of other models for sale outside the United States—most of them unknown to American consumers.

Hanging On: The Beetle Today, in Mexico and Latin America

After dying in the U.S. market, the Beetle found a new—actually, a continued—life south of the border. In Mexico and points south, VWs not only remained in production, but continued to sell strongly, appealing to practical-minded customers whose infatuation with the technology—and the design—never ceased.

Volkswagen de Mexico, S.A. completed this 1,450,000 square-foot factory at Puebla—75 miles east of Mexico City—in 1967. In its early years, about 100 Beetles were turned out each day. (Volkswagen)

Body shells pass overhead, while completed Beetles wait below at the Puebla plant. Mexican-built Beetles in the late Sixties were identical to those produced in factories and assembly plants in more than a dozen countries. (Volkswagen)

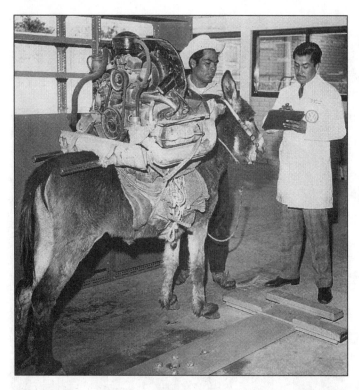

Most engines arrived at Mexican dealerships under their own power, but technicians in 1971 were ready for anything. VW industrial engines performed farm duties that previously had been handled by burro-power, so this hardy creature might have been facing downsizing back at the ranch. (Volkswagen)

Established in January 1964, Volkswagen de Mexico S.A. operated initially as an importing, assembly and marketing facility. Late in 1967, a complete factory was finished at Puebla, situated east of Mexico City.

By 1969, the Puebla plant was shipping replacement parts to the United States, as well as complete vehicles within Mexico and elsewhere in Latin America. Through the 1970s, Mexican-built Beetles even were exported to Germany—a notable irony in VW history. The Puebla facility also turned out buses, Rabbits (called *Caribe*) and Type 181 ("The Thing"), as well as a *Brasilia* passenger car and a basic truck called *Hormiga*.

On May 15, 1981, the 20-millionth Beetle was produced, at Puebla. A special "Silver Bug" went on sale to mark the occasion. In addition to offering individual Mexicans a sensible automobile at moderate cost, the Beetles saw plenty of use as taxis throughout the country.

Labor strife and a sagging economy impaired Volkswagen's Mexican production early in the 1990s. In 1992, a record total of more than a million vehicles were built in Mexico, but Volkswagen failed to share in that success. By spring of 1994, General Motors had leaped to second place in Mexican production, hard on the heels of VW, as the new subcompact GM Joy and Swing began to outsell the Golf.

Volkswagen in Brazil

Biggest of the three plants that produced VWs from scratch in the 1970s was in Brazil. That facility turned out Beetles, Dashers, buses, plus a locally-marketed *Variant* and *Brasilia*.

Writing in the *Chicago Tribune* in 1994, Kerry Luft related his attempt to rent a car in Sao Paolo, Brazil, longtime home of the Brazilian VW plant. "I'm sorry, sir," the rental clerk said, "but all we have is a Fusca...little and sort of funny-looking. And it's noisy.... I'm so sorry."

As Mr. Luft pointed out at the time, no apologies were needed. He was pleased to learn that Beetles still were "putt-putting along in Brazil, 15 years after disappearing from American showrooms and eight years after its first demise in Brazil."

After disappearing from the Brazilian scene in 1986, the Beetle (dubbed *Fusca*, as a Portuguese rendering of "folks," or "volks") resumed manufacture in 1993, due largely to the efforts of Brazilian President Itamar Franco. A one-time Beetle owner himself, Franco offered the company tax incentives to revive production. Facing continual, rampant inflation, Brazil badly needed a moderately-priced automobile if its workers were to remain mobile. Autolatina therefore pumped $35 million into reworking an assembly line for the revived Beetle, even hiring workers who'd built the earlier ones.

Volkswagens first went on sale in Brazil in November 1950, assembled by a local company—Brasmotor—from German-built components. Jose Thomson, a Chrysler importer, saw the merit of VWs early on—a sensible choice for Brazil's poor roads and lack of domestic oil. Heinz Nordhoff visited Brazil with Friedrich Schultz-Wenk, who be-

In Brazil as well as in Mexico and other Hispanic countries, Volkswagen taxis were—and still are—a common sight. Note the swing-open rear side window. (Volkswagen)

came head of new company—and even became a Brazilian citizen.

In 1953, Volkswagen opened its own plant in the state of Sao Paolo, assembling its first car in March. Initially, the plant assembled "kits" sent from Germany, working in a rented shop in the Sao Paulo suburbs. Construction of a permanent factory began in 1956, and the first complete vehicle (a Transporter) left the plant in September 1957, assembled with more than half local content. By 1959, whole cars were being produced in Brazil at the rate of five per day.

Volkswagen do Brasil became the biggest VW manufacturing subsidiary outside of Germany. Not much time passed before VW actually became Brazil's biggest industry, providing nearly two-thirds of the country's private automobiles.

Production of Karmann Ghias began in 1962. All Brazilian VWs were similar to the German cars, but used lower compression engines and stronger suspension components, to cope with the rough roads. In 1963, the half-millionth Brazilian VW was built. Four years later, the millionth (with nearly all local content).

Specific models for the Brazilian market began in 1968, starting with a four-door version of the 1600 sedan. A fastback 1600 emerged in 1971, followed in '72 by an *SP* coupe of Brazilian design, on a modified 1600 chassis with a 1.7-liter engine. The *Brasilia* debuted in 1973, as a two- or four-door sedan or a hatchback. Then came a Brazilian-built Passat (accompanied by a lower-cost *Surf*, targeting younger customers).

Another new model, the *Gol*, used a Beetle engine but front-wheel-drive. Brazil also issued the *Polo*, first intended to be the Beetle's replacement. By 1985, the plant also built the *Voyage*, a water-cooled variant of the Gol, along with a *Parati* station wagon and a posh *Santana*. A year later, production of the Fusca ground to a halt.

Over a 44 year period, more than 3.3 million Volkswagens were sold in Brazil—the best-seller ever in that country. "The official story," said Alexander Gromov to Mr.

Beetles were called "Fusca" (a Portuguese equivalent) in Brazil. This is a 1983 model.

Volkswagen do Brasil produced this Karmann Ghia TC in the mid-1970s. Like many VW models, it never appeared in the U.S. market. (Volkswagen)

Another Brazilian product of the 1970s was this rakish SP-2 coupe. (Volkswagen)

Kerry, was that "nobody wanted to buy them anymore." Head of the 650-member Fusca Clube do Brasil, Gromov noted that VW had not abided by an old saying in his country: "You should not spit in the plate that you're eating from."

In 1993, its first full year as a revived model, only 18,171 Fuscas were sold—about half the 1986 total. In their heyday, in the early 1970s, they'd moved that many in a month.

Volkswagen Globally

In addition to Brazil and Mexico, Volkswagen assembly reached a number of other countries, including Canada (1952), South Africa (1956), Belgium (1970), Argentina (1980), the People's Republic of China (1985), Spain (1986), the Czech Republic (1991), the Slovakian Republic (1991), Poland (1993), Hungary (1994), Taiwan (1994) and Portugal (1995).

By the early 1970s, German plants were turning out the expected varieties of Beetles—series 1200, 1300 and 1302—as well as Karmann Ghias, the 1600 series, and the Type 181. Also assembled in Germany was the K70 sedan, with a 75- or 90-horsepower four-cylinder engine; the 411 series (two- and four-door sedans); and the Volkswagen-Porsche 914. By 1972, Opel ranked ahead of Volkswagen as the top German automaker.

In 1985, a "50th Anniversary" Beetle was produced in Mexico and Brazil.

Passats (derived from the Audi 80) debuted in 1973. Within the following year, Volkswagen's fortunes looked dim, and the work force was sharply cut. The small Polo hatchback arrived in 1975, followed by the Golf GTI and the Derby.

Further into the Seventies, the Wolfsburg plant produced Golfs (the European name for Rabbit), plus the Polo, VW Derby and Audi 50; and later, Rabbit diesels for the

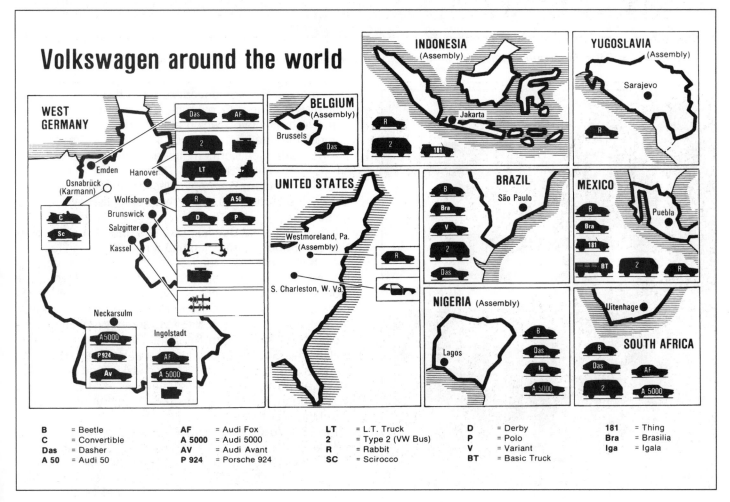

B	= Beetle	**AF**	= Audi Fox	**LT**	= L.T. Truck	**D**	= Derby	**181**	= Thing
C	= Convertible	**A 5000**	= Audi 5000	**2**	= Type 2 (VW Bus)	**P**	= Polo	**Bra**	= Brasilia
Das	= Dasher	**AV**	= Audi Avant	**R**	= Rabbit	**V**	= Variant	**Iga**	= Igala
A 50	= Audi 50	**P 924**	= Porsche 924	**SC**	= Scirocco	**BT**	= Basic Truck		

In 1978, Volkswagen had factories or assembly plants in nine countries. (Phil Hall)

The Volkswagen Polo coupe and sedan were produced in Europe, but failed to reach the American market. (Phil Hall)

Voyage was the name given to one of Volkswagen's Brazilian models of the 1980s, built as a two- or four-door sedan. (Phil Hall)

U.S. market. Beetle convertibles and the Scirocco were built by Karmann in Osnabrück. Buses and Campmobiles came from Hanover, which also produced all air-cooled engines and the front-engined LT truck. The Emden plant on the North Sea, formerly used to produce Beetles for the United States, now did Dashers and Audi Foxes. Plants in southern Germany (Neckarsulm and Ingolstadt) issued the Audi 5000, Fox, Avant and five-cylinder engines.

South Africa did Beetles, Dashers, buses and the Audi Fox and 5000. Nigeria also had a manufacturing facility.

As the Eighties decade began, the list of German-built models included the subcompact Polo, the Derby, the Golf and Jetta, Sciroccos, Passats and luxurious notchback Santanas—plus a Thing-like Iltis. Nigeria continued to turn out 1500 series Beetles, adding versions of the Golf, Jetta, Passat and Santana. Brazil had Fuscas as well as the Golf, Voyage, Passat and Brasilia, with Parati wagons joining a little later. Mexico still issued a few Type 181s, along with its 1200 series Beetles. In Argentina, Volkswagen issued something quite different: a Dodge 1500 four-door sedan.

In 1982, Volkswagen signed an agreement with Seat of Spain, whereby the latter would import (and later build) Polos and Passats, under VW licensing. An agreement was signed with the Chinese that same year, permitting production of Santanas at the Shanghai Motor Works. Santanas also were built in Japan, by Nissan.

Technical Innovations and Future Products

Like other manufacturers, Volkswagen issued the occasional experimental vehicle, typically loaded with engineering innovations. In January 1981, for instance, an Aerodynamic Research vehicle appeared at the Detroit Auto Show. Capable of traveling at 225 mph and delivering fuel mileage of 39 mpg (at 155 mph), this VW set eight world records for diesel vehicles at the Nardo circle track in Italy. Its 2.4-liter diesel six was similar to the engine used in the LT truck, but turbocharged, yielding 173 horsepower.

Moving into the Nineties, an experimental Integrated Research Volkswagen managed to park itself. The system employed independent four-wheel steering with electric motors, along with a laser to measure distance to the curb and adjoining vehicles. Displayed at Detroit's North American International Auto Show in 1991, the Futura—wearing removable gullwing doors—converted into an open recreational vehicle. Display screens showed distance from the vehicle ahead, among other safety-related information.

A year later, the Detroit show featured a multi-fuel concept Jetta, which ran on methanol.

VW announced the Sharan multi-purpose vehicle early in 1995, with the VR6 engine and either front-drive or Syncro

Volkswagen's most luxurious model in 1984 was the Santana GX5 sedan, with a new 2.0-liter engine. (Phil Hall)

four-wheel-drive. Seating up to seven, measuring only two centimeters longer than a Passat, the Sharan featured an engine cover and windshield that blended into a single line, dubbed "one box" styling, with a drag coefficient of just 0.33. At the time of the Sharan's debut, Europe's multi-purpose vehicle market amounted to only 1.4 percent of the total, but was expected to grow—though not likely to the proportion seen in the United States.

The Golf Ecomatic, issued in 1993, brought VW's experimental automatic engine stop-start principle into a standard production automobile. A 64-horsepower diesel engine worked with a special semi-automatic transmission. The engine was switched off automatically when not needed—as when waiting at stoplights. Touch the gas pedal, and it restarted immediately. (Volkswagen)

A Golf Design concept nicknamed "Harlequin" appeared at the Geneva auto show in 1996. Fifty were to be built, for exhibition at events in the United States, after its appearance in Europe. If produced, such a vehicle could be offered in a choice of five basic color lines, from yellow to black, but customers would not know exactly which elements would be painted which color.

A Schatz Heat Battery began to appear in European Golf and Passat models in 1993. Developed by Oscar Schatz, the battery operated by capturing and storing waste heat from the car's engine. This allowed instant release of heat for the heating system.

In May 1996, *Automotive News* reported that Volkswagen was developing a VR5 engine—five cylinders, based on the VR6. For 1997, VW had a Golf GTI at the ready, with a 110 horsepower diesel engine and 120 mph top speed.

Also for sale elsewhere in the world, Volkswagen was developing a new small car, tinier than the Polo, designed for assembly in just seven hours. Based on the concept Chico, exhibited at the Frankfurt auto show in 1991, the new minicar probably will use a three-cylinder engine. Volkswagen AG President Ferdinand Piëch also told the Vienna International Motor Symposium in spring 1996 that the new Polo would eventually take just 14 hours to produce.

Volkswagen as the Century Ends

Under Carl Hahn, head of Volkswagen AG since 1982, the company undertook an ambitious investment program. Ferdinand Piëch took the helm in January 1993, determined to save the company's sagging fortunes by cutting costs—including elimination of 12,500 German workers. (By then, German workers were the highest paid in the world.)

In 1994, what is known as The Volkswagen Group produced nearly 3.3 million vehicles, under Audi, SEAT, Skoda and Volkswagen nameplates. Globally, the company employed 238,000 people (141,000 of them in Germany). Ever since 1985, the Group had ranked as the largest vehicle producer and supplier in Western Europe, accounting for 16 percent of the vehicle market.

Available models ranged from compact Seats and Skodas to deluxe Audis. Commercial vehicles stretched from small pickup trucks to 35-tonners. Volkswagen AG had factories at Wolfsburg, Hanover, Emden, Brunswick, Salzgitter and Kassel, in Germany.

As of the mid-1990s, Volkswagen of America operated through a network of 630 Volkswagen dealers and 280 Audi retailers, having sold more than 10 million cars in the United States.

In 1993, Volkswagen suffered a barrage of unfavorable publicity as a result of the sudden move of purchasing chief Jose Ignacio Lopez from General Motors to VW. Allegations quickly surfaced that Lopez had brought secret GM information with him as he made the move—a charge that Volkswagen denied.

Additional product launches were planned for late 1996 and beyond. "Our joint objective," said Volkswagen board member Dr. Robert Büchelhofer in 1996, "must be to actively shape the future, to meet the quality demands of our customers, and to strengthen the competitiveness of our sales organization." Still, the one new product that's likely to grab at the hearts of VW fans is the New Beetle—a futuristic revival of the original concept—as described in the next chapter.

OWNER COMMENTS: Pat Miketinac

For years, *Small World* magazine reported on Volkswagens whose odometers had reached high figures. Stories of VWs with 300,000, 400,000 or more miles surfaced periodically—perhaps true, perhaps someone's fantasy.

Pat Miketinac has the real thing. Way back in 1970, his wife just happened to buy a 1963 Volkswagen. Not that there was anything special about that Bug, Miketinac recalls. "She was looking for a car for school." Nothing more.

Today, that Beetle has traveled close to 700,000 miles. "I don't have any way of telling" for certain, Miketinac says, because the odometer was broken when his wife bought the car. But he can personally document the last half-million miles or so.

Miketinac has used the car to travel from job to job on his maintenance route, caring for elevators in five cities. In 1995 alone, he drove it 38,000 miles.

"The [front] suspension is original," he says, "except for wheel bearings, tie rod ends and shocks. The transaxle and rear suspension are original except for oil seals and shocks.

Miketinac does engine overhauls and brake jobs about every 100,000 miles. He does at least 90 percent of the work himself. "What's amazing to me," Miketinac says, "is that the transmission is still good. It's never been out."

Unfortunately, that well-traveled '63 suffered a mishap in spring 1996. Its hood and left fender got "wrinkled." Miketinac is in the process of repairing that tireless Beetle, "little by little." That doesn't mean he's driving a Brand X vehicle on his maintenance route. He also has a '65 Volkswagen, doing duty as his "spare" car.

Chapter 22

A Beetle for the 21st Century

Though many still mourned its passing, and a legion of enthusiasts began to grow, the original Beetle and its variants were largely forgotten by the general public. In the Beetle's heyday, as we've seen, millions of people had loved it—while a sizable band of naysayers despised the car.

Many of those who'd owned one or more of the charming machines had mixed feelings, too. Some were unabashed fans in the early days, but retained no interest later. On the other hand, a certain "cult" following began to develop. Or more accurately, to continue—even among people too young to remember the Beetle's glory years.

Concept 1 Takes Detroit by Storm

Surprises don't come easily to the North American International Auto Show, held each January in Detroit. Journalists who cover the event every year grow used to hearing—and often dismissing—claims from manufacturers that their latest product will be the hottest item of the year.

No one had much of an idea what Volkswagen had up its sleeve for the 1994 show—but it turned out to be a stunner. Unveiled to a noisy fanfare was a bright yellow, rounded-contour, cute and cuddly Beetle! Or so it seemed.

An impressive video presentation, aided by a haunting musical score, succeeded masterfully in evoking fond memories of Beetles past, as the Concept 1 emerged in a puff of smoke. Though softer in shape—with a roofline reminiscent of the concept car that evolved into the toned-down Dodge/Plymouth Neon—kinship to the original Beetle was unmistakable. Yet, the car had been styled in California by twenty-something designers. Said one: "It's something that's definitely been thought of for years and years at the studios.... It didn't start as this project, but it evolved into what we see now."

"We want to return to our roots," research/development chief Ulrich Seiffert explained at the show. "We will never bring the Beetle back, but we'd like to come back to an affordable, reliable car." Volkswagen executives were careful not to utter the term Beetle, or Bug, or anything to suggest that the old Beetle was about to be reborn. Nevertheless, anyone who had even a passing familiarity with the original—which includes the bulk of the global population—could hardly miss the resemblance, and perhaps speculate about a scenario or two.

"Volkswagen AG spent years trying to squash the Beetle," wrote *Automotive News* correspondent Arlena Sawyers after the Detroit show; "but the bug is on the way back."

Styled by a team of young artists at VW's design center in Simi Valley, California, the four-seat Concept 1 (sometimes spelled out as "Concept One") sat on a Polo platform. The two-door, front-engine car had a 101-inch wheelbase, standing 60 inches tall and 65.4 inches wide. Weight: just under a ton. Volkswagen exhibited several engines that could conceivably power a revived Beetle: diesel, hybrid diesel-electric or fully electric.

Quite a few reporters who'd attended VW's press conference expressed affection for the Concept 1. Consumers also fell hard for the design. Not everyone—but enough to show that Volkswagen seemed to have something truly special on its hands.

For months after the Detroit show, journalists snorted that it would never be produced. Or if it was, that the design would be toned down so drastically as to lose all of its virtues.

A rousing sensation at the North American International Auto Show in Detroit, in January 1994, the Concept 1 was intended as a show car only.

Exuberant reaction from the press and public to the Concept 1 caused Volkswagen to rethink the idea. After a time, it was announced that such a modern-day Beetle would indeed be produced.

Volkswagen stayed mum for many months, neither confirming nor denying rumors that production was being considered. Finally came an announcement that yes, in response to the surge of favorable public reaction to the Concept 1, Volkswagen really was contemplating the possibility of taking the car all the way to production. Not exactly a "yes," but definitely not a "no."

The Concept 1's instrument panel was just about as simple as that of the early Beetle, but the powertrain had to be dramatically different: namely, a front-mounted, liquid-cooled engine.

Next Up: The 1995 Tokyo Motor Show

The next version of the Concept 1 design study turned up at the Tokyo Motor Show, in October 1995. Only a closed car had been exhibited at Detroit, but Tokyo visitors also got to see a convertible. At least 1,500 orders were taken at the Tokyo show, for the real thing when it finally appears.

Not only did VW announce firmly that production would begin at some future point, it had selected a site. On October 25, 1995, Dr. Ferdinand Piëch, chairman of Volkswagen AG, affirmed that the Concept 1 would be built at its North American production facility in Puebla, Mexico—a factory now used to turn out Golfs for the American market.

"Instead of keeping the car under wraps up to the time of its launch," Piëch explained, "we want the customers to continue to participate in the product development of the Concept 1." Piëch noted that Volkswagen had been "overwhelmed by the positive response" at the previous year's Detroit show. "Since then we have talked to customers and dealers all over the world, and taken careful note of the recommendations of the media and the motoring press. Why? Because we want to put a car on the markets of the world that perfectly corresponds to the requirements, the desires and dreams of our customers."

VW had finally given its rebirthed Beetle—front-drive notwithstanding—a firm "go."

Complete Car, a British motoring periodical, published an account of the latest Beetle design in its January 1996 issue, under the title "Concept Fun." This coming-soon model "manages to evoke memories of the old-timer despite futuristic lines," wrote author Paul Carslake. "Cynics said [the Concept 1] was merely another publicity stunt to try to boost flagging sales of Golfs and Jettas in the U.S.," but they were mistaken.

The dashboard of the production version might even contain an optional flower vase—crafted of fine crystal in the Czech Republic—just like the original Beetles in the Fifties.

Output for the entire world, Carslake reported, would be about the same as that of the Beetle that's been produced for South America: roughly 100,000 per year, about half of those destined for the U.S. market. Because of the car's wide track and narrow body, Carslake noted, "charm takes precedence over interior space." Bulging wheel arches might look sharp, but help restrict the back seat area, despite the car's ample overall width.

The "wacky new replacement" for the old Beetle was "being engineered to share much of the same understructure as the next Golf, which is helping to keep the costs of this car low." Carslake predicted that a hatchback coupe would go on sale in 1998, followed some three years later by a Cabrio (convertible).

"New Beetle" Goes Onstage at Geneva

Billed as "an inspired combination of technology and emotion," what Volkswagen now dubbed the "New Beetle" appeared at the Geneva (Switzerland) Motor Show in March 1996.

Rather than abandon the familiar Beetle designation, as some had predicted, Volkswagen now expects to use that name when the car finally goes on sale.

"Concept 1 *is* the new Beetle," Volkswagen spokespersons insisted. This was the first usage of that name for the Beetle-derived vehicle that's expected late in the 1990s. "Not only does its distinctive design bring back fond memories of the past," the introductory announcement read, "it also reflects its international name." This version was called the "latest technical evolutionary stage."

"Beneath the futuristic yet familiar silhouette," Volkswagen advised of the Beetle at Geneva, "there is a great deal of modern technology." That included dual (driver and passenger) airbags—plus lateral (side) airbags. It will also have anti-lock braking, and a futuristic drivetrain: most likely a powerful—but frugal—TDI engine, coupled with syncro four-wheel-drive.

Development toward production was said to be "forging ahead," as engineers sought to meet all current safety standards and introduce "forward-looking drive technology." That meant "modern, transverse straight-type engines," a far cry from the rear-mounted, air-cooled powerplants of Beetles past.

Instead of that old flat four-cylinder engine out back, the new one is expected to carry a modern inline four, installed transversely. The new Beetle seen at Geneva held

Few could miss the connection between the Concept 1 and the old Beetle, though some of the car's California designers were barely old enough to recall the original. Three possible powertrains were exhibited at the Detroit show, including an electric and a hybrid-electric. A revised version of the Concept 1 appeared at the Geneva (Switzerland) motor show in spring 1995. At the Frankfurt (Germany) motor show in autumn 1995, Volkswagen announced that the Concept 1 actually would be named "New Beetle" when it goes into production, later in the 1990s. A convertible is expected later.

a 1.9-liter TDI (direct-injection turbo-diesel) engine, rated at 90 horsepower—also far removed from the output of even the last Beetles of the 1970s. Two gasoline engines also were in the planning stage, yielding either 105 or 150 horsepower. Those engines might find their way into the Beetle, when it enters production, "if the market demands it." Volkswagen specifically noted that "at customer request, it is conceivable that other engine-transmission units could be fitted."

Volkswagen promotes the fact that the coming-soon Beetle will *not* be a small car. Although the initial version seen in Detroit in January 1993 looked little larger than the original, the real thing will not be a subcompact. The Geneva edition stood 24 centimeters (more than 9 inches) longer than the original Concept 1, due mainly to greater overhang at the rear for more seat and luggage space, and at the front to hold a choice of engines. Unlike the original VW, too, the New Beetle is a hatchback.

With a wheelbase measuring 2.51 meters (98.8 inches), the Geneva version stood 4.06 meters (160 inches) long, 1.51 meters (59.4 inches) high and 1.73 meters (68 inches) wide. In contrast, the original Beetles rode on a 94.5 inch wheelbase, but measured a nearly-identical 160 inches long and 59.1 inches tall. However, they stood only 60.6 inches wide. In its final years on the U.S. market, overall length approached 165 inches—five inches longer than the New Beetle.

Inside the Geneva show car was a light gray/yellow interior, mixing fabric and "leather finish" to give an "impression of lightness and fun." A single large, round instrument cluster contained the speedometer, temperature gauge and fuel gauge—not quite as basic as the first Beetles, yet aimed at "the essential functions." A radio sat in the center of the dashboard. Folding down the rear seat backrest could provide even greater luggage capacity, accessible via a "generously-sized" tailgate.

As one method of obtaining publicity during the Geneva show, the company made use of the Internet. Instead of providing only the usual sort of online information, Volkswagen set up a "live" link between the exhibit area and VW's recently-introduced Worldwide web site. Computer-modem users could dial up the Design Center's Internet address (www.vw.com), and—if the time was correct and communications problems did not interfere—wind up asking questions of Volkswagen people at the show. Thus, enthusiasts all over the world could hook into the exhibit and glean information. They could even ask questions, and present ideas of their own for the car's eventual launch.

The web site offered information in German, English or French. Web "surfers" could get details on the basic idea behind the modern-day Beetle, sign in as an "official Beetle fan," view a 3-D model of the car (or an interior view) and give feedback to the team in Geneva. Although the link-up did operate, communication with the Geneva site often turned out to be even more sluggish than the usual Internet connections. Still, it was an innovative use of contemporary technology to promote an all-new automobile.

The Geneva car differed from its Tokyo predecessor in a couple of crucial ways. For one thing, it was now painted pearlescent cyber green. It also featured a sliding glass sun roof, whose ingenious design was credited to Porsche. For open-air driving, the wide Targa glass roof could open and disappear right into the tail of the car, beneath the large rear window. A fabric roller blind kept direct sunlight from penetrating into the interior when the roof was closed. The glass roof is not expected to continue into production.

Volkswagen has asserted that the "positive response, ideas and wishes expressed by the press and the general public...confirm the correctness of the decision to launch the *New Beetle* into series production by the end of the century." Volkswagen engineers, it believes, "succeeded in retaining the unique, distinctive lines while answering future challenges such as safety, environmental compatibility and typically Volkswagen functionality." The company hopes the new version will "bring back memories of the original VW Beetle, for many people the embodiment of personal mobility." When it goes on sale, it's supposed to demonstrate its new owner's "philosophy on life: individualistic, unhampered, youthful and relaxed."

Well, that's a fair description of the original. Tradition-minded Beetle fans continue to scoff at the idea of a front-drive VW, with a turbodiesel engine and water cooling, no less. Maybe so; but if its reception at that 1994 Detroit show and subsequent appearances are any indication, thousands of Americans will likely line up to be among the first to drive one home. They've already done so, attempting to toss deposit money at dealers for the privilege of buying one of the first examples to roll off the Mexican line.

For the New Beetle, Volkswagen has decided to "take what people found endearing about the old VW," says spokesman Tony Fouladpour, "and just improve upon it." The 21st century edition is "still going to have character," as well as "simplicity" and safety—but with a "fresh approach."

"The Volkswagen is a way of life," wrote Dr. Jean Rosenbaum of the original Beetle, in 1971. "More than that, it is a declaration of a certain attitude toward life and society. The Volkswagen owner is saying that he is concerned about economics, air pollution and good craftsmanship." Beetle owners also were "individualistic [and] almost fiercely loyal to" their cars. Such words just might be warranted, once again, for the Beetle's 21st century successor.

As this is written, most auto analysts believe the car will appear well before the year 2000: more likely, as a 1998 model, with production beginning early in 1997. Even the traditional-minded among VW enthusiasts—those who view the New Beetle's lack of an air-cooled rear engine as virtual heresy—just might decide to take a close look when the car finally arrives at dealerships. Modernization notwithstanding, who can resist that familiar Beetle profile?

SELECTED BIBLIOGRAPHY

Who could begin to count the books and articles that have been written about some aspect of the Volkswagen? Whether the subject is early VW history, technical merits, restoration requirements—the list is nearly endless. Shown below are the printed materials consulted most extensively while researching this book.

BOOKS:

Cropsey, Bob. *Volkswagen "Just the Facts."* Bobalu Enterprises, 1995.

Etzold, Hans-Rutiger. *The Beetle: The Chronicles of the People's Car, Volume 1: Production and Evolution Facts & Figures.* Haynes Publications Inc., 1988.

Etzold, Hans-Rutiger. *The Beetle: The Chronicles of the People's Car, Volume 2: Design and Evolution—the story.* Haynes Publications Inc., 1990.

Flat 4 Project. *Vintage Volkswagen.* 1984.

Flammang, James M. *Standard Catalog of Imported Cars 1946-1990.* Krause Publications, 1992.

Fry, Robin. *The VW Beetle.* David & Charles, 1980.

Hopfinger, K. B. *The Volkswagen Story.* Robert Bentley Inc. 1954, 1971.

Keats, John. *The Insolent Chariots.* J. B. Lippincott Co., 1958.

Marcantonio, Alfredo; Abbott, David; and O'Driscoll, John. *Is the Bug Dead? The Great Beetle Ad Campaign.* Stewart, Tabori and Chang, 1983.

Meredith, Laurence. *Original VW Beetle.* Bay View Books, 1994.

Morgan, G. R. (Dick). *Souping the Volkswagen.* Floyd Clymer Publications (undated).

Muir, John and Gregg, Tosh. *How To Keep Your Volkswagen Alive.* John Muir Publications, 1969 to 1979.

Nelson, Walter Henry. *Small Wonder: The Amazing Story of the Volkswagen.* Little, Brown and Company, 1967.

Nicholson, Geoff. *Still Life with Volkswagens.* The Overlook Press, 1994-95.

Norbye, Jan. *VW Treasures by Karmann.* Motorbooks International, 1985.

Reichert, Nikolaus and Klersy, Hans Joachim. *VW Beetle—An Illustrated History.* Motorbuch Verlag and Haynes Publications Inc., 1986.

Rosenbaum, Jean, M. D. *Is Your Volkswagen a Sex Symbol?* Hawthorn Books, 1972.

Seume, Keith. *California Look VW.* Motorbooks International, 1995.

Steinwedel, Louis. *The Beetle Book: America's 30-year Love Affair with the "Bug."* Prentice-Hall Inc., 1981.

Vack, Peter. *Illustrated Volkswagen Buyer's Guide.* Motorbooks International, 1993.

Volkswagen of America. *Think Small.* 1967.

Wilson, Bob. *The 1949-1959 VW Beetle: Authenticity Series.* Beeman Jorgensen, Inc., 1994.

PERIODICALS:

Various issues of the following magazines, from the 1950s to recent years, were consulted:

Advertising Age
Automotive News
Brandweek
Business Week
Car and Driver
Changing Times
Complete Car (British)
Consumer Guide
Consumer Reports
Dune Buggies and Hot VWs (1990s)
The Economist
Foreign Car Guide (1960s)
Life
Look
Mechanix Illustrated
Motor Trend
Newsweek
Popular Mechanics
Popular Science
Road & Track
Small World (issued by Volkswagen of America; 1960s to '80s)
Time
U.S. News & World Report
Volkswagen World (issued by Volkswagen of America; 1990s)
VW Trends (1990s)

VOLKSWAGEN COMPANY LITERATURE:

Also consulted during the research for this book were hundreds of items issued by Volkswagen AG (in Germany), Volkswagen of America or other Volkswagen subsidiary organizations. They include sales brochures and literature (from the 1950s to the present day), press releases and press kits (1960s to current), promotional materials, print advertisements, technical bulletins, auto show and dealer items, videotapes and more.

CLUB AND ENTHUSIAST PUBLICATIONS:

VWAutoist. Volkswagen Club of America.

VVWCA Newsletter. Vintage Volkswagen Club of America.

Zündfolge. Central Ohio Vintage Volkswagen Club.

The Wolfsburg Edition. Northeast Illinois Volkswagen Association.

The VW Connection. Connecticut Volkswagen Association.

German Air Sucker Society. Troy L. Heitzenrater, director.

APPENDIX

Volkswagen Clubs and Organizations

Vintage Volkswagen Club of America
VVWCA, Inc.
5705 Gordon Drive
Harrisburg, PA 17112
Phone: (717) 540-9972 (call between 6:00 and 10:00 p.m., Monday-Friday, or all day Saturday)
Internet address: vvwca@primenet.com
VVWCA has close to 40 regional chapters.

Volkswagen Club of America
P.O. Box 154
North Aurora, IL 60542-0154
VCOA also has several dozen regional chapters.

Late Model Bus Organization, International (LiMBO)
(For 1968-up Transporters)
9 Golden Hill Avenue
Shrewsbury, MA 01545-3042

German Air Sucker Society
927 Liberty Street
Salem, OH 44460
Phone: (216) 332-1865 (9:00 a.m. to 5:00 p.m., EST)

In addition to the above groups, dozens of local and regional VW clubs are flourishing, in the United States and Canada as well as elsewhere in the world.

Parts, Service and Information Sources

Because hundreds of companies and individuals offer Volkswagen parts and service, this is an abbreviated list, provided for information only. A mention here does not imply an endorsement by the author.

Barrett Enterprises
701 E. Arrow Highway
Azusa, CA 91702
Phone: (818) 967-5171

Boston Engine
Bob Donalds
8 Production Road
Walpole, MA 02081
Phone: (508) 668-2676

Bugstuff
709 Jefferson Avenue
West Brownsville, PA 15417
Phone: (800) 752-2847

The Bug Works
Noel Clemmer
Route 4, Box 323
Morgantown, WV 26505
Phone: (304) 599-9801

Bus Boys
18595 E. Lake Blvd.
Redding, CA 96003
Phone: (800) 792-2697

California Import Parts
1120 Yew Avenue
Blaine, WA 98230
Phone: (604) 434-8300

California Pacific VW Parts & Accessories
2040 Oceanside Blvd.
Oceanside, CA 92054
Phone: (619) 722-2535

Car Custom
915 W. Foothill Blvd.
Azusa, CA 91702
Phone: (818) 969-7967

Chirco VW Super Centre
9101 E. 22nd Street
Tucson, AZ 85710
Phone: (602) 722-1987

Chuck's Convertible Parts
Box 246T
Corona del Mar, CA 92625
Phone: (714) 673-5123

Classic-Antique & More Auto Parts
Jerry Coia
P.O. Box 161
Palmer, MA 01069
Phone: (413) 283-5772

D&G Foreign Auto Parts Inc.
Route 9, Lover's Lane
P.O. Box 256
Elizabethton, TN 37643
Phone: (800) 568-9001

Eurorace
2899 W. 190th Street
Redondo Beach, CA 90278
Phone: (800) 722-8678

Gene Berg
1725 N. Lime Street
Orange, CA 92665-4187
Phone: (714) 998-7500

The Guild
P.O. Box 4116
Long Beach, CA 90804
Phone: (310) 434-1255

House of Ghia
2626 Three Lakes Road
Albany, OR 97321
Phone: (503) 926-6513

JBUGS Car & Truck Depot
14222 S. Prairie Avenue
Hawthorne, CA 90250
Phone: (310) 978-0926

Jim's Custom VW
219 State Route 7
Columbiana, OH 44408
Phone: (216) 482-0018

Johnny's Speed & Chrome
6411 Beach Blvd.
Buena Park, CA
Phone: (714) 994-4022

Karmann Ghia Parts & Restoration
P.O. Box 58
Moorpark, CA 93020-0058
Phone: (805) 529-4442

Koch's
26943 Ruether Avenue, Unit M
Canyon County, CA 91351
Phone: (805) 252-9264

Latest Rage
3321 E. Artesia Blvd.
Long Beach, CA 90805
Phone: (310) 220-1140

Mark V Fiberglass
1650 Foothill Drive
Boulder City, NV 89005
Phone: (702) 293-5329

Marty's VW Service
203 Center Street
New Milford, NJ
Phone: (201) 261-4244

Mull's VW Farm
4838 Cat Creek Road
Valdosta, GA 31602
Phone: (912) 244-3814

NOPI Imported Car Parts
486 Main Street
Forest Park, GA 30050
Phone: (800) 277-6674

OKRASA
Vintage VW Performance Engine Specialist
Joe Ruiz
P.O. Box 2975
Anaheim, CA 92814
Phone: (714) 491-7574

Ray Betz Volkswagen Service
8877 Columbus Road
Mount Vernon, OH 43050
Phone: (614) 397-0293

The Real Source
4201 Airport Road
Cincinnati, OH 45226
Phone: (513) 871-9400

Rusty Bug Restorations
Greg Curello
1034 Prospect Road
Cheshire, CT 06410
Phone: (203) 250-7322

Street Bugs
43418 N. I-94 Service Drive
Belleville, MI 48111-2468
Phone: (313) 699-4220

Strictly Foreign
6800 Crater Lake Highway 62
White City, OR 97503
Phone: (503) 830-4141

Troy Hill Auto Service
Rege Stephens
1500 Lowrie Street
Pittsburgh, PA 15212
Phone: (412) 321-5503

Unique Supply Inc.
610 Tennessee Street
Redlands, CA 92374
Phone: (909) 793-0212

V-Dub Restoration Parts
Box 31555
Broad Street Complex
Richmond, VA 23294
Phone: (804) 747-0198

Vee Dub Parts Unlimited
17404 Beach Blvd.
Huntington Beach, CA 92647
Phone: (714) 848-8868

Vintage Parts Inc.
317 N. Victory Blvd.
Burbank, CA 91502
Phone: (818) 848-2863

West Coast Metric Inc.
24002 Frampton Avenue
Harbor City, CA 90710
Phone: (310) 325-0005

Wolfsburg West
1051 N. Grove Street
Anaheim, CA 92806
Phone: (714) 630-9653

VW SPECIFICATIONS

1945 "BEETLE" (TYPE 1) SPECIFICATIONS

Engine:

Type	Four-cylinder, four-stroke
Arrangement	Horizontally-opposed, overhead-valve
Mounting	Rear
Displacement	69.0 cubic inches (1131 cc)
Bore x Stroke	2.95 x 2.52 inches (75 x 64 mm)
Horsepower	25 at 3600 rpm
Compression ratio	5.8:1
Carburetor	Solex (no accelerator pump)
Battery	six-volt

Engine Note: Prewar Beetles used a 985-cc horizontally-opposed engine.

Chassis:

Frame	Central backbone with steel platform
Front suspension	Independent; torsion bars
Rear suspension	Independent; transverse torsion bar
Steering	Worm and roller
Transmission	Four-speed, non-synchromesh
Brakes	Mechanical, four-wheel

Dimensions:

Wheelbase	94.5 inches
Length	160 inches
Width	60.5 inches
Height	61.0 inches
Front track	50.8 inches
Rear track	49.2 inches
Tires	4.50x16 (1946: 5.00x16)

Performance:

Acceleration	0-30 mph in 9.7 seconds; 0-60 in 37.2 seconds
Top speed	66 mph

1949 "BEETLE" (TYPE 1) SPECIFICATIONS

Engine:

Type	Four-cylinder, four-stroke
Arrangement	Horizontally-opposed, overhead-valve
Mounting	Rear
Displacement	69.0 cubic inches (1131 cc)
Bore x Stroke	2.95 x 2.52 inches (75 x 64 mm)
Horsepower	30 (SAE) at 3300 rpm
Compression ratio	5.8:1
Cooling	Air; automatic thermostat control
Battery	six-volt
Carburetor	Solex 28 PCI downdraft

Gearbox/Final Drive:

Speeds	Four forward, one reverse; unsynchronized
Final Drive	4.43:1

Chassis:

Frame	Channel-shaped center section; welded-on platform
Front suspension	Independent; kingpins with upper/lower trailing arms and transverse torsion bars
Rear suspension	Independent; swinging half axles with trailing arms and torsion bars on each side
Steering	Worm and nut
Braking	Mechanical, front/rear drum
Tires	5.00x16
Fuel tank	8.8 gallons (1.1 gallon reserve)

Dimensions:

Wheelbase	94.5 inches
Length	160 inches
Width	61.0 inches
Height	60.5 inches
Track	51.0 inches (front), 49.2 inches (rear)
Weight	1,600 lbs.

1954 "BEETLE" (TYPE 1) SPECIFICATIONS

Engine:

Type	Four-cylinder, four-stroke
Arrangement	Horizontally-opposed, overhead-valve
Mounting	Rear
Displacement	72.74 cubic inches (1192 cc)
Bore x Stroke	3.031 x 2.52 inches (77 x 64 mm)
Horsepower	36 (SAE) at 3700 rpm
Compression ratio	6.6:1
Piston speed	1,427 feet per minute at 3400 rpm (68 mph)
Oil capacity	5.3 pints
Cooling	Air; automatic thermostat control
Battery	six-volt
Air cleaner	Oil-bath type
Carburetor	Solex 28 PCI downdraft

Gearbox/Final Drive:

Speeds	Four forward, one reverse; top three gears synchronized
Ratios	Deluxe model: (1st) 3.60:1; (2nd) 1.88:1; (3rd) 1.23:1; (4th) 0.82:1; (reverse) 4.63:1. Standard model: (1st) 3.60:1; (2nd) 2.07:1; (3rd) 1.25:1; (4th) 0.80:1; (reverse) 6.60:1
Final Drive	4.4:1

Chassis:

Frame	Channel-shaped center section; welded-on platform
Front suspension	Independent; kingpins with upper/lower trailing arms and transverse torsion bars
Rear suspension	Independent; swinging half axles with trailing arms and torsion bars on each side
Shock absorbers	Double-acting telescopic type

Turning radius	18 feet (approx.)
Foot brake	Deluxe model: hydraulic, front/rear drums. Standard model: mechanical
Handbrake	Mechanical, on rear wheels only
Tires	5.60x15
Fuel tank	10.6 gallons including 1.1-gallon reserve

Dimensions:

Wheelbase	94.5 inches
Length	160.2 inches
Width	60.6 inches
Height	59.1 inches
Track	50.8 inches (front), 49.2 inches (rear)
Unladen weight	(sedan) 1,609 lbs.; (convertible) 1,764 lbs.

Performance:

Fuel mileage	32 mpg
Acceleration	0-60 mph in 39 seconds
Cruising speed	65-68 mph
Climbing ability	(1st gear) 20.5 degrees (37% grade); (4th gear) 3.5 degrees (6% grade)

1954 TRANSPORTER SPECIFICATIONS

Engine:

Type	Four-cylinder, four-stroke
Arrangement	Horizontally-opposed, overhead-valve
Mounting	Rear
Displacement	72.74 cubic inches (1192 cc)
Bore x Stroke	3.031 x 2.52 inches (77 x 64 mm)
Horsepower	30 (SAE) at 3400 rpm
Compression ratio	6.1:1
Piston speed	1,378 feet per minute at 3300 rpm (50 mph)
Lubrication	Pressure-type, with oil cooler
Cooling	Air; automatic thermostat control
Battery	six-volt
Carburetor	Downdraft with accelerator pump

Gearbox/Final Drive:

Speeds	Four forward, one reverse; top three gears synchronized
Ratios	(1st) 3.60:1; (2nd) 1.88:1; (3rd) 1.23:1; (4th) 0.82:1; (reverse) 4.63:1.
Final Drive	6.2:1

Chassis:

Front suspension	Independent; two square-section torsion bars
Rear suspension	Independent; circular torsion bars on each side
Shock absorbers	Double-acting hydraulic
Turning circle	39 feet
Foot brake	Hydraulic, front/rear drums
Handbrake	Mechanical, acting on rear wheels only
Tires	5.50x16
Fuel tank	10.5 gallons including 1.25 gallon reserve

Dimensions:

Wheelbase	96 inches
Length	161.5 to 168.1 inches
Width	67 to 68.8 inches
Height	74.5 to 79 inches
Track	53.4 inches (front), 53.5 inches (rear)
Load-carrying or passenger space	79 inches long, 59 inches wide and 53 inches high
Loading space	141 cubic feet (plus 21 cubic feet of additional load space)
Unladen weight (incl. driver)	(Kombi) 2,260 lbs.; (Micro Bus) 2,403 lbs.; (delivery van) 2,204 lbs.
Payload	(Kombi) 1,708 lbs.; (Micro Bus) 1,565 lbs.; (delivery van) 1,764 lbs.
No. of seats	(Kombi/van) 2-3; (Microbus) 8

Performance:

Fuel consumption	25 mpg
Cruising/maximum speed	50 mph (at 3300 rpm)
Climbing ability	(1st gear) 13.5 degrees (24.5% grade); (4th gear) 2.5 degrees (4% grade)

1959 KARMANN GHIA SPECIFICATIONS

Engine:

Type	Four-cylinder, four-stroke
Arrangement	Horizontally-opposed, overhead-valve
Mounting	Rear
Displacement	72.74 cubic inches (1192 cc)
Bore x Stroke	3.031 x 2.52 inches (77 x 64 mm)
Horsepower	36 (SAE) at 3700 rpm
Compression ratio	6.6:1
Lubrication	Force-feed, oil cooler in air stream
Cooling	Air; automatic thermostat control
Battery	six-volt
Carburetor	Downdraft with accelerator pump

Gearbox/Final Drive:

Speeds	Four forward, one reverse; top three gears synchronized
Final Drive	4.43:1

Chassis:

Frame	Tubular center section, forked at rear, with welded-on platform
Front suspension	Independent; upper/lower trailing arms with square torsion bars
Rear suspension	Independent; swinging half axle-shafts; trailing arms with torsion bars
Shock absorbers	Double-acting hydraulic
Foot brake	Hydraulic, front/rear drums
Handbrake	Mechanical, on rear wheels only
Tires	5.60x15 tubeless super balloon
Fuel tank	10.6 gallons including 1.3 gallon reserve

Dimensions:

Wheelbase	94.5 inches
Length	163.0 inches
Width	64.3 inches
Height	52.4 inches
Track	51.4 inches (front), 49.2 inches (rear)
Unladen weight	1,790 lbs.

Performance:

Fuel mileage	32 mpg
Maximum and cruising speed	71 mph
Climbing ability	(1st gear) 19 degrees (34% grade); (4th gear) 3 degrees (5.5% grade)

1962 VOLKSWAGEN "BEETLE" SPECIFICATIONS

Engine:

Type	Four-cylinder, four-stroke
Arrangement	Horizontally-opposed, overhead-valve
Mounting	Rear
Displacement	72.7 cubic inches (1192 cc)
Bore x Stroke	3.031 x 2.52 inches (77 x 64 mm)
Horsepower (SAE)	40 at 3900 rpm
Compression ratio	7.0:1
Cooling	Air; automatic thermostat control
Battery	six-volt
Air cleaner	Oil-bath type
Carburetor	Solex 28 PCI downdraft

Gearbox/Final Drive:

Speeds	Four forward, one reverse; top three gears synchronized
Ratios	Deluxe model: (1st) 3.60:1; (2nd) 1.88:1; (3rd) 1.23:1; (4th) 0.82:1; (reverse) 4.63:1. Standard model: (1st) 3.60:1; (2nd) 2.07:1; (3rd) 1.25:1; (4th) 0.80:1; (reverse) 6.60:1
Final Drive	4.4:1

Chassis:

Frame	Channel-shaped center section; welded-on platform
Front suspension	Independent; kingpins with upper/lower trailing arms and transverse torsion bars
Rear suspension	Independent; swinging half axles with trailing arms and torsion bars on each side
Shock absorbers	Double-acting telescopic type
Steering	Worm and nut
Foot brake	Hydraulic, front/rear drums
Handbrake	Mechanical, on rear wheels only
Tires	5.60x15
Fuel tank	10.6 gallons

Dimensions:

Wheelbase	94.5 inches
Length	160.2 inches
Width	60.6 inches
Height	59.1 inches

Track	51.4 inches (front), 50.7 inches (rear)
Weight	(sedan) 1,565 lbs.; (convertible) 1,698 lbs.

Performance:

Fuel mileage	28-32 mpg
Cruising speed	72 mph
Acceleration	0-60 mph in 22 seconds

1966 FASTBACK AND SQUAREBACK SPECIFICATIONS

Engine:

Type	Four-cylinder, horizontally-opposed, overhead-valve, four-stroke
Mounting	Rear
Displacement	96.66 cubic inches (1584 cc)
Bore x Stroke	3.37 x 2.72 inches (85 x 69 mm)
Horsepower (SAE)	65 at 4600 rpm
Torque (SAE)	87 pound-feet at 2800 rpm
Piston speed	1,923 feet/minute at maximum speed
Carburetion	Two Solex 32 PDSIT downdraft carburetors
Air cleaner	Oil-bath type with pre-heated air intake
Oil capacity	5.3 pints
Cooling	Air; automatic thermostat control and crankshaft-mounted fan
Battery	six-volt

Gearbox/Final Drive:

Speeds	Four forward (synchronized) plus reverse
Ratios	(1st) 3.80:1; (2nd) 2.06:1; (3rd) 1.32:1; (4th) 0.89:1; (reverse) 3.88:1
Final Drive	4.125:1

Chassis/suspension:

Frame	Semi-unitized body with platform frame
Front suspension	Two torsion bars with trailing arms and stabilizer
Rear suspension	Two transverse torsion bars with trailing arms and swinging half shafts (plus auxiliary spring in Squareback sedan)
Shock absorbers	Double-acting telescopic type
Steering	Worm and roller
Turning circle	36.5 feet (2.8 turns, lock-to-lock)
Foot brake	Hydraulic; front discs, rear drums
Handbrake	Mechanical, on rear wheels only
Tires	6.00x15 tubeless
Fuel tank	10.6 gallons

Dimensions:

Wheelbase	94.5 inches
Length	166.3 inches
Width	63.2 inches
Height	58.1 inches
Track	51.6 inches (front), 53.0 inches (rear)
Ground clearance	5.9 inches (fully loaded)
Curb weight	1,962 lbs. (Fastback); 2,029 lbs. (Squareback)

Performance (claimed):

Fuel mileage	28 mpg
Cruising speed	84 mph
Acceleration	0-50 mph in 12.5 seconds
Climbing ability	(1st gear) 41.5% grade with half payload; (2nd) 21.5%; (3rd) 12.5%; (4th) 7.5%

1971 SUPER BEETLE SPECIFICATIONS

Engine:

Type	Four-cylinder, four-stroke
Arrangement	Horizontally-opposed, overhead-valve
Mounting	Rear
Displacement	96.6 cubic inches (1585 cc)
Bore x Stroke	3.36 x 2.72 inches
Horsepower (SAE)	60 at 4400 rpm
Compression ratio	7.5:1
Oil capacity	5.3 pints
Cooling	Air; automatic thermostat control
Battery	12-volt
Air cleaner	Oil-bath type with thermostatic-controlled preheating of intake air
Carburetor	Solex downdraft, with automatic choke

Manual Gearbox/Final Drive:

Speeds	Four forward, one reverse; all forward gears synchronized
Ratios	(1st) 3.80:1; (2nd) 2.06:1; (3rd) 1.26:1; (4th) 0.89:1; (reverse) 3.61:1.
Final Drive	4.125:1

Optional Automatic Stick Shift Transmission:

Speeds	Three forward, one reverse
Ratios	(Low) 2.06:1; (Drive 1) 1.26:1; (Drive 2) 0.89:1; (reverse) 3.07:1
Final Drive	4.375:1

Chassis:

Frame	Tubular center section; forked and welded-on platform
Front suspension	Independent; MacPherson struts with shock absorber/coil spring combination
Rear suspension	Independent; trailing arms with diagonal links and half-axles
Turning circle	31.2 feet (approx.)
Foot brake	Hydraulic, front/rear drums
Handbrake	Mechanical, on rear wheels only
Tires	5.60x15 on 4J x 15 hump-type safety rims
Fuel tank	11.0 gallons

Dimensions:

Wheelbase	95.3 inches
Length	160.6 inches
Width	62.4 inches
Height	59.1 inches
Track	54.3 inches (front), 53.2 inches (rear)
Ground clearance	6 inches
Curb weight	(sedan) 1,918 lbs.; (convertible) 2,028 lbs.

Luggage capacity	9.2 cubic feet (front compartment); 4.9 cubic feet (rear compartment, behind seat)

Performance:

Fuel mileage	26 mpg (at half payload at steady three-fourths of top speed on level road); 25 mpg with automatic
Cruising speed	81 mph (78 mph with automatic)

Standard Equipment:

Padded dashboard; front armrest; sun visors; one outside mirror; day/night mirror; seatbelts all around; dual braking system; electric rear defogger; two-speed wiper with pneumatic washer system; front passenger grab handle; glove compartment (sedan); fold-down rear seat; tool kit; coat hooks (sedan); door pocket; courtesy light; front/rear ashtrays; assist straps; rubber floor mats.

Optional Equipment:

Automatic Stick Shift transmission; leatherette upholstery; whitewall tires; hinged rear side windows; sliding steel sun roof; radio; rear speaker; air conditioner; cigarette lighter; vent shades; gravel guards; tissue dispenser; and more.

1975 CAMPMOBILE SPECIFICATIONS

Engine:

Type	Air-cooled, rear-mounted
Construction	Four-cylinder, horizontally-opposed
Displacement	120.2 cubic inches (1970 cc)
Horsepower	67 at 4200 rpm (SAE)
Fuel/air supply	AFC fuel injection
Electrical system	12-volt; 55-amp alternator

Transmission/Differential:

Type	Fully synchronized transaxle
Speeds	Four forward, one reverse
Final drive	Rear-wheel-drive with double-jointed axles
Clutch	Single disc

Chassis/Suspension:

Frame	Unitized body/chassis; box-shaped side and cross-members
Front suspension	Independent; torsion bars with trailing arms and stabilizer
Rear suspension	Independent; torsion bars with trailing and diagonal arms
Steering	Roller-type
Brakes	Dual diagonal circuit; power-assisted; front disc, rear drum
Parking brake	Cable-operated on rear wheels
Tires	185R14 on 5-1/2J x 14 rims

Dimensions:

Wheelbase	94.5 inches
Length	177.4 inches
Width	67.7 inches
Height	77.2 inches (unloaded)
Ground clearance	7.9 inches (loaded)
Turning circle	41.0 feet (wall to wall)

Performance:

Top speed	79 mph (manual), 76 mph (automatic)
EPA fuel mileage	26 mpg highway, 16 mpg city (manual shift)

ENGINE CHANGES
BEETLE AND KARMANN GHIA

Model Year	Introduced during	Displacement cc	cu. in.	BHP (SAE)	Comp. Ratio
1945	1945	1131	69.0	30	5.8:1
1953	Dec. 1953	1192	72.7	36	6.1:1
1954	Aug. 1954	1192	72.7	36	6.6:1
1961	1960	1192	72.7	40	7.0:1
1966	1965	1285	78.4	50	7.3:1
1967	1966	1493	91.1	53	7.3:1
1970	1969	1585	96.7	57	7.5:1
1971	1970	1585	96.7	60	7.3:1

SQUAREBACK AND FASTBACK

1962	1961	1493	91.1	53	7.2:1
1964*	1963	1493	91.1	66	8.5:1#
1966*	1965	1585	96.7	65	7.7:1

  * Dual carburetors.
  # Premium fuel required.

Note: Not until August 1, 1955, did Volkswagen have a separate "model year."

VOLKSWAGEN PRODUCTION (1945-1969)

Year	Total Output	Cars	Trucks
1945	1,785	1,785	—
1946	10,020	10,020	—
1947	8,987	8,987	—
1948	19,244	19,244	—
1949	46,154	46,146	8
1950	90,038	81,979	8,059
1951	105,712	93,709	12,003
1952	136,013	114,348	21,665
1953	179,740	151,323	28,417
1954	242,373	202,174	40,199
1955	329,893	279,986	49,907
1956	396,690	333,190	62,500
1957	472,554	380,561	91,993
1958	553,399	451,526	101,873
1959	696,860	575,407	121,453
1960	865,858	725,939	139,919
1961	1,007,113	838,513	168,600
1962	1,184,675	1,004,338	180,337
1963	1,209,591	1,020,297	189,294
1964	1,410,715	1,210,390	200,325
1965	1,542,654	1,352,778	189,876
1966	1,583,239	1,391,866	191,373
1967	1,290,328	1,127,587	162,741
1968	1,707,402	1,453,483	253,919
1969	1,830,018	1,556,884	273,134

VOLKSWAGENS BUILT FOR EXPORT (1947-1969)

	Export			U.S. Registrations		
Year	Total	Cars	Trucks	Total	Cars	Trucks
1947	1,656	1,656	—	—	—	—
1948	4,464	4,464	—	—	—	—
1949	7,128	7,128	—	2	2	—
1950	29,387	27,816	1,571	157	157	—

	Export			U.S. Registrations		
Year	Total	Cars	Trucks	Total	Cars	Trucks
1951	35,742	32,185	3,557	390	390	—
1952	46,884	38,829	8,055	611	601	10
1953	68,757	55,449	13,308	1,013	980	33
1954	108,842	86,635	22,207	6,614	6,343	271
1955	177,657	147,319	30,338	30,928	28,907	2,021
1956	217,685	180,153	37,532	55,690	50,457	5,233
1957	270,987	210,544	60,443	79,524	64,803	14,721
1958	315,718	248,777	66,941	104,306	79,038	25,268
1959	404,187	324,183	80,004	150,601	120,442	30,159
1960	489,272	397,046	92,226	191,372	159,995	31,377
1961	533,420	438,487	94,933	203,863	177,308	26,555
1962	627,613	525,080	102,533	222,740	192,570	30,170
1963	685,763	573,562	112,201	277,008	240,143	36,865
1964	797,468	—	—	343,263	307,173	36,090
1965	851,114	—	—	388,592	383,978	4,614*
1966	964,576	—	—	423,645	420,018	3,627*
1967	812,959	—	—	456,231	452,937	3,294*
1968	1,104,752	—	—	567,975	563,522	4,453*
1969	1,098,893	—	—	540,623	537,933	2,690*

*Starting in 1964, station wagons were counted as passenger cars instead of trucks.

RETAIL SALES (1949-1981) - VOLKSWAGEN OF AMERICA

	Cars			Trucks	
Year	Type 1	Type 3/4	Front-drive	(Type 2)	Total
1949	2	—	—	—	2
1950	328	—	—	2	330
1951	367	—	—	50	417
1952	887	—	—	93	980
1953	1,139	—	—	75	1,214
1954	8,086	—	—	827	8,913
1955	32,662	—	—	3,189	35,851
1956	42,884	—	—	6,666	49,550
1957	54,189	—	—	18,366	72,555
1958	61,507	—	—	24,478	85,985
1959	96,892	—	—	32,423	129,315
1960	127,159	—	—	34,878	162,037
1961	162,960	—	—	23,300	186,260
1962	194,508	—	—	32,141	226,649
1963	232,550	—	—	38,238	270,788
1964	276,187	—	—	37,239	313,426
1965	314,625	4,723	—	37,796	357,144
1966	318,563	57,954	—	35,439	411,956
1967	339,971	69,292	—	34,247	443,510
1968	423,008	95,528	—	50,756	569,292
1969	403,016	95,527	—	52,823	551,366
1970	405,615	99,012	—	65,069	569,696
1971	354,574	105,056	—	63,025	522,655
1972	358,401	80,386	—	46,858	485,645
1973	371,097	62,542	—	42,656	476,295
1974	243,664	23,307	37,625	23,307	334,515
1975	92,037	6,552	147,594	21,547	267,730
1976	27,009	—	155,197	19,464	201,670
1977	19,245	—	215,349	26,108	260,702
1978	9,932	—	206,046	23,322	239,300
1979	10,681	—	265,437	15,901	292,019
1980	4,572	—	275,856	13,167	293,595
1981	33	—	267,498	10,882	278,413

RETAIL SALES (1982-1995) - VOLKSWAGEN OF AMERICA

Year	Total Sales	Year	Total Sales
1982	171,281	1989	133,650
1983	166,915	1990	136,357
1984	177,709	1991	96,723
1985	218,042	1992	75,873
1986	217,231	1993	49,533
1987	191,705	1994	97,043
1988	168,800	1995	59,227

LOW-COST IMPORTED CARS AVAILABLE IN THE U.S. IN 1958

Prices for the least-expensive models are listed.

Make	Model	Origin	Base Price
Austin	A-35	Britain	$1,557
Austin	A-55 Cambridge	Britain	2,214
Borgward	Isabella	Germany	2,495
Citroën	2CV	France	1,298
Datsun*	PL210	Japan	1,799
DKW	3-6	Germany	1,995
Fiat	500	Italy	1,098
Fiat	600	Italy	1,298
Fiat	1100	Italy	1,683
Ford	Anglia	Britain	1,441
Ford	Prefect	Britain	1,490
Ford	Taunus 17M	Germany	2,017
Goggomobil	T400	Germany	1,095
Goliath	1100	Germany	1,945
Hillman	Minx Special	Britain	1,699
Isetta (BMW)	300	Germany	1,048
Isetta (BMW)	600	Germany	1,398
Lloyd	600	Germany	1,295
Messerschmidt	KR200	Germany	1,073#
MG	Magnette	Britain	2,740
Morris	Minor	Britain	1,705
NSU	Prinz	Germany	1,398
Opel	Rekord	Germany	1,957
Panhard	Dyna	France	1,995
Peugeot	403	France	2,175
Renault	4CV	France	1,345
Renault	Dauphine	France	1,645
Saab	93B	Sweden	1,895
Simca	Aronde	France	1,595
Skoda	S440	Czechoslovakia	1,687
Standard	Vanguard	Britain	—
Sunbeam	Rapier	Britain	2,499
Toyota*	Toyopet Crown	Japan	2,187
Triumph	TR10	Britain	1,699
Vauxhall	Victor	Britain	1,957
Vespa	400	France	1,080
Volkswagen	Beetle	Germany	1,545
Volkswagen	Karmann Ghia	Germany	2,445
Volvo	PV444	Sweden	2,239
Wartburg	311	East Germany	1,686

* First year of availability in U.S.
  # Price in 1956.

FOREIGN CAR SALES, 1958-1959

Americans bought and registered 609,500 foreign cars in 1959—one-tenth of the total, and up from 378,500 in 1958. Listed below are the top 15 sellers in 1959. (Source: *Advertising Age*)

Make	1959	1958
Volkswagen	119,850	78,550
Renault	90,500	48,100
British Fords	42,500	33,500
Opel	39,000	15,500
Fiat	38,000	21,000
Simca	35,000	17,000
Hillman	27,800	19,000
Triumph	23,000	16,000
Vauxhall	22,500	17,300
Volvo	18,300	14,000
MG	17,500	16,000
Austin-Healey	16,500	5,500
Morris	15,000	9,000
Metropolitan	14,500	12,000
Mercedes-Benz	13,700	8,000

MAJOR MODERATE-COST IMPORTED CARS AVAILABLE IN THE U.S. IN 1967

Make	Model	Origin	Base Price
BMW	1600	Germany	$2,477
Citroën	AMI-6	France	1,703
Citroën	ID19	France	2,669
DAF	44	Holland	1,795
Datsun	PL411	Japan	1,666
Fiat	124	Italy	1,798
Fiat	1100R	Italy	1,564
Fiat	600D	Italy	1,237
Fiat	850	Italy	1,795
Ford	Anglia 1200	Britain	1,569
Ford	Cortina 1500	Britain	1,815
NSU	Prinz	Germany	1,510
Opel	Kadett	Germany	1,695
Peugeot	404	France	2,595
Renault	Dauphine	France	1,409
Renault	R-10	France	1,647
Saab	96	Sweden	1,795
Simca	1000	France	1,614
Skoda	1000MB	Czechoslovakia	1,480
Sunbeam	Arrow	Britain	2,172
Sunbeam	Imp	Britain	1,495
Toyota	Corona	Japan	1,760
Toyota	Crown	Japan	2,305
Triumph	1200	Britain	1,665
Volkswagen	Beetle	Germany	1,639
Volkswagen	Karmann Ghia	Germany	2,250
Volkswagen	1600	Germany	2,148
Volvo	122S	Sweden	2,755

ABOUT THE AUTHOR

James M. Flammang is a full-time automotive writer/editor, based in Chicago. In addition to writing about new and used vehicles for various consumer periodicals and buying guides, including those issued by Consumer Guide and Edmund Publications, he publishes *Tirekicking Today*, a monthly automotive newsletter.

Collectible and historic vehicles also command a major share of Flammang's editorial attention. He is the author of two prior Krause books, *Standard Catalog of American Cars 1976-1986* and *Standard Catalog of Imported Cars 1946-1990*, and has contributed articles to *Old Cars Weekly News & Marketplace* since the mid-1970s. Flammang also has authored a large number of automotive history books for Consumer Guide, including the *Ford Chronicle*, *Chrysler Chronicle*, *Great Book of Dream Cars* and *Chronicle of the American Automobile*.

No Volkswagens occupy the Flammang garage at this time, but he retains fond memories of a faded red 1957 Beetle sedan and a light green '61 Microbus. Split- and oval-window Beetles are his favorites, but he wouldn't mind owning an old Karmann Ghia, and especially enjoyed road testing the current Cabrio. Having attended the debut of the "New Beetle" for the 21st century, at Detroit's auto show in 1994, he is eagerly awaiting a test drive when that car finally goes into production.

INDEX